STUDIES IN A CHRISTIAN WORLD VIEW

Sponsored by the Institute for Advanced Christian Studies
Carl F. H. Henry, Editor-in-chief

Available

vol. 1: Contours of a World View, by Arthur F. Holmes
vol. 2: Christianity and Philosophy, by Keith E. Yandell

In preparation

vol. 3: Christianity and psychology (Mary Stewart Van Leeuwen)
vol. 4: Christianity and economics (Brian Griffiths)
vol. 5: Christianity and natural science (V. Elving Anderson)
vol. 6: Christianity and Eastern religions (John B. Carman)
vol. 7: Christianity and the arts (Nicholas Wolterstorff)
vol. 8: Christianity and history (Robert Eric Frykenberg)
vol. 9: Christianity and contemporary God-concepts (Alvin Plantinga)
vol. 10: Christianity and literature (David L. Jeffrey)

The Institute for Advanced Christian Studies is a non-profit corporation dedicated to the development of Christian scholarly writing for our times. Mailing address: Box 95496, Chicago, IL 60690

CHRISTIANITY AND PHILOSOPHY

by

KEITH E. YANDELL

INTER-VARSITY PRESS,
LEICESTER, ENGLAND

WILLIAM B. EERDMANS PUBLISHING COMPANY
GRAND RAPIDS, MICHIGAN

For Merritt
Who introduced me to Gummy Bears

Inter-Varsity Press
38 De Montfort Street, Leicester LE1 7GP, England

Wm. B. Eerdmans Publishing Company
255 Jefferson Ave. S.E., Grand Rapids, Michigan 49503

Printed in the United States of America

First published 1984
IVP EDITION 0-85110-726-5

Library of Congress Cataloging in Publication Data

Yandell, Keith E., 1938–
Christianity and philosophy.

(Studies in a Christian world view; v. 2)
1. Christianity—Philosophy. 2. Theism. I. Title.
II. Series.
BR100.Y36 1983 201 83-14226
ISBN 0-8028-1964-8 (pbk.)

Inter-Varsity Press is the publishing division of the Universities and Colleges Christian Fellowship (formerly the Inter-Varsity Fellowship), a student movement linking Christian Unions in universities and colleges throughout the United Kingdom and the Republic of Ireland, and a member movement of the International Fellowship of Evangelical Students. For information about local and national activities write to UCCF, 38 De Montfort Street, Leicester LE1 7GP.

CONTENTS

INTRODUCTION

This volume is an exercise in the philosophy of religion. It concerns theism in general, and Christianity in particular. It asks whether (i) theism is "cognitively meaningful"—whether it is either true or false—and (ii) whether there is any reason to think it true.

Theism is a conceptual system, and, as one kind of theism, Christianity is also a conceptual system. Christianity presents a variety of types of claims, and so is accessible to a variety of types of evidence. No doubt it is in some sense more than a conceptual system, but certainly it is not *less* than that (though such is the depth of current confusion and sophistry that some have even denied that Christianity has a theology). For the purposes of this discussion, Christianity is understood to involve such claims as the following:

- God created the world; everything else that exists depends on God, and not conversely. The world that God created is real, not illusory, and that it exists is a good rather than an evil state of affairs: matter is not evil.
- God is holy in the dual sense that he is unique (alone worthy of being worshiped) and that he is morally pure, or righteous. Thus, worship is not a preliminary religious exercise to be later transcended; its appropriateness is built into the nature of the Creator/creature distinction, which cannot be dissolved.
- God is providential in the sense that he governs the course of history, moving it toward an end (the kingdom of God), so that time and the historical process are one-directional (not cyclical), and time and historical events are real, not illusory; it is a good, not an evil, that there are temporal and historical processes.

- God loves all persons in the sense that he wills their ultimate good and acts to bring it about. Central to our being made in God's image is our capacity to love ourselves and others in this sense of willing their ultimate good and acting to bring it about. Love in this sense is thus primarily volitional rather than primarily emotional.
- God is all-knowing, all-powerful, and all-good. Inasmuch as they are made in his image, human beings have some knowledge, some power, and some capacity for goodness. This is, of course, quite different from human nature being "inherently good" in the sense that persons cannot help being good moral agents; inherent value is not the same as inherent goodness.
- Persons are created by God and in God's image, with the dual consequence that every person (in Kant's terms) has dignity rather than price (that is to say, every individual has a unique worth derived from the fact of being created in God's image), and that ethics is based upon our making actual the potential mature goodness that being created in the image of God makes possible by imitating the behavior ascribed to God (insofar as this is possible to creatures). Human individuality is real, not illusory; and it is good, and not evil, that individual persons exist.
- Because God is righteous, he judges sin (sin being understood as that which persons freely do to thwart their own and others' *summum bonum,* or greatest good). God loves all persons, and his intolerance of sin derives from the nature of divine love. Human sin and guilt are real, not illusory, and it is better that persons act freely as moral agents than that they be unable to sin.
- God has acted in history at real times and in real places to reveal himself to real persons and actually to act on their behalf. Religious doctrine *essentially* concerns certain persons and contains essential reference to historical events.
- Religious knowledge is primarily gained through revelation (a process initiated by God) rather than through reflection, meditation, self-abasement, good works, yoga, or any other such means. Revelation involves both words and actions; propositional revelation without redeeming events would be empty, and redeeming events without propositional revelation would be unintelligible.
- The basic religious problem is sin rather than merely ignorance, and the basic religious need is for forgiveness rather than merely information or enlightenment. Salvation, the solution of the basic

religious problem, is by grace (God's unmerited favor) rather than merely by human effort.

Now these claims, however rich in material for clarification, amplification, reflection, and controversy, do not descend into the particulars of Christianity. For that, one can turn to Paul's famous summary of the gospel that he "received" when he turned to Christianity and then "delivered" to others—namely, "that Christ died for our sins in accordance with the scriptures, that he was buried, that he was raised on the third day in accordance with the scriptures" (1 Cor. 15:3-4). Here one comes to Christianity's core. Let us, then, refer to these claims of St. Paul as *core* claims, and let us refer to those more general claims cited earlier as *context* claims, since they are presupposed by, and provide the context for, the core: if the context claims are neither true nor false—if they *lack truth value*—then so do the core propositions. Many philosophers have held exactly this view concerning context claims and so have held it also about the core claims (namely, that both lack truth value): if the proposition *God exists* does not even manage to rise to the dignity of falsehood, then it is pointless to worry about the core, and the same holds if the proposition is false. Many philosophers of religion, as well as some professed theologians, have held such views as these, and such notions as Christian atheism, and a "secular meaning" of the gospel (which even Logical Positivists can accept), have been forwarded as viable interpretations of Christianity.

The core logically presupposes the context; yet many philosophers have claimed that the context lacks truth value. Understandably, then, contemporary philosophers of religion have concerned themselves more fully with the context; this has meant that their focus has been more on what might be described as a "basic monotheism" than on the features distinguishing Judaism, Christianity, Islam, or any other monotheistic perspective. To that general emphasis this volume is no exception. Indeed, the context claims will not be examined individually. The focus will instead be on the basic monotheistic claim that God exists. It is not the purpose of this volume to present an argument for the Christian core claims, or even of the context claims in their details.

The basic question in the philosophy of religion is whether religious claims can be rationally assessed—and if so, how. If religious claims cannot be assessed, then the philosophy of religion has completed its task when it demonstrates this to be the case. If, on the other hand, religious claims *can* be assessed, then it is the task of the philosophy of religion to show that this is so, stating the constituents of the assessment procedure and applying that procedure—a task that will involve coming to terms with various competing religious and nonreligious conceptual systems, offering a fair and accurate analysis of their contents, considering what can be said for and against their truth, and considering possible reformulations of such systems in the light of objections. If rational assessment of religious claims is impossible, the philosophy of religion is a matter of dispelling conceptual fog. If such assessment is possible, the philosophy of religion is a matter of constructing a conceptual vessel, or perhaps of finding that one already constructed is built well enough for safe travel.

It is the aim of this volume to provide a defense of the view that religious claims can indeed be rationally assessed, that theism is either true or false and that there is reason to think that theism is true. Chapter One argues that (given an assumption which is beyond the scope of this volume to assess) there is experiential confirmation for theism. Chapter Two suggests that theism has some explanatory force. Chapters Three and Four challenge various perspectives that are incompatible with the conclusions defended in the earlier chapters.

Chapter Five argues against moral skepticism and moral relativism—views that are incompatible with theism's having any positive connections with morality. Chapter Six argues that the existence of evil is not evidence against God's existence. Chapter Seven criticizes some varieties of nontheistic ethical systems and suggests some ways in which theism comports nicely with plausible views in ethics.

Finally, Chapter Eight offers a proposal regarding the rational assessment of religious (and nonreligious) conceptual systems—one that notes various ways in which conceptual systems can go wrong, epistemically speaking, and suggests that Christian theism manages to avoid these pitfalls (asserting also, however, that this is a matter for inquiry in particular cases).

In these ways the cognitive status and the plausibility of theism in general (and of Christian theism in particular) are discussed and defended.

The overall aim of this volume, then, is to deal with at least the basic topics most closely related to the questions of whether religious claims can be rationally assessed and whether theism is true or false. Each chapter could easily expand into a volume of its own, but the decision was made to pursue a breadth of coverage; as a result, perhaps the argument more resembles a mural than an etching.

The arguments are addressed to those who already have some acquaintance with philosophy—to college juniors and seniors with some background in philosophy on up (if that is the right direction), and to those who are interested enough in the topics discussed to be willing to work to follow an attempt to deal with them.

Keith E. Yandell
Madison, Wisconsin
1983

PART ONE
THEISM AND EVIDENCE

ANALYTICAL TABLE OF CONTENTS TO CHAPTER 1

CHAPTER 1

DOES NUMINOUS EXPERIENCE PROVIDE EVIDENCE THAT GOD EXISTS?

SENSORY EXPERIENCE AND NONSENSORY EXPERIENCE

The term "experience" is hardly the most lucid in the language. *Seeing that a contradiction cannot be true* is an experience, yet it need involve no imagery whatever; the notion of a *nonsensory* experience, then, is perfectly coherent. Yet "experience" is often used as shorthand for "sensory experience"; "knowledge gained from experience" often does duty for "empirical knowledge" or "knowledge gained through the senses." As a convenience, the practice is harmless; as supposed grounds for the view that all experience is sensory, it is worthless.

Some experiences which are not purely sensory have sensory components; the recognition of the beauty of a painting or a symphony is not "purely sensory," if a "purely sensory" experience is one in which (assuming the experience to be veridical)[1] the experience's subject recognizes, or comes to know, only that an object has observable properties—properties that can be seen, heard, felt, tasted, or smelled.[2]

Some experiences which are not sensory presuppose that the

1. Roughly, an experience is veridical if things really are as they seem to the experiencing subject to be.

2. With "seen" used in its literal and visual sense, as in "I see the red in the sunset," not its metaphorical sense, as in "I see the point of your remark."

one who had them has had sensory experiences; if one feels an obligation to help a student who requests it, or a duty to tell a friend the truth, or regret that one forgot an important appointment with the dean, or remorse over harsh words unthinkingly spoken to an acquaintance, one has an experience which one would not have had were one not to have had any sensory experience of student, friend, dean, or acquaintance; yet to feel an obligation, duty, regret, or remorse is not the same as (though it presupposes) having sensory experience.

According to a long tradition, there are five senses: sight, hearing, taste, touch, and smell. This list can be expanded to include senses of heat, cold, dizziness, hunger, pain, and so on; whether it is useful to do so depends on one's purposes, and it is not important here to establish, by nature or convention, exactly how many senses there are.

SENSORY SEEMING AND JUDGMENTAL SEEMING

It is important for our purposes to distinguish between two *sorts* of experience. Suppose Ralph, riding in the desert, at least seems to see an oasis and feels dizzy. His feeling dizzy is not a matter of it at least seeming to him that an object, which exists quite independent of himself if it exists at all, does exist and has certain observable properties. One might say: this experience only has content, but no object. By contrast, his at least seeming to see an oasis is a matter of its at least seeming to him that an object, which exists quite independent of himself if it exists at all, does exist and has certain properties. One might say: this experience has an object.[3] Ralph at least seems to see an oasis; thus either he sees one or else he "sees a mirage." To see a mirage is not to see something; "see" in "see a mirage" is a courtesy verb, so to say, reflecting the fact that the experience so named is qualitatively similar or identical to that of actually encountering an oasis. It will be convenient, in discussing experiential evidence, to have a way of expressing this similarity; a standard way of doing so talks of how things *seem* or *appear*. Unfortunately, "seems" and "appears" have various senses. Sticking to forms of "seems," *It seems to me that he is unreliable* expresses an

3. It has content, too, but not *only* content. One might express this by saying that *seeing an oasis* is *subject-consciousness-object* in structure, and *being dizzy* is merely *subject-consciousness* in structure.

opinion or judgment; *It seemed to me to be safe* contrasts with *It was safe,* explaining a mistake. Neither use of a form of "seems" need reflect any role of sensory experience in forming the opinion or making the mistake. What we need is a sense of "seems" which has two features: (i) what seems may, or may not, be so; and (ii), the seeming is *sensory.* The first feature is clear enough; the second requires explanation. For convenience restricting ourselves to the traditional five senses—these being in any case the ones most relevant to our gaining information about the "external world"—how things *sensorily seem* to a person at a time **t** is how things *look, smell, taste, feel,* and/or *sound* to that person at **t**, whether things are so or not.

It might appear that we can construct analogous senses of "seems." For example, if aesthetic judgments can be true or false—that is, if there are such things as aesthetic judgments—and if it is possible to be aesthetically mistaken in the sense of taking some such judgment to be true when in fact it is false, then it makes sense to say such things as *All ruins seem ugly to me* in a sense of "seems" which only says how ruins aesthetically seem to one. Similarly one could report *Requiring a teaching assistant to paint one's garage seems to be exploiting him* as only a way of saying how this morally seems to one. But how things seem aesthetically, or morally, to one is how one judges them to be; so in fact these are not analogous to "sensorily seems" though they may (nonsensorily) seem to be analogous.

"PURELY SENSORY" EXPERIENCE

The notion of a "purely sensory" experience—one in which (assuming the experience to be veridical) the experience's subject comes to know only that an object has observable properties—was used earlier; it was noted that various experiences were not, in that sense, purely sensory. Suppose Ralph sees a red apple on the table, and not unreasonably therefore believes the proposition *There is a red apple on the table.* Ralph ascribes the property *being red* to the apple; he also ascribes the property *falling under the concept "apple"* to the item on the table. The former property is observable; determinate colors are proper objects of a sensory modality. The latter property is not an observable property; falling under a determinate concept is not proper to any sensory modality, nor is it common to two or more sensory modalities. Further, apples are substances; they endure through time, have dispositional properties, and *have* (as opposed to *being merely sets of*) properties. In *The apple is red,* "is" is the "is of predication" rather than the "is of class membership"; a quality is ascribed to an owner rather than an item being included in a set, and even implicitly coming to know that this is so is not merely a matter of coming to know that an object has an observable quality. Thus the rather ordinary sensory experience in which one comes to know that a red apple is in view—a matter of having a "purely sensory" experience in the sense described above—is a rather more complex affair than one might suppose. It involves having a set of intimately entangled concepts (*substance, observational property, dispositional property, enduring object,* etc.), though of course it does not require that one be conscious of having them in such manner that one has sorted them out and noted their connections. Not everyone who can spot a contradiction in a professor's lecture has explicitly formulated the principle of noncontradiction, and not everyone who has identified an apple has explicitly formulated the notion of a substance or continuant. One might object to the notion of a "purely sensory experience" by saying that any experience in which one learns that an observable object has an observable quality is one in which one has learned that some observable object exists, and thus has dispositicnal properties not now being observed; one might also say, as is done here, that a "purely sensory experience" is more complex than it might appear.

EXPERIENCES WITH, AND EXPERIENCES WITHOUT, OBJECTS: THE "FILLING" OF SENSORY EXPERIENCE

Experiences which have content but no (even apparent) object do not purport to present information about mind-independent objects; they provide information—to the effect that one is dizzy, or feels tired, or feels nauseous, or the like, and if one knows what physiological conditions are associated with these feelings, one can infer that one's body is in whichever condition is associated with one's feelings, though such conclusions may be mistaken. Experiences which have objects do purport to present information about those objects; they do seem to their subjects to be experiences of objects, and those objects seem to those subjects to have certain properties—properties which vary from experience to experience. Had "experiences with only content" not already been used contrastively with "experiences which have objects," one could say "properties which vary as the contents of the experiences vary."

Suppose that at time **t** Ralph sees a white circle on a red background, and at **t + 1** sees a red circle on a white background; these experiences differ in an obvious way—one might say that they have different *sensory fillings,* indeed that the second experience has a reverse sensory filling from that of the first. Experiences which have objects, then, purport to present information about those objects; they do seem to their subjects to be experiences of objects, and those objects seem to those subjects to have certain properties, properties which vary as the sensory fillings of the experiences vary.[4]

SENSORY EXPERIENCE AS EVIDENCE

If there can be experiential evidence—if experience can provide evidence in favor of, or against, a proposition—then if it now sensorily seems to Ralph that there is a large dalmatian in his garden, he has evidence for the proposition *There is a large dalmatian in my garden now.* Of course Ralph may be mistaken; this does not mean that the experience is not evidence for the proposition in question. Nonetheless, that one at time **t** has an experience **E** which has a sensory filling of a sort appropriate to **E** being evidence for proposition **P** does not entail that one takes **E** to be evidence for **P**. **P** might not cross one's mind at **t**, or ever cross one's mind. One may believe (correctly or not) that **P** is false, or know that **P** is false, and so not take **E** to be evidence for **P**. Ralph might do this if he resides in Illinois and unreservedly if incorrectly believes that all dalmatians reside in Russia. One may believe (correctly or not), or know, that **E** is caused in such a way that **E**'s occurrence is not evidence for **P**—that **P**'s being true is in no way relevant to explaining **E**'s occurrence even though **E**'s sensory filling is appropriate to its being evidence for **E**.[5] The circumstances described (save for the first) provide epistemologically interesting conditions under which, so to say, potential evidence does not become actual evidence; in that respect, they differ from one's being too confused, or distracted, or tired, to take **E** to be evidence for **P**.

4. In a technical use of the term, experiences of this outer-directed sort often are called "intentional."

5. Alternatively, one may have, or think one has, evidence that **P** is false, which at **t** is parried by **E,** so that one is unsure whether to think **P** is true—but then one is taking **E** to be evidence for **P**.

SENSORY EXPERIENCE AND EXPERIENCE OF GOD

No one, the Bible says, has seen God at any time; Judeo-Christian monotheism does not regard God as a proper object of any sensory modality, or as an object common to any two or more. So no sensory experience, whatever its sensory filling, can be an experience of God.[6] Unless, then, there is some sort of experience, other than sensory, which presents itself as being an experience of something that is distinct from, and independent of, the subject of the experience, no experiential evidence for the existence of God is available.

In fact, people have claimed to experience God. Some of them, no doubt, have been insane. But then, no doubt, all of those who have been insane have claimed to experience physical objects, and only some of them have claimed to experience God. Presumably this does not discredit the claim that there are objects, or that people encounter them.

THE "FILLING" OR PHENOMENOLOGY OF NUMINOUS EXPERIENCE

A standard term for alleged experience of God is *numinous* experience, and its classic characterization goes something as follows. The subject, on the one hand, has a sense of being in some manner in the presence of a being who at least seems to have certain properties; on the other hand, the subject has certain responses to this sense of being in the presence of a being who at least seems to have these properties. The former is the core of the experience; the responses are conditioned by, or are functions of, the at least apparent existence of a being who seems worthy of attention. Perhaps, then, an accurate, more specific description of numinous experience—at least in its fullest manifestation—can be given in these terms. Using "seems" again so that what seems to be so may not, but also may, be so, the subject of a numinous experience in which the features of such experience are rather fully manifested—the subject, one might say, of a paradigmatic or *standard* numinous experience—seems to experience an awesome being, one who is absolutely unapproachable save on terms he dictates, to whom the appropriate response is not simple fear, but reverence or awe; the subject seems to experience a majestic and overpowering being and the subject

6. It does not follow that no experience with sensory components can be experience of God. Cf. Isaiah 6 or Exodus 3.

seems to be dependent on this being, and thus has a feeling of being a creature in the presence of the creator, a feeling which includes humility as well as dependency; the subject seems to experience a being who is unique in kind and intensely alive, whose presence is compelling, fascinating, positive, welcoming, and yet fearsome and in no way to be toyed with or taken for granted, and to whom worship is the appropriate response; the subject seems to experience a morally pure and righteous being, and feels a sense of guilt and sinfulness.

Numinous experience, then, is a complex phenomenon; the subject seems to experience a being which[7] it would be laughable to regard as somehow the product, and not the object, of the experience; whatever the facts of the matter, the subject seems to be aware of something—more carefully, someone—distinct from and independent of himself or herself.

Numinous experience, then, has what one might call, not a sensory, but a *theistic* or at least a *numinous* filling; it is a sense of the presence of a numinous being which a theist who supposes such experiences to be veridical will identify as God. There is no strict entailment from *A being exists which has the properties the object of standard numinous experience appears to have* to *God exists*; theism ascribes to God properties which the object of standard numinous experiences does not appear to have.[8] Theological description goes beyond the theistic filling of numinous experience, a fact to be dealt with at the appropriate time. Setting this fact aside for the moment, experiences do occur which have a "filling" of a nonsensory kind and which seem[9] to be experiences of a being who is awesome, living, majestic, overpowering, unique, righteous, and the like.

The fairly standard way of referring to how things seem to the subject of an experience is to talk of the *phenomenology* or *phenomenological description* of an experience; a phenomenological description of one's experience E gives an account of how things seem to one to be while one is having E.[10] Perceptual experience has one

7. At least "from within the experience," or while one was having the experience.

8. Which is not the same as ascribing to God properties which the object of standard numinous experiences appears *not* to have.

9. In the sense of "seems" which is compatible with things being, but also with their not being, as they seem.

10. The fairly standard way of putting the point made above by using a particular, neutral sense of "seems" is made by talk of "bracketing"—i.e., remaining neutral concerning the veridicality—of the experience.

sort of phenomenological description, numinous experience has another. As noted, both sorts of experience involve their subjects seeming to be aware of a type of entity—one sort in the case of sensory, another sort in the case of numinous—which exists distinct from, and independent of, the subject of experience and distinct from, and independent of, the experience. So there are experiences which are candidates for being evidence for God's existence, or at least the existence of a numinous being.[11]

SENSORY AND NUMINOUS EXPERIENTIAL EVIDENCE: A CRITIQUE AND A REPLY

If there is experiential evidence for any existential proposition, perceptual experiences provide evidence that there are physical objects; it is arbitrary not to add that if perceptual experiences provide evidence that there are physical objects, numinous experience provides evidence that God exists, unless there is some epistemically relevant difference between sensory and numinous experience. The crucial similarities are that both sorts of experience are "intentional" and have phenomenologies, or can be expressed via "intentional" phenomenological descriptions. That perceptual experiences have sensory fillings or phenomenologies, and numinous experiences do not, by itself seems no more reason to think that numinous experience in no way supports the proposition *There is a God* than does the fact that numinous experiences have theistic fillings or phenomenologies, and perceptual experiences do not, by itself provides reason for thinking that perceptual experience in no way supports the proposition *There are physical objects.*

It is true that not everyone has numinous experiences, while everyone has perceptual experiences. But not everyone has *visual* perceptual experiences, or *auditory* ones, or *tactual* ones, and so on. So long as many persons have had numinous experiences, and so long as numinous experiences occur to persons at various periods of human history, in a wide variety of cultures—so long as they are spread across much of space and time, so to speak—the fact that everyone has (some variety of) perceptual experience and, apparently, not everyone has numinous experience seems nothing like a sufficient reason for thinking that numinous experience in no way

11. Since the fact that theological description outruns the phenomenology of numinous experience has been noted, and will be discussed, the qualifying phrase following "or" hereafter will be dropped.

supports *God exists.* After all, *God exists* is true only if one particular being exists; otherwise, it is false. But *There are physical objects* is true if, not only any one of an indeterminable if not infinite number of objects exists, but if any of a very large set of *types* of objects has at least one member. It may well be that more persons have seen their hands than have had numinous experiences, but perhaps more persons have had numinous experiences than have seen albino elephants; it would be silly to rank *There are hands, There is a God,* and *There are albino elephants* in descending order of plausibility on these grounds. Sheer cardinality of experiences seems basically irrelevant here.

A more reasonable cause for concern is this. Suppose Ralph sees a table in the corner. If this experience is veridical, then presumably (assuming Ralph and Ruth to be perceptually normal) if Ruth looks in the same corner, Ruth will see a table; if this does not happen, then either Ralph hallucinated or there is some explanation as to why Ruth fails to see what Ralph saw—but the expectation is that Ruth will see the table. But suppose Ralph, perhaps upon having prayed for one, has a numinous experience; one cannot presume that Ruth, even if Ruth offers prayer to the same purport, will have a numinous experience. Of course, that Ruth has no such experience is (in principle) explicable, but there is no (justified) expectation that Ruth will have a numinous experience. Nor can it be presumed that Ralph can repeat his numinous experience at will, though Ralph can look at the table again and again, as often as he wishes.

There are these differences; why do they obtain? The explanations concerning numinous experience differ depending on whether the experience is veridical. Suppose Ralph's numinous experience is in fact an experience of God. Then presumably the explanation will be that God is sovereign, making himself known to whom he will, when and as he wills; were one able to guarantee his presence in numinous experience by asking to have such an experience, God would not be sovereign—he would be like the genii who came, and had to come, when Aladdin rubbed his lamp. But such a being would not be God. On the other hand, suppose Ralph's experience is not veridical, and, further, that no one's is. Then presumably the explanation refers purely to the natural causes of numinous experience. The explanation may be very complex, and perhaps we never shall know how to state it fully. These possible explanations are relevant to both the differences noted—the fact Ruth may not have a numinous experience, and yet Ralph may have one, even though at the same time and in the same place both pray to have one, and the fact that Ralph may have a numinous experience at time **t** and not have one at **t + 1**, even though Ralph is in the same place, and offers the same prayer on both occasions. Indeed, numinous experiences tend just to come, unbidden and unsought by those who have them.

The net effect of all this is that, in one respect, perceptual experience is public or shared, and numinous experience is private or unshared, and that while one can predict what will happen when one perceives a physical object—what one will perceive if one changes the perceptual perspective or uses others of one's sensory modalities or does one thing or another with the object—no similar predictions are possible regarding numinous experience or its putative object. Perceptual objects are public and predictable, God is private and unpredictable; so the critique goes, and it has a point.

Suppose, however, that Ralph's numinous experience **E** at **t** is veridical; roughly, that God exists, and is object (and so cause) of **E**. Then what can one rationally expect? What one can expect was noted above; God will be sovereign, and will not be known save on his terms. Revelation cannot be coerced; genuine knowledge follows the contours of its object rather than forcing the object into contours of its own. As God differs from physical objects, experience of God will differ from experience of physical objects; the latter set of differences will be a function of the former. So the reply goes, and it has a point.

THE SITUATION AFTER CRITIQUE AND REPLY

Both critique and reply have a point; with what result? It is true that absence of predictability in the case of numinous experience—absence of ability to project from one particular or specific numinous filling at time **t** to another particular or specific numinous filling at time **t1**—appears to mean the absence of one way of checking the veridicality of numinous experience. One cannot argue *If Ralph's numinous experience* **E1** *at time* **t** *has filling* **F1** *and is veridical, then at* **t + 1** *Ralph (or Ruth) will have a numinous experience* **E2** *such that* **E2** *has filling* **F2** in the way one can argue *If Ralph's perceptual experience at time* **t** *in which it seems to Ralph that there is an apple on the table is veridical then at* **t + 1** *Ralph (or Ruth) will feel a firm smooth object when he (or she) puts his (or her) hand where the apple seems to be.* But this is decisive, or even particularly important, only if there is no adequate way to check and see whether a numinous experience is veridical.

TWO QUESTIONS ABOUT EXPERIENTIAL EVIDENCE

Two questions should be distinguished: (i) is there any way of telling whether some numinous experience or other—whether *at least one* numinous experience—is veridical? and (ii), is there any way of telling whether some particular numinous experience—whether *this* numinous experience—is veridical? Comparable queries of course can be raised regarding perceptual experience: (i) is there any way of telling whether some perceptual experience or other is veridical: whether *at least one* perceptual experience is veridical? (ii) is there any way of telling whether some particular perceptual experience—whether *this* perceptual experience—is veridical? In each case, the first question asks whether *a certain sort* of experience has cognitive value or provides reliable information about what there is; the second question asks whether *a certain experience* has cognitive value or provides reliable information about what there is. Just as one who supposes perceptual experience has cognitive value can admit that some perceptual experiences are not veridical, and indeed must do so if, given various perceptual experiences, the same thing seems to have incompatible properties, so one who supposes numinous experience has cognitive value can admit that some numinous experiences are not veridical, and indeed must do so if, given various numinous experiences, God seems to have incompatible qualities.

Each question (i) is distinct from, but also related to, its corresponding question (ii). Suppose one finds that if one supposes that some numinous experience is veridical[12] one can distinguish between genuine and counterfeit numinous experiences. Among the ways actually appealed to are these: genuine, or veridical, numinous experiences conform to, at least by way of being consistent with, if not by way of involving descriptions which embody, orthodox doctrine; their phenomenology has a positive tone or "sweetness"; they lead to conduct which is morally elevated[13] and their subjects are morally good persons; counterfeit, or nonveridical, numinous

12. Which is tantamount to supposing that God exists, provided one can deal with the gap noted above between *There is a being who is the object of numinous experience* and *God exists*.

13. Given the criteria accepted by the tradition within which the experiences occur, or the subject of experience lives.

experiences involve descriptions of God which do not conform to orthodox doctrine, their phenomenology has a negative tone or "sourness," they lead to morally unacceptable conduct, and their subjects are not morally good persons. So long as orthodox theology and ethics are true, and the then very plausible proposition *Experience of God will corrupt neither orthodox theology nor ethics* is accepted, some such criteria as those mentioned, not surprisingly, are appropriate. The epistemically interesting questions concern how the theology and ethics were justified. An answer to question (ii) which in effect reads *there is an affirmative answer to (ii) provided there is one to (i)* is not very satisfactory unless one can offer an affirmative answer to question (i). This is so for the (i)/(ii) questions concerning perception, as well as the (i)/(ii) questions concerning numinous experience.

"INTENTIONALITY"

There is something about the perceptual version of (i) which, if not exactly perverse, is at least puzzling. Suppose that at **t** Ralph seems to see a duck-billed platypus. There is a way to test whether this experience Ralph has at **t** is veridical; Ralph can look again, or try to carefully pick the creature up or stroke its back, or listen for platypus noises, or sniff for platypus odors, or even run his tongue gently over its forehead in search of a platypus taste. But suppose one wonders whether any of these perceptual experiences is veridical; suppose one questions whether *any* perceptual experience has cognitive value. Suppose, that is, one really presses the formulation of (i) that concerns perception. What will rationally assuage this sceptical thirst?

Various attempts have been made. One involved trying to "translate" statements about the existence and properties of physical objects into statements about only ideas (conceived as mental states) or about only qualities (conceived as physical states or processes which required no enduring substance or continuant); such "translations" would be successful only if they met the condition that the physical-object-statement was true if and only if the translating statement was true, and the consensus is that this condition was never met. Analogously, attempts have been made to "translate" statements about God into statements about human feelings and beliefs, or the like; their success would require that they meet the same condition just noted (identity of truth-conditions between translat*ing* and translat*ed* statements), and the condition, again, was not met. Or one simply tried to replace physical-object-language by sense-data language, or language only about ideas or the like, with no pretense of translation, the basic claim being that one can describe the sensory fillings of perceptual experiences as well without making use of physical object-concepts as one can with them. The analogous claim regarding numinous experience is that one could describe its numinous filling—even at its fullest or most developed—as well without as with the concept of God. The most important problem with these claims is that they simply seem false; our perceptual experience has sensory filling and seems to be of objects, and numinous experience has theistic filling and seems to be of God. The *seeming-to-be-experience-of-something-distinct-from-and-independent-of-oneself* feature of perceptual experience, noted earlier, is often called[14] "intentional"; perceptual experiences have an intentional phenomenology. This feature prevents the "translation" and replacement strategies from being successful. Numinous experience also is intentional; the different "fillings" or phenomenologies of perceptual and numinous experiences provide the grounds for different phenomenological descriptions of their putative objects.

INTENTIONALITY AND EVIDENCE

One might argue that, by itself, the intentionality of perceptual and numinous experience does not guarantee their cognitive value or veridicality as sorts of experience; it does not necessitate an affirmative answer to the (i) questions raised above. Perhaps this can be defended by considering the following argument. Suppose that one discovers, living in the center of Transylvania, a timid creature named Fearful. Fearful lives in a one-room house whose single room is lined with mirrors. The room is rife with bookcases which are packed with books whose content can be surmised by noting the title of a representative volume: *History and Habits of Vampires: Dracula and His Household.* Fearful never goes out at night. He keeps revolvers loaded with silver bullets, on each bookcase, on his desk, and under his pillow. Each day he shops for his loaf of bread, bottle of wine, pound of cheese, and bag of apples, and, on his way home, purchases water and wafers from the Transylvanian National Church near his home; he daily pours the water over his doorstep and stuffs

14. After Franz Brentano's technical use of the phrase.

the wafers in the cracks around his windows. He requires that the shopkeeper, the priest, and anyone else with whom contact, alas, is unavoidable, look into a mirror at an angle from which he devoutly hopes he will see their reflection, and every word and movement reveals his constant terror. It seems fair to conclude that Fearful is afraid, and that his fear is fear of vampires in general, and Dracula in particular. His fear is intentional; it is outer-directed or is a fear of something, not being merely a case of generalized anxiety, and its being a fear of Dracula is what gives it its peculiar flavor and force. For all that, Fearful's unhappy autobiography is not proof, or even evidence, that among the things that are, Dracula is to be found.

Between Fearful's fear of Dracula on the one hand, and perceptual and numinous experience on the other, there is a relevant similarity and a relevant difference. The relevant similarity is that as use of the concept of Dracula, or at least of a vampire, is essential to describing the fear—to faithfully representing the experience's phenomenology—so use of the concept of a physical object is essential to describing perceptual experience and use of the concept of God is essential to describing numinous experience. The relevant difference is that fear of Dracula does not present itself as experience of Dracula, whereas perceptual experience does present itself as experience of objects and numinous experience does present itself as experience of God. This phenomenological fact is reflected in the corresponding fact that S *fears* X does not entail X *exists,* whereas S *has perceptual/numinous experience of* X does entail X *exists.*

THE DENIAL OF "INTENTIONALITY" TO PERCEPTUAL AND NUMINOUS EXPERIENCE

If neither translation nor replacement strategies remove perceptual evidence for objects or numinous experience as evidence for God, one nonetheless might bite the bullet and simply deny that any experience is ever evidence for any existential claim, or at least for any such claim other than those concerning one's own existence and states. One way to ground this denial would be to assert these experiences do not have intentional phenomenologies; but the fact seems to be that they do, as is reflected by the use of substantival concepts[15] to describe that phenomenology and by the entailments noted in the preceding paragraph. Another way to ground it would be to deny that one's having experiences which seemed to be experiences of objects or God ever was evidence that there are objects or is a God; it is hard to distinguish this from the denial that experience ever is evidence for the existence of anything other than oneself or one's states. And this denial seems mistaken.

Perhaps this can be seen in the following way. Suppose Ralph seems to see a black cat walking down the hall. There are many ways in which whatever evidence this experience provides for *There is a black cat in the hall* might be overcome; the relevant point is that one who, in the circumstances noted, wishes to contend that the hall is free of cats has something of epistemic relevance to overcome. Put generally and positively, the point is: *If one seems to experience an* **x**, *then this is some evidence that there is an* **x**; put generally and negatively, the point is: *if Ralph seems to experience an* **x** *and Ruth denies that there are any* **x***'s, and Ruth wishes to justify this denial, then Ruth must present weightier grounds for the denial than Ralph's experience provides against it.*

In sum: if one has experience **E**, and **E** has an intentional phenomenology such that it phenomenologically seems to one that one is experiencing **x**, this is some evidence that **X** *exists* is true. If the "filling" is perceptual, "X" will be replaced by some term referring to a physical object; if the filling is numinous, "X" will be replaced by "God," or at any rate by some such locution as "a numinous being." At least, this seems correct; it seems so even though there are the differences between numinous and sensory experiences noted above—differences regarding a publicity and predictability which sensory experiences possess and numinous experiences lack, because if numinous experience is veridical, then it will differ in that sort of way from perceptual experience. Were numinous experience like perceptual in those ways, it would not be very plausible to take it to be veridical, since a numinous being—a being of the sort one encounters in numinous experience, if that sort of experience is veridical—is not one which is predictable and experimentally accessible. Or, if one prefers, an experience of a predictable and experimentally accessible being would not be a numinous experience after all.

15. Concepts of substances or continuants.

DISTINGUISHING VERIDICAL FROM NONVERIDICAL "INTENTIONAL" EXPERIENCES

Yet one may be forgiven for not yet being persuaded. How, exactly, will one tell if a numinous experience is nonveridical, and isn't it possible that all numinous experiences are just that? Indeed, isn't that plausible as well as possible, since one can produce numinous experiences by the use of drugs?

THE POSSIBILITY OF ERROR

It is logically possible that all numinous experiences are nonveridical; it also is logically possible that all sensory experiences are nonveridical. Unless some variety of the ontological argument succeeds, *God does not exist* is not a contradiction. Both *There is no numinous being* and *There are no physical objects* are logically consistent; so are *No one ever experiences God (or any numinous being)* and *No one experiences any physical object.* But that the denials of these propositions are logically contingent is no reason to deny that these denials enjoy experiential support.

COMPETING EXPERIENTIAL EVIDENCE

What sometimes defeats a sensory experience, or shows it not to be veridical, is other sensory experiences which (i) seem to be experiences of the same object as the one they defeat, and (ii) cannot be veridical if the defeated experience is. Correspondingly, it seems possible that some numinous experiences defeat others, and something like this happens when there is a series of numinous experiences in which the object appears to have one character in the earlier experiences but in the later ones seems both to have a different character and to explain that the earlier experiences, at least in part, were given to instruct, or test, their subject.

DRUG INTAKE AND EXPERIENTIAL EVIDENCE

Further, while it is true that within limits, and under controlled conditions, it seems that if a person is given the right sort of drug dosage, he or she is far more likely to have a numinous experience (or its carbon copy, or at least its experiential cousin) than if he or she is in the same sort of conditions and is not given any drug, it is also true that within limits, and under controlled conditions, it seems that if a person is given the right amount of "white lightning," he or she is far more likely to have a perceptual experience of vermin crawling over the walls (or its carbon copy, or at least its experiential cousin) than if he or she is in the same sort of conditions and is not given any white lightning.

From all this, it seems to follow that if Ralph has been given the right sort of drug dosage to produce a numinous, or near-numinous, experience, the occurrence of that experience will not do much to epistemically enhance the claim that there is a numinous being or that God exists, for we (and he) will be in a good position to explain that experience without our making any reference to God, just as it follows that if Ralph has had enough alcohol to produce the perceptual, or near-perceptual, experience of seeming to see vermin, the occurrence of that experience will not do much to epistemically enhance the claim that the walls are covered with vermin, for we (and he) will be in a good position to explain that experience without our making any reference to vermin. Ralph, in these cases, may experience God or the vermin, but the experiences (numinous in the former case, perceptual in the latter) will not be *evidence* that this is so. But it is not clear why any of this should affect the epistemic status of cases in which numinous experience occurs without drugs having been taken, or walls are seen as vermin-infested without any white lightning having been imbibed.

EXPLANATIONS OF NUMINOUS EXPERIENCES

Still, this fact that if we can explain a numinous experience by reference to drug intake, we are in a good position to set aside the notion that it has evidential force, or supports the claim that God exists, may well suggest a more general line of reasoning. Various explanations have been offered of the fact that persons have had numinous experiences. Some have been psychological, perhaps noting that persons have a deep-seated need to live in a comfortable and sympathetic cosmic environment, and positing a complex of psychological mechanisms which both transmute this need into an experience which appears to be of a being who fulfills it and disguise the process of transmutation from those in whom it occurs. Some are sociological, perhaps contending that the sense of objective authority attaching to mores and patterns of living, an authority which indeed is external to the individual but is objective only in the sense that it resides in the society, nonetheless is given a status as attaching to a superperson who is allegedly experienced on occasions of special importance. Others are anthropological, or economic, or whatever. There are no such explanations of the fact that persons have sensory experiences—that persons seem to walk on sidewalks and open doors and taste salads. So sensory experience must be in one epistemic condition, and numinous experience in another; we are able to offer explanations of the existence of numinous experience which can be completely true even if God does not exist, but we are not in a position to explain the occurrence of sensory experiences in ways which do not require the existence of physical objects. Further, this difference is absolutely crucial, for what it means is that while sensory experience indeed is evidence that there are physical objects, numinous experience is not evidence that God exists; still further, no amount of appeal to the intentional phenomenology of numinous experience will set aside this critique, for the critique grants that numinous experience has that phenomenology, but notes that delirium tremens experiences (such as the white lightning-inspired perception of vermin), plus alleged sightings of ghosts and leprechauns and trolls and all manner of "little people," also have an intentional phenomenology without this fact doing very much for the epistemic credibility of such experiences. Unless this argument, too, can be met and defeated, the status of numinous experience as evidence seems minimal at best.

"EXPERIENCE OF" AND "EXPERIENCE WHICH PROVIDES INFORMATION ABOUT"

One might attempt to evade rather than meet this argument by some such line of reasoning as this. An experience can provide information about God without being an experience of God. For example, suppose that at the moment of creation, or at some time t^n long prior to time **t**, God determined that at **t** Ralph should have an experience in which Ralph reflects for the first time in his life about whether there is a God or not, and finds welling up within him a deep conviction that there is. Under the supposition noted, at **t** Ralph had an experience which provided him with information about God, but which was not an experience of God. One, then, might claim that either a numinous experience is an experience of God, or else it is experience which provides information about God, and it does not really matter which.

The notion of an "experience which provides information about God" is ambiguous. It might mean that there are experiences whose occurrence provides evidence that some proposition about God is true; then Ralph's hypothetical experience, just recounted, is not such an experience, for, by itself, a person's thinking about *God exists* and coming to have a conviction that it is true is not *evidence* that it is true. It might mean that there are experiences in which persons come to believe propositions about God which are true although those experiences are not evidence for those propositions; but then there will have to be some reason to believe that the propositions in question in fact are true. The first sense, then, seems to be the relevant one, and if any numinous experiences are veridical, *experiences of God* seem to be a subclass of *experiences which provide information about God* if there are instances of the latter which are not instances of the former; otherwise, their extension presumably will be identical, even if it is null. The problem with this attempt to evade the argument just presented is this: numinous experience, viewed as experience of God, or at least of a numinous being, potentially provides evidence that God, or at least a numinous being, exists. The argument recited above challenges that claim. In order to escape the brunt of the argument, the "defense," such as it is, suggests that perhaps numinous experience is experience which "provides information about God," and the relevant sense of that phrase seems to be "provides evidence for some proposition about God" (albeit, in this case, not by being an experience of him). But then we need some reason for thinking that a numinous experience provides information about God, without its being construed as being an experience of God. That line of reasoning is not very promising; probably it is better that one deal with the critical argument directly.

THE EPISTEMOLOGICAL CONSEQUENCES OF EXPLANATIONS OF NUMINOUS EXPERIENCE

The relevant explanations of numinous experience all share this feature: they require the truth of neither *God exists* nor *God does not exist.* Also, they must be complex enough to account for the fact that not everyone ever has a numinous experience; perhaps more do not have such experiences than do. Yet presumably those who do, and those who do not, may have the same deep need to live in a comfortable and sympathetic cosmic environment, or the same sense of objective authority, or whatever.

In those who do not have numinous experience, presumably

something blocks the functioning of the relevant mechanisms (or whatever) which would otherwise produce the experience. It is treacherously easy to suppose that this must be the superior rationality, or greater maturity, of those who lack the experience, though if one considers some of those who have had such experiences and some of those who have not, this contention becomes highly implausible, so the temptation will be to choose irrational and immature persons as representatives of those who have had numinous experiences and rational and mature persons as representatives of those who lack the experience. This strategy is easily reversed. The fact that some persons do, and others do not, have numinous experience, and the further fact that a psychological (or sociological, or whatever) theory intended to account for numinous experience in such a manner that it is not construed as experience of God, or any independently existing numinous being, must account for this lack of universality, of course does not show, or even tend to show, that no such explanation can succeed. But it will be necessary that these facts be explained not only (i) without supposing that God does not exist but also (ii) *without supposing that it is unreasonable to think that he exists, unless this is shown to be true* and (iii) *without supposing that those who have numinous experiences are somehow less mature (or the like) than those who do not—unless this is shown, using a standard for maturity which is either itself part of, or entailed by, theism, or else independently established on its own.* Sensitive to (i), some such explanations are utterly insensitive to (ii) and/or (iii), as they betray not the faintest recognition that theistic belief should be *shown* to be unreasonable if the explanation requires that it be so, or that some standard of the sort mentioned in (iii) be established if the alleged emotional immaturity (or the like) on the part of those who have numinous experiences is assumed by the explanation. This is not relevant to an explanation which simply claimed that all numinous experiences are produced by drugs; but that claim is historically false.

Explanations of numinous experience which are intended in any fashion to discredit theism[16] tend to include some violation of (i), (ii), or (iii). The appearance of such violations within the scope of explanations of the occurrence of religious experience is to make

16. Or to discredit numinous experience as evidence for theism. Explanations which are not of this sort, however interesting in themselves, are irrelevant here.

them dubious, for they include, at crucial points, commitment to propositions—to judgments about the reasonableness of beliefs or the maturity of persons (or the like)—which are not obviously true or themselves justified by the theory. This situation is analogous to one (or more) premises of an argument being such that we have no good reason to accept it (or them).

This leads to some features that all actual explanations of religious experience seem to possess. These explanations occur within the context of, or themselves partly comprise, general theories in the discipline within which they occur. These theories, in turn, tend to have one, or else both, of two features. One is that they are not universally accepted within the field, but have rivals which are of roughly equal plausibility and which (if they deal with the matter) offer different and competing explanations of religious experience and belief; and in this last respect they are potentially if not actually in conflict as well with theories from other disciplines which also endeavor to explain religious phenomena. The other, not unrelated, feature is that they contain propositions about the structure of human nature, or of society, or of the primitive mind, or of mythology and language, or of sexuality, or whatever, which are both highly theoretical and hardly on solid epistemic ground. These propositions (which are not likely to be identical to those referred to in (ii) and (iii) above, but may be part of what motivated the acceptance of those propositions) are crucial to, and in large part may be, the theory which is used to explain the occurrence of numinous experience; but the observational evidence for such propositions may be scant or nonexistent and the complex of inferences involved in arriving at them rather than other, incompatible propositions not so clear and cogent as to be very convincing to a defender of a competing theory or to an honest doubter. One even can be forgiven for comparing such propositions to the propositions of a theology, and wonder whether the former are any more easily assessed, or more firmly tied to empirical evidence, or more clearly founded on valid inference from premises known to be true, or the like, than the latter.

It, then, is not clear that the explanations offered for the occurrence of numinous experience have particularly impressive epistemic credentials. Nor is there any generally accepted theory of this sort, though that there were would be relevant only if the agreement was produced by good reasons for thinking the explanation true. The argument presented here has not been a matter of noting that there are various theories so that each is improbable; rather, attention has been focused on the features of the theories which cause their critics to hesitate to accept them. The relevant question is not how many explanations there are, but rather whether any of them lacks the sorts of defects we have been considering; none seems to do so.

NONEPISTEMIC CONTRIBUTING CAUSES

A different feature of explanations of numinous experience deserves attention. An explanation of this sort typically refers to something that is said to be the cause of a numinous experience—to something which allegedly produces the experience, not always, but under certain conditions. Usually, perhaps always, it is not clear that what is said to produce the experience is more than a contributing cause; the effect of discovering a contributing cause of numinous experience on the epistemic status of numinous experience is not clear, even though the contributing cause be utterly nonepistemic in the sense of not providing evidence for the belief to whose occurrence it contributes (as it will be). So the effect of the explanation which enshrines the discovery on the epistemic status of numinous experience is not clear either.

CAUSALLY NECESSARY CONDITIONS

This point can be understood in contrast to a similar-sounding, but actually quite different, contention. Sometimes, causality is defined in terms of causally necessary conditions;[17] when this occurs, the idea is as follows. A causally necessary condition of something **x** at time **t** is anything whose failure to occur would result in **x**'s not existing at **t**. A necessary condition of Ralph's being alive at **t** is that oxygen be present at **t** in Ralph's environment; another is that Ralph not have been decapitated at **t-1**. Suppose Ralph's great-grandparents were both very shy and a bit eccentric; his grandfather took walks only on the prairie under a full moon and his grandmother took a walk only on the prairie on the evening when the first frost of the year was on the ground. Happily for Ralph, the first frost came on a night when the moon was full, for if his future

17. After this fashion: **x**'s cause = **all** of the causally necessary conditions (= the causally sufficient conditions) of **x**.

grandparents were going to meet, it would be as they both walked on the prairie.

EXHAUSTIVE, COMPLETE, AND ADEQUATE EXPLANATIONS

One might distinguish, then, between an *exhaustive,* a *complete,* and an *adequate* explanation of Ralph's existence. An *exhaustive* explanation would refer to all the necessary conditions of Ralph's existence, and *their* necessary conditions, and so on, without end, to the beginning, or else forever; an explanation of this sort would include reference to the concurrence of the full moon and the first frost in the year when Ralph's grandparents met, and so on and on. A *complete* explanation will not go back to Ralph's grandparents, let alone beyond them; it will specify only those phenomena which obtain at **t** which are such that, if they fail to obtain at **t**, *Ralph exists* will be false at **t** (or, perhaps: those phenomena which are such that, had they not obtained at **t-1**, *Ralph exists* would be false at **t**); it will include all the necessary conditions that are contemporaneous with (or, perhaps, are immediately precedent to) the phenomenon being explained; this presumably would yield the contemporaneous (or immediately precedent) sufficient conditions[18] of that phenomenon. In fact, of course, it is not reasonable to expect either an exhaustive, or a complete, explanation of anything. To accuse an explanation of numinous experience of failing to be exhaustive or complete will be to utter a truth without launching a critique. An explanation is *adequate* if it is offered within a discipline (physics, anthropology, psychology, history, theology, etc.) whose standards it meets; this will involve both the explaining phenomenon (or *explicans*) and the phenomenon explained (or *explicandum*) being described in the language of the theory, the relation between the *explicans* and the *explicandum* being of the sort that the theory regards as explanatory (e.g., *attraction* in Newtonian physics, *sublimation* in Freudian psychology), and it will require that the *explicans* refer only to entities and relations the theory treats as primitive or be able itself to become the *explicandum* in an explanation (or series of explanations) which refers only to such items. Adequacy, then, is discipline-relative, and, no doubt, time-relative within a disci-

18. That is, those conditions of an event **x** such that if they obtain, then **x** obtains.

pline. The most that can be expected of an explanation of numinous experience is that it be, not exhaustive or complete, but adequate. Such explanations will isolate one sort of phenomenon the occurrence of which, in the presence of "background conditions," will be accompanied by numinous experience. What will not be clear, however, is whether the occurrence of that phenomenon, in the presence of background conditions, is sufficient to explain the occurrence of the experience; that is not decided, even if it is decided that the explanation is adequate.

SUFFICIENT EXPLANATIONS

"Sufficient" in the sentence immediately preceding cannot mean "exhaustive" or "complete," for explanations of that sort are never available; what can it mean? Suppose one learns that a colleague who ordinarily is compassionate to a fault has refused to provide help of a sort only he can give to a student who needs it badly. One then meets the colleague's insurance agent in the hall and discovers that the colleague's son has just "totaled" the family car, escaping with minor injuries, but that unfortunately the insurance coverage lapsed for a few days, during which the accident occurred; upon hearing of the colleague's uncharacteristic lack of compassion, the agent (who hates animals in general, and cats in particular) explains the refusal to provide help by the fact that the colleague had just learned that he will have to bear the cost of the accident himself; that is the sort of explanation that "rings true" to one of her business (and anti-cat) orientation. One sees the relevance of the explanation, but wonders whether even the prospect of bearing the full cost of the accident is enough to explain the refusal. Shortly after talking with the agent, one runs into a colleague who loves cats (and is completely unconcerned about finances). She reveals that the Siamese cat our normally compassionate mutual colleague loves vanished two days ago and has not been seen since, and she explains the uncharacteristic unwillingness to provide help by his deep concern over the whereabouts of his cat; this is the sort of explanation that "rings true" to one of her animal-loving (and unconcern-about-finances) orientation. One then encounters one's colleague himself, who has just phoned the student to offer the previously withheld aid, and sadly reports that neither the financial setback nor the absence of the Siamese would have been enough to cause him to act like that, but, coming together as they did, they were "just too much." Relative to the financier's perspective, the fiscal explanation was adequate; relative to the animal-lover's perspective, the feline explanation was adequate. In the sense of providing an account of all that is relevant, against background conditions, to yield the temporary refusal to provide help, neither the fiscal nor the feline explanation was sufficient.

An explanation offered from a psychological perspective may be adequate in the sense characterized above, and yet a sociologist is likely to fault it. The sociologist may fault it for referring to the wrong sorts of things in the *explicans* (to personal feelings rather than social institutions, for example). But the sociologist may fault it for being "adequate so far as it goes"—*adequate within psychology*, as it were—but for leaving out things that in fact are also relevant in the coming-to-be of the phenomenon being explained, and thus for being *insufficient* in that sense. This can be viewed, not without plausibility, as a consequence of the complexity of the phenomenon under discussion.

Supervised injection of a drug will not automatically or always produce a numinous (or numinous-like) experience; even when the subject of the experiment is placed in circumstances which seem likely to encourage attitudes and feelings sensitive to worship, it may be that no such experience occurs. Perhaps it is not surprising, then, that when no injection is given, it is hard to produce an explanation of the occurrence of a numinous experience which does not appear insufficient in the sense just characterized. But where does all this leave us?

A REVIEW OF SOME RELEVANT POINTS

Various claims relevant to answering this question have been discussed. One is that numinous experience (like perceptual) has an intentional phenomenology. Another is that while perceptual experience can be checked in ways involving publicity (if Ruth and Ralph are in the same sensory environment and Ralph seems to see **x**, the veridicality of Ralph's experience is called in doubt if Ruth does not see **x**) and predictability (if Ralph seems to see **x**, then Ralph will have certain other sensory experiences of specific sorts if Ralph changes visual perspective, touches **x**, etc., or else the veridicality of his experience is called into question), numinous experience cannot; but if numinous experience is veridical, it is not surprising that it lacks publicity and predictability. Still another is that attempts to describe the intentional phenomenology of numinous experience without use of the concept of God (or, at least, of a numinous being), and attempts to translate *God exists* into statements about only the psychological (or other) states of numinous experiencers, fail for the same sorts of reasons as do attempts to describe the intentional phenomenology of perceptual experience without the use of the concept of a physical object, or translate *There are physical objects* into statements about only the sensory (or other) states of perceivers. Again, as some perceptual experiences seem to be of the same object, but cannot all be veridical since then the object would have incompatible qualities, so perhaps some numinous experiences seem to be of the same object, but cannot all be veridical, since then the same God would have incompatible properties.

ASSESSMENT OF PERCEPTUAL AND NUMINOUS EXPERIENTIAL EVIDENCE

This point requires development. Consider that very familiar example of perceptual illusion, a straight stick that appears bent in water. Suppose one looks at the stick twice, once out of the water (it appears to be straight), once partially submerged in the water (it appears to be bent); one also feels it twice, once in and once out of the water, and it feels straight. One joins the rest of humanity in supposing the stick to be straight. This conclusion is poorly defended if it rests only on a vote of 3-1 among the tests one ran; that could change by one's looking twice more at the partially submerged stick. Nor is it a matter, or merely a matter, of objects having, or more often having, the shape they feel like they have rather than the one they visually appear to have, if visual and tactual testimony conflict. A crucial fact is that one can explain the fact that a straight stick will appear to be bent when it is partially submerged, but we cannot explain what a bent-stick-theory proponent would want to be a fact, namely that a bent stick will look straight out of the water (or when fully submerged), nor is this a fact. Another important consideration is that the stick, out of water and fully submerged, visually appears to be straight, and feels straight out of the water, partially submerged, and fully submerged. If we try to discount how it feels, and claim that only how it looks is relevant to deciding what its shape really is, not only do we treat our data arbitrarily, but we have to explain the fact that then the stick changes from straight to bent to straight as it goes from not being submerged to being partially submerged to being fully so, and here, too, we have no theory to help us; so we cannot hold that a stick always is as it visually appears, and must admit that some visual perception or other of the stick is nonveridical. So in the case of claims about objects we can appeal to various sensory modalities; to how things appear to the same modality from different perspectives; to what plausible theories there are which will help us in deciding between experiences **A** and **B** by virtue of its being the case (given some such theory) that we can explain why **A** occurs even though it is not veridical provided we suppose that **B** is veridical but cannot explain why **B** occurs even though it is not veridical provided we suppose that **A** is veridical; and to reports of various perceivers. In the case of claims about God, insofar as they are based on numinous experience, one can appeal to the reports of various persons who have had such experience, comparing their accounts of the nature of the object of their experiences. It is not clear that one has some actual parallel to a perceiver's being able to shift perspective or appeal to other sensory modalities; there will be an analogue to appeal to relevant, plausible theories only if one rationally can decide between competing theological or religious conceptual systems, a matter to be discussed later.[19] One might argue that something analogous to shifting one's perceptual perspective is available in two ways. One is through comparing descriptions of numinous experience which occur within various religious traditions (Judaism, Christianity, Islam, Bhakti Hinduism, etc.). Another, which involves some of the same materials, but involves appeal to a different criterion for selection, is to compare reports of numinous experience from different cultures, and from within the same culture at different periods. Whether or not this is particularly analogous to change of perceptual perspective, such comparisons do seem crucial for any discussion of the question as to whether numinous experience is veridical, and provide relevant considerations as to the epistemic status of any one numinous experience.[20]

THE ARGUMENT FROM RELIGIOUS EXPERIENCE

Given all this, it seems that numinous experience may provide evidence that God exists—at any rate, that its differences from

19. In Chapter 8.
20. Considerations of space prevent this being done here, and to that degree the argument is incomplete.

sensory experience do not preclude its doing so. The argument that it does provide such evidence can be put, somewhat more formally than previously, and in terms of "axioms" of experiential evidence, as follows.

AXIOM ONE: THAT THERE IS EXPERIENTIAL EVIDENCE

It seems true that (A1)* *If it seems to one that one experiences* **x**, *then one who claims that there is no* **x** *or that one perceives no* **x**, *has something of epistemic relevance, some evidence contrary to the claim, to overcome.* "Seems" in (A1)*, it will be remembered, is used phenomenologically in contrast to its use just prior to (A1)* in which it expresses a judgment. (A1)* is true if experiences with intentional phenomenologies ever provide evidence for existential claims regarding items other than their subjects or their subjects' conscious states.

RELEVANCE CONDITIONS

One's seeming to experience an **x** is not a matter of one's having the opinion that one's experience supports some claim. A person who, upon examining the entrails of an unfortunate sparrow, decides that the world will end tomorrow in an attack of omnivorous locusts which devour everything else and then self-destruct, forms an opinion. In the relevant sense of "seems," no such thing has seemed to him to be the case. Not just any experience can count as evidence for just any claim; there are epistemic proprieties. It is not easy to state these proprieties with precision, but perhaps something like the following will suffice. One might have a perceptual, or a numinous, experience which one did not take to be evidence for anything. But suppose one does take such an experience to be evidence for a claim—roughly a claim about what seems to be the object of the experience to the effect that this object has the character that "within the experience" it seems to have. Then we can say something of this sort: (A2) *If one has an experience* E *in which it seems to one that* **x** *has character* N *(i.e., has properties* **P1**, **P2**, *etc.), and if one takes* E *to be evidence for the claim* C *that "***x** *has* N*," then* E *meets the relevance conditions with respect to* C *(and* C *meets the relevance conditions with respect to* E*).*

If one considers (A1)* and (A2) together, then it seems clear that if both of them are true, it is also true that: (A3) *If one has an experience* E *which meets the relevance conditions with respect to claim* C, *one has something of epistemic relevance to overcome, some evidence to the contrary, if one supposes that* C *is false, or that one has no grounds for thinking* C *true.* Having an experience which meets the relevance conditions with respect to a claim puts one in this position with regard to that claim: if one's only information relative to the claim's truth value is one's experience, one's information is to the effect that the claim is true.

AXIOM TWO: WHEN AN EXPERIENCE MEETS RELEVANCE CONDITIONS

That one has an experience which meets the relevance conditions with respect to a claim does not guarantee that one is justified if one accepts the claim. For one thing, one might have other experiences which suggest that the claim is false. As defined in (A2), "relevance conditions" apply only in cases in which one has evidence *in favor of* a claim; further, the claim must be about the alleged character of the alleged object of the experience. But suppose X *has nature* N entails, not only X *does not have nature not-*N, but also X *lacks nature* N1; won't the experience that confirms the claim X *has* N also disconfirm X *has* N1? And suppose theory T is well confirmed and includes the proposition *Anything that has* N *also has* Q. Then X *has nature* N, plus T, will confirm X *has* Q. Under these circumstances, so long as one allowed for the possibility that the distinction, as they say, is only of degree and not of kind, one might say that E is *directly* (and negatively) relevant to X *has* N1 and *indirectly* (and positively) relevant to X *has* Q.

These considerations can be captured by rephrasing (A2) along these lines: one will need (A2a) *If one has an experience* E *in which it seems to one that* x *has character* N *(i.e., has properties* A1, A2, *etc.), and if one takes* E *to be evidence for the claim* C *that* "X *has* N," *then* E *(directly and positively) meets the relevance conditions with respect to* C *(and* C *(directly and positively) meets the relevance conditions with respect to* E*), and* E *(directly and negatively) meets the relevance conditions with respect to any proposition that is logically contradictory or contrary to* C; one will also need: (A2b) E *(indirectly and positively) meets the relevance conditions with respect to any proposition* C1 *such that a well-confirmed theory* T, *plus* C, *entails* C1 *and (indirectly and negatively) meets the relevance conditions with respect to any proposition* C2 *such that a well-confirmed theory* T1, *plus* C, *entails the negation of* C2. This allows that a proposition which *directly* met the relevance conditions with respect to an experience might *indirectly* meet the relevance conditions with respect to two propositions which could not both be true, though that would be due to two well-established theories being incompatible rather than to some epistemic defect in the proposition or the experience. It will be convenient to combine (A2a) and (A2b) into one "axiom" (A2)*.

AXIOM THREE: THAT EXPERIENCES WHICH MEET RELEVANCE CONDITIONS PROVIDE EVIDENCE

In the light of (A2)*, one can rephrase (A3) along these lines: (A3a) *If one has an experience which positively (directly or indirectly) meets the relevance conditions with respect to claim* **C**, *one has something of epistemic relevance to overcome, some evidence to the contrary, if one supposes that* **C** *is false, or that one has no grounds for thinking* **C** *true.* Further, (A3b) *if one has an experience which negatively (directly or indirectly) meets the relevance conditions with respect to claim* **C**, *one has something of epistemic relevance to overcome, some evidence to the contrary, if one supposes that* **C** *is true, or that one has no grounds for thinking* **C** *false.* It will be convenient to combine (A3a) and (A3b) into (A3)*. (A1)*, (A2)*, and (A3)* seem equally appropriate with regard to perceptual or numinous experience.

Suppose that at time **t**, one has a numinous experience which (directly) meets the relevance conditions with respect to *God is holy,* where **X** *is holy* entails something like **X** *is unique, or ontologically set apart from other things,* and **X** *is righteous, or morally pure.* Suppose, however, one has reason to think that one's having the experience at **t** may be explicable in terms of an explanation that meets these conditions: (i) it is compatible with *God exists* and with *God does not exist*; (ii) its *explicans* refers to *natural, nontheistic* conditions **Q** known to obtain relative to one at **t** (or at **t-1**); (iii) its *explicans* refers to generalizations which are well confirmed and are of some such form as *If* **Q** *obtains relative to a person at some time* **t** *(or:* **t-1**) *then that person will (or: is likely to) have an experience of kind* **K** *at* **t**; (iv) while *kind* **K** is described in the (nonnuminous, nontheistic) language of the discipline in which the explanation finds its conceptual context, it is plausible that an experience which is of kind **K** have a "numinous filling" or be phenomenologically numinous. Then one may decide that the experience was not veridical, or one may not be able to decide whether it was veridical or not. After all, one might argue, the sheer "psychological force" of a numinous experience by itself is not evidence that it is veridical; were the "psychological force" of experiences evidence of their veridicality, nightmares would rank higher than they do on the scale of direct evidence about what there is, and while the "psychological force" of the experience might linger on, that is not relevant to the question of the experience's veridicality. On the other hand, the "phenomenologically patent intentionality" of the experience might be distinguished from the experience's "psychological force" and viewed as the cause of that force, and it might be appealed to as evidence. Perhaps, then, one in the circumstances described is just in a quandary about whether the experience was veridical; at any rate, this would seem to be a reasonable state for one to be in under the circumstances described. Weighing the occurrence of the experience on the one hand, against the fact of one's having an explanation of the sort described on the other, is no easy epistemic task.

AXIOM FOUR: EVIDENCE AND EVIDENCE-CANCELING EXPLANATIONS

One might capture part of the source of one's quandary in some such fashion as this: (A4)* *If, at time* t, *one has an experience* E *such that* E *(directly and positively) meets the relevance conditions with respect to claim* C, *and one is aware of an explanation* A *of experience* E *such that (i) "*A *is true" does not entail "*C *is true" or "*C *is false," (ii) together "*A *is true" and "*E *occurs" do not entail or, on balance, provide evidence for "*C *is true," (iii) if* A *is false, and so is every other explanation which, like* A, *satisfies (i) and (ii), then "*E *occurs" does provide evidence for "*C *is true," and (iv) one has better reason to think* A *true than to think* E *veridical, then one has reason to think that, on balance, one's having had* E *is not reason to think that* C *is true.* Decisions as to whether numinous experiences provide evidence that God exists are likely to require that one weigh competing epistemic considerations; in that respect, they resemble a great many epistemic assessments.

At best any actual explanation which satisfies (i)–(iv) in (A4)* will be adequate relative to a discipline. If a numinous experience is veridical, then its theistic explanation, which might be expressed as *God is object, and cause, of the experience,* is true; if a perceptual experience (say, of a redwood) is veridical, the "realistic" explanation, which might be expressed as *A redwood is object, and cause, of the experience,* is true. The "realistic" explanation of a veridical perceptual experience is not "news" to one who has had the experience and accepts it as veridical; an account which traces light waves from object to retina might be "more informative." The theistic explanation of a numinous experience is not "news" to one who has had the experience and accepts it as veridical; an account which specified psychological characteristics found universally or frequently among those who have such experiences, and not among those who do not, might be "more informative." "More informative" here means something like "provides new, and perhaps unexpected, information to the experience's subject." The "natural" explanation, from the subject's viewpoint, of perceptual experience is the "realistic," and of numinous experience is the theistic; but the theoretical context of the natural explanation is often neglected whereas the theoretical context of other explanations looms large. If the theoretical contexts of other explanations are highly plausible, or at least highly prestigious, the "natural" explanation will be, or at least seem, less cogent. On the other hand, it usually is easier to see that an experience directly and positively meets the relevance conditions with respect to a claim C1 than it is to tell that an experience indirectly and positively meets the relevance conditions with respect to a claim C2.

AXIOM FIVE: THEORETICAL CONTEXTS, EXPERIENTIAL EVIDENCE, AND RELATIVE PLAUSIBILITY

Numinous experience has its own theoretical context or contexts, (the varieties of) theism. Call an explanation that is adequate and meets (i–iv) in (A4)* an *evidence-canceling* explanation. If (A4)* is true, then so is something like: (A5)* *If explanation* A1 *of one's experience* E *is at least as plausible as explanation* A2, *where if* A1 *is true, then* E *is veridical with respect to* C *and* A2 *is evidence-canceling with respect to* E *and* C, *and* E *meets the relevance conditions with respect to* C, *and one knows this, then one has better reason to accept than not to accept* C, since the experience itself provides evidence for C, and A2 no more calls it into question than A1 supports it.

Call an explanation A of one's experience E such that A is adequate and if A is true, E is veridical with respect to claim C, *evidence-confirming* with respect to E and C.[21] One might argue that

21. This, of course, assumes that E meets the relevance conditions with regard to C.

if one has experience E, explanation A is evidence-confirming with respect to E and C, and explanations A1 and A2 are evidence-canceling with respect to E and C, and A, A1, and A2 are competing and equiplausible, then since the proposition A1 *or* A2 is more likely true than is A, one (who knows all this) is more reasonable to reject than to accept A. Perhaps this is so; it will be important only if one has a surfeit of evidence-canceling explanations which are equiplausible with a smaller number—perhaps just one—of evidence-confirming explanations. If A and A1 are evidence-confirming, and A2 is evidence-canceling, and A1, A2, and A3 are competing and equiplausible, it will be reasonable for one who knows this to opt for A1 *or* A2 over A3. But this is important only if there is more than one competing evidence-confirming explanation.*

SUFFICIENT EXPLANATION AND CAUSAL DUPLICATION

It is the case that the claim that numinous experience is veridical is not incompatible with perceptual experience being a reliable source of information or that particular sensory experiences be veridical. That theism be true is not incompatible with the truth of psychological or sociological or anthropological explanations. It also seems to be the case, for any single social science explanation (or conjunct of same) that it is not a *sufficient* explanation (in the sense noted above). This last point can be put as follows. Suppose an executive unjustly fires both her secretaries, and both resent it so deeply that they independently conclude that the ultimate revenge is called for. Each independently sets an appointment for the same time and place to treat the executive to coffee, "just to show that there are no hard feelings," and the three meet and sit together in the coffee shop. As the executive talks to one secretary, the other secretary puts enough strychnine to kill several persons into the executive's untouched coffee. As the executive turns to talk to the other secretary, the first puts enough arsenic to kill several persons into the executive's untouched coffee. Then, as always, the executive drinks the whole cup at one gulp. Here is a case of *causal duplication.* Causal duplication occurs when it is true that, given background conditions C, it is true that *If* A *obtains,* D *will obtain* and A *obtains,* and *If* B *obtains,* D *will obtain* and B *obtains.* In these circumstances, D will obtain, and two states of affairs—A and B—

*For an alternative account of Axiom Five, see Appendix.

are such that if either occurs, D will and both A and B obtain. It is not clear, in the case of any social science explanation W, and theistic explanation T, of one's numinous experience E, that *both* T *and* W *are true* provides causal duplication regarding E *occurs.*

One reason for this is that various social science explanations of one's numinous experience E, at least insofar as they issue from different disciplines, need not be competing; if explanations A1, A2, and A3 issue from different disciplines, all three may be true, and it is very likely that there will be no reason to think that their conjunct is sufficient in the sense characterized above, or that their conjunct is such that it, plus the theistic explanation, provides causal duplication regarding E. Part of the reason, in turn, for this is that it is not clear what conditions would be sufficient (in that sense of "sufficient" which is distinct from the sense of either "exhaustive" or "complete") to explain one's numinous experience. Insofar as this is not clear, it is not clear that the theistic explanation is competitive with various social science explanations in the sense that their truth is incompatible with its truth or renders its truth less likely. Any such explanation may provide only a contributing condition to E's occurrence; there is little if any reason to think it provides more. If this is correct, then these explanations will not be evidence-canceling explanations; the social science explanations, not being incompatible with, or evidence against, theism, are not explanations of that sort. Thus they do not counter, or overturn, the evidence numinous experience provides for theism. But even if this is correct, two qualifications should be noted. One concerns a point already raised, namely that *Numinous experience is veridical* entails *A numinous being exists,* but does not entail *God exists.* The other is that the plausibility of *Numinous experience is veridical* is not logically or epistemically unrelated to the plausibility of theism.

THE "UNDERDETERMINATION" OF THEOLOGY BY NUMINOUS EXPERIENCE

God is described as all-knowing, all-powerful, and all-good, as creator and providence, and Lord and savior and judge. These descriptions may be grounded in numinous experience, in one fashion or another, but they clearly are not mere reports of how the object of numinous experience appears to its subject. It seems to the subject of a standard numinous experience that he experiences a holy being, where X *is holy* entails something along the lines of X *is unique in kind* and **X** *is morally pure or righteous*; Isaiah's famous response to holiness, rendered into King James English, was "Woe is me, I am undone, for I am a man of unclean lips and dwell in the midst of a people of unclean lips."

A sense of dependence upon an overwhelmingly powerful being; a sense of guilt before an overwhelmingly righteous being; a sense of forgiveness before an overwhelmingly loving being; a sense of awe before an overwhelmingly majestic being: it is not hard to see how a sense of experiencing a being of this sort should give rise to something like the concept of God. Roughly, one might put things in this way: dependence suggests creation; guilt suggests holiness; forgiveness suggests love; awe suggests worship-worthiness; this way of putting the matter attaches the concepts of theology to the reactions to the at-least-intentional object, of numinous experience. Roughly, one might put things this way: an overwhelmingly powerful being resembles an omnipotent one more than your ordinary person does; an overwhelmingly righteous being is a good candidate for being a cosmic judge, or an overwhelmingly loving being for being a savior, or an overwhelmingly majestic being for being the Lord of nature and history. The phenomenological content of numinous experience is *relevant to but not sufficient for* the traditional concept of God; otherwise stated, the experience *underdetermines* the concept.

THEOLOGICAL AND EXPERIENTIAL CONSTRAINTS

Another way of putting this is to note that there are theological as well as experiential constraints on the concept of God. A deity who lacked power (or knowledge) might well lack just that power (or knowledge) required to save us, and there may be no such thing as *being unable to do just one thing* or *there being only one thing one does not know*; an omnipotent being is not simply one capacity for action better than a very powerful nonomnipotent one or an omniscient being one proposition wiser than an almost omniscient one. If God creates persons in his image because it is better that he do so than not, and loves them, then he cannot condone what thwarts the realization of their nature, and so will condemn their sins, but may also not simply leave them alone to drink their punishment to its last dregs, but love them to the extent that he provides a way of their being not only forgiven but also brought to maturity as persons.

This illustrates some conceptual, theological constraints on the concept of God. Working out such considerations is not the basic concern here; it is sufficient for present purposes if the connections very roughly traced in the preceding paragraph are clear enough so that one can see how theological constraints may shape the development of concepts to which the phenomenology of numinous experience also contributes.

Another feature of (some) numinous experiences should be mentioned in this regard. These experiences often, perhaps usually, involve visual and/or auditory imagery; in particular, some of them involve what seems to the subject of the experience as propositional communication—it seems to the subject that God is speaking to him in such a manner that information about God is conveyed. Among the information so conveyed in biblical descriptions of numinous experience is a substantial part, at any rate, of the concept of God.

WHICH COMES FIRST, EXPERIENCE OR TRADITION?

This, in turn, raises a "chicken and egg" type of question: which comes first, experience or tradition? The answer is to challenge the question. The inelegant fate of the claim that something or other is ineffable applies to numinous experience as fully as to anything else. Thus no experience is aconceptual.[22] Further, numinous experience has a "theistic filling," a particular sort of intentional phenomenology. Hence, for both these reasons, it is not the case that people have experiences which are somehow neutral or contentless and then bring concepts or interpretations to bear on them; there are no such "bare" or "pure" experiences. In the "filling," or phenomenology, of numinous experience, tradition or theology is latent. The tradition does not produce the experience, though claims about the world, based on numinous experience, no doubt will be filtered through theistic tradition in one or another of its varieties.

NUMINOUS EXPERIENTIAL EVIDENCE AND DETERMINATE CONCLUSIONS

If, then, one asks "What is the object of numinous experience, supposing there is one (i.e., supposing this sort of experience to be veridical)?" a determinate, specific answer is possible only if two things can be accomplished. It must be possible at least to decide

22. See Chapter 4, below.

that some numinous experiences are more accurate, or more adequate to their object, and others less, if not that some are veridical, and others are not; this will assume at least that standard numinous experiences have a single object if they have any. Also, it must be possible to decide between competing varieties of theism, or to reduce any competition among varieties so that there is significant overlap in the remaining concepts of God as these relate to numinous experience.

Suppose, however, that theism itself is implausible; suppose that the existence of evil shows that *God exists* is false, or that it is unreasonable to think it true? Then we will face the situation in which we have, or are alleged to have, reason to think numinous experience nonveridical; we will have, or be alleged to have, one or more evidence-canceling explanations.

Positively put, then, a theology, or a theistic conceptual system, places constraints on how numinous experience may be interpreted, renders the description of numinous being determinate, and (providing it is plausible, or there is reason to think it true) provides epistemic support for the claim that numinous experience is veridical. But should there be no way of finding sufficient common ground between the concepts of God held in different theistic perspectives without rationally assessing them and also no way of assessing them in such a fashion as to eliminate those whose concepts of God are in crucial respects not very similar, we shall not be able to answer the question as to what being numinous experience is experience *of*. If there is reason to think theism false, independent of numinous experience, then this, by itself or together with explanations of numinous experience which by themselves are epistemically neutral, may yield one or more evidence-canceling explanations of numinous experience after all, whereas if, independent of numinous experience, there is reason to think some form of theism true, that will render the claim that numinous experience is veridical more plausible. There is no way that is epistemically very satisfactory to explore the question as to whether numinous experience is veridical without also exploring the question as to whether theism, independent of appeal to such experience, has much plausibility.

PHENOMENOLOGICAL UNITY, THEORETICAL UNITY, AND UNITY OF DESCRIPTION

Where does all this leave us regarding our question "Does numinous experience provide evidence for religious belief?" Given the discussion to this point, the answer seems to be as follows. It may be that, upon a rather full examination of cross-cultural descriptions of numinous experiences, we would find that they on the whole agreed about the properties which are to be ascribed to the object of that experience if at least some of those experiences are veridical. We, that is, might discover what one might call a *phenomenological unity* among such descriptions, which in turn generated a *unity of description* concerning the putative object of the experiences in question.[23] There might, and might not, be unity among *reactions to* the properties the putative object of the experiences possessed; that would be considerably less important, save as difference in reaction was reason to suppose significant difference also in the properties that the "intentional" object seemed to possess.

The sort of phenomenological unity thus far discussed would be discovered simply by comparing a substantial number of descriptions of numinous experience from as diverse as possible a set of cultures, places, and times. Suppose, however, this not to be available; suppose the initial diversity to be too great. Still, it might be that something like the following was true. Suppose one found that the material—the collected descriptions of numinous experiences—could be divided into strands **A**, **B**, and **C**. It seems likely that there be *some* phenomenological unity, but suppose it to be thin, and that only property **P1** is ascribed to God in all three strands. Strand **A**, perhaps, ascribes properties **P2–P5** to God, and **B** ascribes properties **P6–P10**, and **C** ascribes properties **P11–P15**. But suppose also one finds that the persons whose descriptions fall into **A** are within one theistic subtradition, or assent to one particular variety of theism, whereas those persons whose descriptions fall into **B** assent to another, and those persons whose descriptions fall into **C** assent to a third variety of theism. Call these varieties T^A, T^B, and T^C. Suppose, further, that upon examination T^A is rationally superior to T^B and to T^C, and that one can see how holding T^B or T^C might distort the description of an experience that could also be described along

23. There need not be phenomenological *uniformity* in order to produce unity of description, since it might universally or usually be the case that the object of a numinous experience seemed to have properties **P1**, **P2**, and **P3**, whereas it only sometimes or rarely seemed (in some cases) that the object had **P4**, and (in other cases) that it had **P5**, or lacked **P4**. Such divergences of description occur regarding perceptual experience, and perhaps would cause no more difficulty in the case of numinous experience than in that of perceptual.

the lines of descriptions in **A**, and distort it just the sorts of ways one finds present in descriptions in the **B** and **C** strands.[24] Then one might properly grant descriptive preference to those descriptions in the **A** strand. In this, or some similar, way one might *argue to* a phenomenological unity which required that some sorts of descriptions be rejected, or edited, or corrected, or the like; call the result of such a process *theoretical unity.* Theoretical unity, in effect, is *critically elicited* phenomenological unity. Theoretical unity, too, could generate unity of description of the putative object of numinous experiences.

NONTHEISTIC ALTERNATIVES, RELIGIOUS AND SECULAR

Ultimately, the veridicality of numinous experience is essentially connected to the rational plausibility of theism, and anything relevant to the latter is also relevant to the former. As the overall plausibility of a scientific theory which refers to a theoretical entity **x** is relevant to the question of whether to describe experimental observations in terms of seeing an **x**, thereby providing confirmation for *There are* **x**'*s* (the phenomenology of the observation also being relevant), so the overall plausibility of theism is relevant to the question of whether to describe numinous experiences as experiences of God, thereby providing confirmation for *God exists* (the phenomenology of the numinous experiences also being relevant).

Obviously, there are religious alternatives to theism—for example, Theravada Buddhism and Jainism. And there are varieties of secularism which are alternatives to theism—for example, a rigorously stated materialism. Perspectives such as Marxism and humanism are also alternatives to theism, and perhaps fall somewhere between being religious and being secular. In any case, one important factor in determining the plausibility of theism is its own internal coherence. Another is how it fares in comparison with its

24. In principle the distortions might rise from differences in philosophical, or scientific, views, or in some combination of these with theological perspectives, or in some features peculiar and idiosyncratic to persons whose descriptions appeared in the **B** and **C** strands, or in other discernible ways.

alternatives, if some comparative rational assessment can be made. But these matters go beyond the concerns of this chapter.[25]

CONCLUSION

Suppose that there is either a phenomenological, or else a theoretical, unity among descriptions of numinous experiences.[26] Then, if the overall argument of this chapter is correct, the occurrence of numinous experiences in widely divergent cultures, places, and times does provide some confirmation of the claim that God exists. The meaning of the term "God" in this claim in part will be determined by the unity of description which the phenomenological, or theoretical, unity generates, and in part determined by the sort of theological constraints alluded to earlier.[27]

SUGGESTIONS FOR FURTHER READING

Alston, William P. "Psychoanalytic Theory and Theistic Belief." In *Faith and the Philosophers,* edited by John Hick. New York: St. Martin's Press, 1964.

Baillie, John. *Our Knowledge of God.* New York: Scribner's, 1939.

______. *The Sense of the Presence of God.* New York: Scribner's, 1962.

Broad, Charlie Dunbar. "Religion." In *Religion, Philosophy, and Psychical Research.* New York: Harcourt, Brace, 1953.

Evans-Pritchard, E. E. *Theories of Primitive Religion.* Oxford: Clarendon Press, 1965.

James, William. *The Varieties of Religious Experience.* New York: Longmans, Green, 1902.

James's work is of course a classic in the field, as is Rudolf Otto's *The Idea of the Holy,* below.

Katz, Steven T., ed. *Mysticism and Philosophical Analysis.* New York: Oxford University Press, 1978.

25. A possible methodology for such assessment is discussed in Chapter 8.

26. And so at least a significant degree of phenomenological unity among the experiences themselves.

27. The assumption that there is phenomenological, or else theoretical, unity of the sort the overall argument of this chapter requires if its title question is to receive an affirmative answer is a complex one, and I hope soon to offer a book-length treatment of it which considers numinous, but also other religious, experiences.

Lewis, Hywel David. *Our Experience of God.* London: Allen & Unwin, 1959.

Martin, Charles Burton. *Religious Belief.* Ithaca, NY: Cornell University Press, 1959.

Martin presents a fairly standard "reductionistic" treatment of religious experience.

Mavrodes, George I. *Belief in God: A Study in the Epistemology of Religion.* New York: Random House, 1970.

This volume is valuable both as a reply to Martin's thesis and in its own right.

Otto, Rudolf. *The Idea of the Holy.* London: Oxford University Press, 1936.

Smart, Ninian. *Doctrine and Argument in Indian Philosophy.* London: Allen & Unwin, 1969.

______. *Philosophers and Religious Truths.* London: SCM Press, 1964.

______. *The Philosophy of Religion.* New York: Oxford University Press, 1979.

______. *Reasons and Faiths: An Investigation of Religious Discourse, Christian and Non-Christian.* New York: Humanities Press, 1959.

______. *The Yogi and the Devotee: The Interplay between the Upanishads and Catholic Theology.* London: Allen & Unwin, 1968.

Wainwright, William J. *Mysticism: A Study of Its Nature, Cognitive Value, and Moral Implications.* Madison, WI: University of Wisconsin Press, 1981.

Yandell, Keith E. "Experience and Truth in Religion." In *Basic Issues in the Philosophy of Religion.* Boston: Allyn and Bacon, 1971.

______. "Hume on Religious Belief." In *Hume: A Re-evaluation,* edited by Donald Livingston and James T. King. New York: Fordham University Press, 1976.

______. "Hume's Explanation of Religious Belief." *Hume Studies,* 5 (Nov. 1979).

ANALYTICAL TABLE OF CONTENTS TO CHAPTER 2

26. It seems that it is only if theism is true that these tragic states of affairs do not occur, however, and inasmuch as this version of the moral argument merely assumes rather than establishes this to be true, it also seems not to be a proof. 92
27. The positive significance of the proofs, then, seems to come not by way of their showing that the proposition *God exists* is true, but by virtue of the fact that they suggest ways of articulating the various relationships between the existence of God (if God does exist) and the various phenomena to which their premises refer. 92

CHAPTER 2
DO THE TRADITIONAL ARGUMENTS SHOW THAT GOD EXISTS?

An argument consists of premises, which proffer evidence, and a conclusion, which is the target of the evidence. An argument is a *proof* only if it meets certain conditions: its premises must be true, and together they must entail the conclusion in the sense that to affirm the premises and deny the conclusion constitutes a contradiction. Arguments will show that God exists only if they are proofs.

Purposes for offering an argument will differ. I might offer an argument in order to see whether its conclusion is true, or to show myself or someone else that its conclusion is true, or to see if the epistemic status of a conclusion I have already accepted can be improved by being founded on more secure premises than before, and so on. For an argument to serve any of these purposes, however, the one to whom the proof is offered (myself or another) must *know* that its premises are true, and *know* that its premises entail its conclusion.

WHEN IS AN ARGUMENT A PROOF?

An argument, then, is a *proof* only if its premises not only are true, but are *known* to be true, and these premises not only entail the conclusion, but are *known* to entail the conclusion. Since premises can be true and entail a conclusion, independent of anyone knowing this, while knowledge is possessed by some person if it exists at all, this notion of a proof has the consequence that what is a proof for one person need not be a proof for another, and that nothing is a proof unless someone knows it to be one.

Let us suppose that we are presented with an argument whose premises are A and B, and whose conclusion is C, and that our knowledge of A is dependent on our knowledge of C. An argument of this sort could satisfy the conditions of having premises that are known to be true and that are known to entail the conclusion. Yet if our knowledge that A is true depends on our knowledge that C is true, the argument A *and* B, *so* C does not serve to establish C in any way that extends our knowledge or renders our knowledge of the conclusion more secure.[1] Similarly, if we suppose A and B entail C, but A or B or the conjunct of A and B is epistemically less secure than is C itself, then even if A *and* B, *so* C is a proof of C in the sense of satisfying the conditions noted, it will not serve to give C more secure epistemic status than it previously enjoyed.

Taking account of these considerations, we can say that an argument is a proof only if (i) its premises are not only true, but known to be true, and (ii) these premises not only entail the argument's conclusion but are known to entail it, and (iii) our knowledge of each of its premises as well as their conjunct is not dependent on our knowledge of the conclusion, and (iv) each of its premises as well as their conjunct is better known than the conclusion.

Is there any argument whose conclusion is *God exists* and which is a proof? Short of a proof (or proof-independent knowledge) that God does not exist, there is no definitive reason for answering negatively. Short of actually discovering a proof that God does exist, there is no definitive reason for answering affirmatively, and there is no way of telling whether there is such a proof short of examining plausible candidates.

THE ARGUMENT FROM CONTINGENCY

One candidate for being a proof that God exists is the *argument from contingency*, or *cosmological argument*. Distinguish between logically necessary propositions, which are either themselves contradictory and so are necessarily false, or whose denials are contradictory and so are necessarily true, and logically contingent propositions, which are neither themselves contradictory nor possess contradictory de-

1. At any rate, an argument of this sort does not put us in the position of knowing that C is true if we did not know it before.

nials. Define a being as logically necessary if and only if the proposition that it exists is a necessary truth, and a being as logically contingent if and only if the proposition that it exists[2] is logically contingent. Clearly, there are logically contingent beings, among them author and reader. It is not logically impossible that there never have been any such, and it is appropriate to ask why there are any.[3] If we explain the existence of one contingent being at one time by its being caused by another such being at a prior time, the existence of that prior being does not answer our questions; when we ask *Why are there any contingent beings at all?* it is not a sufficient answer to say *Later contingent beings are caused by earlier ones.* But there must be an explanation of there being contingent entities. So there must exist one or more necessary beings.

IT IS NOT A NECESSARY TRUTH THAT THERE ARE CONTINGENT BEINGS

Any version of the argument from contingency requires that some such claim as *That there are contingent beings has an explanation* be known to be true, either as a premise, or as a conclusion of a subproof within the proof. For if this claim is false—if it is false that the existence of contingent beings has an explanation, then it is also false that their existence requires (and has) explanation by reference to a noncontingent being. And if the claim is true, but the cosmological arguer does not know (or reasonably believe) the claim, its being true is of no epistemic use to him. It is a necessary truth that some contingent propositions are true. Consider any contingent proposition and its denial, represented by **p** and **not-p**. *Necessarily, either* **p** *or* **not-p**[4] is true. Since **p** and **not-p** are contingent, and it is necessarily the case that of **p** and **not-p** one is true, it is necessarily the case that some contingent proposition or other is true. But what might be true is that, of any pair of propositions one of which affirms and the other denies the existence of a contingent

2. For the purpose of the argument from contingency, any proposition whose truth requires that an item **x** exists (and which for that very reason is logically contingent) will do as "the" proposition that **x** exists.

3. In asking this question, we are interested not in the *purpose,* but simply in the *explanation* for the existence of contingent beings.

4. This should not be confused with *Either necessarily* **p** *or else necessarily* **not-p**.

being, it is the denial that is so. So while it is a necessary truth that some contingent propositions are true, it is not a necessary truth that there are contingent beings.

That it will not do to explain the fact that there are contingent beings by reference to the existence of one or more contingent beings perhaps can be seen in another way; in any such purported explanation, *explicans* and *explicandum* would be identical.[5]

NECESSARY BEING AND CONTINGENT BEING

Suppose, then, one instead tries to explain the fact that there are contingent beings (for convenience, assume there is just one such, named Catherine) by deducing Catherine's existence from that of a necessary being (for convenience, let us assume there is just one such, named Nellie). This, too, will fail, because the proposition *Nellie exists* states a necessary truth, and if *Nellie exists* entails *Catherine exists,* then *Catherine exists* must be a necessary truth as well, and so Catherine is not a contingent, but a necessary being. If **p** entails **q**, and it is possible that **q** be false, it is then possible that **p** be false. Thus, if it is possible for any contingent proposition to be false, it must also be possible for any proposition that entails a contingent proposition to be false. Thus, a necessarily true proposition, which cannot be false, cannot entail any contingent proposition, even a true one, which can be false. So the claim *Nellie exists* cannot entail, and thus explain, the claim *Catherine exists.*

Perhaps it is not the *existence* but rather some *activity* of Nellie that explains Catherine's existence; perhaps it is *Nellie produces Catherine* that explains Catherine's existence. If so, *Nellie produces Catherine* must be a contingent proposition: it must be possible that Nellie not do so, since otherwise Catherine will be a necessary being. This result is curious: the fact that there are contingent beings is to be explained by reference to a necessary being, but the point of explanatory reference cannot be the existence of the logically inevitable activity of a logically necessary being, but rather must be the logically contingent activity of such a being.[6]

5. In an explanation, the *explicandum* is "that which is to be explained," and the *explicans* is "that which explains the *explicandum.*"

6. Thus, if *God exists* is a necessary truth, it cannot entail *Ralph exists* (assuming "Ralph" to be a human being); nor can *God, who necessarily exists, creates Ralph,* if it is a necessary truth, entail *Ralph exists.* This assumes, of course, that human beings are logically contingent beings—but that seems plainly true.

Does this, then, render an argument from contingency without force, since its intent is to establish that there is a necessary being, while it must rest its final explanation in contingent truths about the activity of such a being? Is it not at least equally plausible simply to take the existence of contingent beings as a brute fact?

NECESSARY EXISTENTIAL INDEPENDENCE

Further, is it the case that *only* a logically necessary being is such that its existence requires no explanation? Suppose there is a being that meets the following two conditions: (i) the proposition asserting its existence is contingent and true, and (ii) the proposition asserting that it is caused to exist, or depends on something else for its existence, is a contradiction. Such a being would be contingent, but it would be logically impossible that it had been caused to exist, so *if* it exists, its existence will require no causal explanation, even though it is logically possible that it not exist. If the notion of a being that satisfies conditions (i) and (ii) is coherent, then a being that does so need not be a logically necessary being. If we say that a being **x** has *necessary existential independence* in the event that the proposition **x** *is caused to exist by, or is dependent on, the existence of some other being* is a contradiction, then a being satisfying conditions (i) and (ii), though logically contingent, will possess *necessary existential independence.* (A logically necessary being also will possess this property.)

A REFORMULATION OF THE ARGUMENT

This last point, if correct, seems to suggest less an abandonment than a reformulation of the argument, to the effect that there is, perhaps not a logically necessary being, but at least a necessarily existentially independent being. Such an argument would explain the fact that there are contingent beings that fail to possess necessary existential independence by reference either to a logically necessary being (which will automatically possess necessary existential independence) or to another contingent being that possesses necessary existential independence. What superiority, if any, has this over saying that the fact that there are contingent beings is simply a brute fact, or one having and needing no explanation?

The superiority, one might suggest, lies in this. Let us say that a fact or state of affairs is *existential* if it includes the existence of some being, and that it is a necessary truth that if any existential state of affairs *can* be explained, then it *has* some explanation.[7] Existential states of affairs that include only the existence of necessarily existentially independent beings, whether these beings be logically necessary or logically contingent, can have no explanation, nor do they require any. Existential states of affairs that include contingent beings lacking necessary existential independence will require, and have, explanations—which is to say that the fact that there are such contingent beings will require, and have, an explanation,[8] and that explanation will involve the logically contingent activity of a necessarily existentially independent being.[9] So, the suggestion concludes, there is a necessarily existentially independent being. (Positing more than one necessarily existentially independent being would explain no more than is explained by positing one, and so would be superfluous.)

A SPECIFIC FORMULATION OF THE ARGUMENT FROM CONTINGENCY

The discussion thus far suggests that the argument from contingency (the cosmological argument) be put along some such lines as these: (1) There are beings that are not necessarily existentially independent. (2) If there are such beings, then it will be logically possible that there is an explanation of this fact. (3) If it is logically possible that there is an explanation of this fact, then there will be an explanation of it.

From premises (1) to (3), it follows that (4) there is an explanation of there being items that are not necessarily existentially independent. (5) The fact that there are beings that are not nec-

7. Along the lines of this suggestion, that there be no such explanation in an alleged world would render that world, in a certain sense, irrational; the fact that there were contingent beings in such a world would be unexplained but not inexplicable. There would be nothing about that fact that made it logically impossible that it have, and so false that it required, an explanation. There just would be no explanation of that fact. Perhaps it is not obvious that this is correct, as it is not obvious that the proposition to which this note is appended *is* necessarily true; see below.

8. Assuming that *It is logically possible that no contingent being exists* and that *If a logically contingent being which lacks necessary existential independence exists, it is not logically impossible that its existence be explained*.

9. This activity will have to be such that it needs no explanation in terms of other states of the being whose activity it is, or of the existence or states of other beings; we will discuss this condition at greater length at a later point, in the context of the *Cosmologico-Teleological Argument*.

essarily existentially independent, or the fact that some particular being exists that is not necessarily existentially independent, does not constitute a (sufficient) explanation of the fact that there are beings that are not necessarily existentially independent. (6) The fact that there are beings must always be explained by the fact that there are other beings (existential conclusions require existential premises). (7) A being that is not necessarily existentially dependent is necessarily existentially independent.[10]

From premises (4) to (7), we can draw the conclusion that (8) there is some being (or beings) that is (or are) necessarily existentially independent. (9) If phenomena can be explained as well by the existence of one thing of kind **K** as by the existence of more than one thing of kind **K**, explaining the phenomena requires the existence of only one thing of kind **K**. (10) That there are beings that are not necessarily independent can be explained as well by reference to the existence of one necessarily independent being as by the existence of many. So it follows that (11) there is some being that is necessarily existentially independent, and we are not entitled by the argument that proves this to conclude that there is more than one.

EXISTENTIAL INDEPENDENCE AND OMNICOMPETENCE

Being necessarily existentially independent is a property that an item will have (if it has it at all) because of other properties that it has. But no set of physical properties that a thing has will entail that it has necessary existential independence; that an item has some set of physical properties (i.e., some set of properties described in the language of physical theory) will at most imply that that item is not dependent on any other if some physical theory is true. Then the proposition *If theory* **T** *is true, then item* **x** *is not dependent on anything else* will be true; but the proposition **T** *is true,* even if it is true, is not *necessarily* true, so **x** cannot be said to have necessary existential independence. Perhaps only omnicompetence (i.e., om-

10. One might object that a being might be (de facto, but not necessarily) existentially independent—that is to say, it might not depend on anything else for its existence, though this were not a *necessary* truth. But then the proponent of the cosmological argument will insist that nonnecessary existential independence itself requires explanation by reference to something that has necessary existential independence.

niscience, omnipotence, and omnibenevolence) on **x**'s part will entail, or explain, or provide an adequate basis for *necessary* independence. So perhaps the proposition *If* **x** *is necessarily existentially independent, then* **x** *is omnicompetent* is true after all: perhaps the cosmological argument is capable of proving more than it is often thought to be capable of proving in the sense that more follows from its conclusion than is often thought to follow. Further, if X *is necessarily existentially independent* presupposes X *is omnicompetent* (i.e., if **x** *is omnicompetent* entails **x** *is necessarily existentially independent*), then if there cannot be more than one omnipotent being, then a fortiori there cannot be more than one necessarily existentially independent being.

LOGICALLY CONTINGENT BEING, NECESSARY EXISTENTIAL INDEPENDENCE, AND OMNIPOTENCE[11]

A brief review of some relevant points may be helpful. If a being is logically necessary, or has logically necessary existence, then it is logically impossible that it be caused to exist. If it is logically impossible that something be caused to exist, let us say that it has necessary existential independence. A being might have necessary existential independence—NEI, for short—even though it is not a logically necessary being. Suppose, for instance, that there is a being such that (i) it exists, and (ii) it is a necessary truth that if it exists, then it has not been caused to exist. Thus it has NEI, but it need not be logically necessary. Further, suppose that adding (iii) it is not a logically necessary being (i.e., it is a logically contingent being) to (i) and (ii) does not produce a contradiction.

If the cosmological argument is successful, something has NEI. Suppose that if it is successful, it shows that *one* thing has NEI, on the grounds that nothing in the argument shows that more than one such being must exist, even if it shows that *If something contingent exists, then something that has NEI exists.* Nevertheless, that a being has NEI is something that itself seems to require explanation. The explanation in the case of a logically necessary being, as noted above, is easy: **x** *is logically necessary* entails **x** *has NEI.* But a being

11. The reasoning in this section is more abstract and complex than that of the preceding and following sections, and some readers may wish to pass on to the next section.

that meets conditions (i) to (iii) will be such that its having NEI must have some other explanation, inasmuch as it is not a logically necessary being, but has NEI. What might that other explanation be?

We might suppose that the simplest explanation would be that it is everlasting. This, in turn, might mean (a) it is a necessary truth that the being is everlasting, or (b) it is a necessary truth that if the being exists, it is everlasting, or (c) it is contingently true that the being is everlasting. Now (a) will be true only of a logically necessary being, so only (b) and (c) can be relevant here. But if (c) is true of a being, then presumably we would still have to explain that this is so: the question of why (c) should be true of this being is one to which there should be an answer (at least, there should be an answer if the perspective on explanation and rationality of the proponent of the cosmological argument is true). That (c) is true, then, will itself require further explanation. This leaves (b). Let us say that a being of which (b) is true has *conditional necessary everlastingness.* But it is logically possible that a being have conditional necessary everlastingness, and yet also be such that it is a necessary truth that if it exists, it depends on something else for its existence. Hence, that a being has conditional necessary everlastingness does not entail (and thereby explain) that being's having NEI.

Perhaps, then, a different sort of attempt at explanation should be made. Let us suppose that a being is omnicompetent (i.e., omnibenevolent, omnipotent, and omniscient); then one might argue as follows: if the being is omnibenevolent, then its existence is an unsurpassed (perhaps unsurpassable) good, and it will not choose or act wrongly, unless it lacks some knowledge or power. If it is omniscient, it will not act wrongly due to lack of knowledge, and it will be aware of any course of action, by itself or another, that would lead to its own demise. If it is omnipotent, it will not act wrongly due to lack of power. If it is omnipotent and omniscient it will not be open to actions by others that would lead to its demise unless it wishes its own demise. It would be a great evil for an omnibenevolent being to cease to exist, or to cease to be omnibenevolent, or to wish its own demise, so it will not allow or cause its own demise save through ignorance or impotence (which omniscience and omnipotence preclude). So if a being is omnibenevolent, omnipotent, and omniscient, then it will be everlasting and have NEI, whether it is logically necessary or not. If this line of reasoning is correct, and no other explanation of possessing NEI is available, then it follows that, should the cosmological argument be successful, it proves some such conclusion as the following: either a logically necessary being (which may be omnicompetent) exists, or else a being exists who is not logically necessary, who has NEI, and whose having NEI is to be explained by its being omnicompetent.

The gist of the cosmological argument, then, will run along these lines: (1) Some things exist that do not have NEI. (2) If there is a sufficient explanation of there being things that do not have NEI, then there will be at least one being that has NEI. (3) There is a sufficient explanation of there being things that do not have NEI. From premises (1) to (3), it follows that (4) there is at least one being that has NEI. (5) A being has NEI if and only if either it is logically necessary or (if it is not logically necessary) it is omnicompetent (i.e., omniscient, omnipotent, and omnibenevolent). So from all of this it follows that (6) there is at least one being that is either logically necessary (and may be omnicompetent) or is not logically necessary and is omnicompetent.

When the cosmological argument is put in this form, it is advantageous to the proponent who wants to establish classical theism that there be something incoherent about the notion of logically necessary existence, since then the existence of an omnicompetent being will follow. But while various empiricists have thought that there is something incoherent about the notion of logically necessary existence, it is not at all clear that the case for this position has ever been made out successfully.

It seems fairly clear that a being could be omnipotent and omniscient without being omnibenevolent. Further, whether a being that was omnipotent and omniscient was omnibenevolent or not would presumably depend on how that being acted—on what use it made of its knowledge and power. Further still, we can define "**x** is omniscient" along some such lines as "for any proposition **P**, if it is logically possible that **P** be known and that **x** know that **P** is true, then **x** does know that **P** is true"; similarly, we can say that "**x** is omnipotent" if it is true that "if it is logically possible that **P** be the case, and logically possible that **x** make **P** be the case, then **x** can make **P** be the case"; but it is not clear that we can define omnibenevolence along similar lines. We might, for instance, propose that "**x** is omnibenevolent if and only if (i) for any proposition

P describing a right action, **x** has made **P** true, or (ii) if **S** is the maximum set of compossible propositions such that S's members describe right actions, **x** will make **S** true, or (iii) if **A** is the set of propositions whose truth will make the most valuable possible state of affairs, then **x** will make **A** true"—but it is not at all clear what (i) or (ii) or (iii) means, or that any of them mean anything coherent. If on the other hand we say that "**x** is omnibenevolent" if it is true that "**x** has never acted wrongly, and never missed an opportunity to do what is right through ignorance or impotence," then we could conclude that an omnipotent and omniscient being can be (but presumably need not be) omnibenevolent.

For theism, then, a benefit of the cosmological argument construed along the lines noted above is that it may link omnipotence and omniscience with omnibenevolence in a way that is not wholly arbitrary.

A SECOND VERSION OF THE COSMOLOGICAL ARGUMENT

Before an assessment of the cosmological argument is offered, it will be useful to consider one more version of the argument that casts the cosmological considerations in a somewhat different language and light: (1) There are beings that are not necessarily existentially independent. (2) Necessarily, nothing causes its own existence. (3) Necessarily, if *What caused* **x**? is an appropriate question to ask about **x**, then there is a (philosophically) sufficient answer to this question. (4) Necessarily, *What caused* **x**? *is* an appropriate question to ask about anything that *is not* necessarily existentially independent.[12] (5) Necessarily, *What caused* **x**? *is not* an appropriate question to ask about anything that *has* necessary existential independence. (6) Necessarily, regarding any explanation **E** of the existence of some item **x**, **E** is not (philosophically) sufficient if **E** explains the existence of **x** in terms of the existence of **y** if one can appropriately ask *What caused* **y**? So, from (2-6) it follows that (7) necessarily, if there are only beings that are not necessarily existentially independent, there is no sufficient explanation of the existence of anything. But (8) necessarily, for anything that exists, there is a sufficient

12. It is not, however, an appropriate question to ask about a being that is, since it is logically impossible that any such being be caused; the question *could not have* an answer.

explanation of its existence. So, from premises (1), (7), and (8) it follows that (9) it is false that there are only beings that are not necessarily existentially independent (i.e., some being *is* necessarily existentially independent). (10) The fact that there is one necessarily existentially independent being explains the existence of beings that are not necessarily existentially independent as well as the fact that there are two or more. So, from premises (9) and (10) it follows that (11) there is one necessarily existentially independent being (or, at any rate, the argument provides no reason for thinking there is more than one such being).

TWO SENSES OF "SUFFICIENT EXPLANATION"

The cosmological argument, in these and other versions, rests on a particular strong understanding of what constitutes an explanation, or at least what constitutes a *sufficient* explanation: *a sufficient explanation is one whose explicans cannot be further explained*—that is, its *explicans* has the property of *being logically impossible that it be explained,* and whatever has this feature *needs* no explanation. Nor is this possibility theory-relative in the sense that although the *explicans* can be explained within the context of one given theoretical framework, it cannot be explained within the context of another. The metaphysical claim—which is sometimes said to rest on an "insight" or "intuition" (although presumably this is so only if the claim is *true*)—is that (i) the world is rational, (ii) the world contains things whose existence can be explained, and (iii) if the world contains things whose existence can be explained, and is rational, then the world also contains something whose existence cannot be explained (and so requires no explanation).[13] Let us call this sense of "explanation" *strong explanation* and the corresponding sense of "rationality" *strong rationality.*

We should note that the alternative to *strong* rationality is not *no* rationality at all, but rather *weak* rationality. Suppose for instance that we hold a perspective characterized by the following claims: (a) there is a correct theory **T** within which everything that exists is either such that its existence is explained in **T** by deriving

13. In (iii), "the world" means "all that exists"; if in saying "the world" one instead means "the physical universe," then the latter portion of (iii) should instead read "the world depends for its existence on something whose existence cannot be explained (and so requires no explanation)."

it from the laws of **T** plus the existence of those entities which are primitive or "given" within **T**, or its existence is itself primitive or "given" within **T**; (b) there is no entity such that it is logically impossible that it not exist, or logically impossible that it be caused to exist—that is to say, there are no necessarily existentially independent beings, but only necessarily existentially dependent beings[14] (some of which are, and some of which are not, primitive within **T**); (c) if the world is to be rational, then (a) and (b) will be true; and (d) science seeks a theory of the sort (a) refers to. Let us then call an explanation of the sort that is possible in terms of the perspective outlined by these four conditions a *weak explanation*, and the corresponding sort of rationality *weak rationality* (with nothing disparaging being meant by the term "weak").[15]

TWO QUESTIONS

For all the sometimes considerable complexity and sophistication of the varieties of cosmological arguments, they seem always to require some variety of the claim that the world is such that there are things in it whose existence can be explained, and whose existence requires sufficient (in the sense of "strong") explanation, and so requires that the world is strongly rational. Consider, then, two questions. The first is as follows: Is either the proposition *That anything exists requires strong, and not merely weak, explanation* or the proposition *The world is strongly, and not merely weakly, rational* one that we know to be true, or such that we are somehow more reasonable if we accept it rather than the proposition *That anything exists requires merely weak, and not strong, explanation,* or the proposition *The world is merely weakly, and not strongly, rational?* While some philosophers claim that the notions of *strong explanation* and *strongly rational* are "meaningless" or "without content," the theories of meaning on which such claims rest do not present very impressive rational credentials; but granting that the former two propositions in the question are perfectly intelligible, it is hard to see any grounds that would justify the claim that we do know that one or the other

14. Or there are beings some of which, while not *necessarily* existentially independent, are (de facto) existentially independent, whereas other beings are existentially dependent.

15. *Weak explanation* and *weak rationality* can be described in ways other than that suggested by conditions (a) to (d), but one variety of *weak explanation* and *weak rationality* is sufficient for our present purposes.

of those propositions is true, or that we are somehow more reasonable in accepting one of the former pair than one of the latter pair. The answer to our first question is in the negative. Perhaps it is *as* reasonable to think that one of the former pair is true as it is to embrace one of the latter pair, and so perhaps it is as reasonable to accept the conclusion of the cosmological argument as not to do so—but this does not help in the assessment of theism: it tells us nothing about its truth.

The second question is as follows: Is either the proposition *That anything exists requires strong, and not merely weak, explanation* or the proposition *The world is strongly, and not merely weakly, rational* one that we know to be true, whereas we do not know that the proposition *God created the world* is true—or is one of the former propositions such that we are more reasonably confident that it is true than we are that *God created the world* is true? It is true, after all, that the fact that God created the world would explain that there is a world, and that the fact that God created beings that lacked necessary existential independence would explain there being such entities. The proposition *If God exists, then he has no cause of existence* and the proposition *If God exists, then he does not depend for his existence on anything else* are necessary truths. Why is one worse off, epistemically, in beginning by holding *God created the world* to be true than in beginning by holding the propositions about *strong rationality* and *strong explanation* to be true, or in deriving those propositions from it rather than in deriving it from them?

NECESSARY EXISTENTIAL INDEPENDENCE AND DEITY

If *being necessarily existentially independent* is conceptually connected with *being omnicompetent* in some way as that suggested earlier, then holding that a being has the former property is tantamount to holding that a being has the latter. If this is not the case, then neither is it clear that the cosmological argument holds much promise as an argument for God's existence. It is true that accepting the proposition *God created the world* at least seems to commit us to a much more specific and explicit claim than does accepting the proposition *There is a necessarily existentially independent being.* To the degree that this is so, it is so because "God" has particular connotations within one or another variety of monotheism, and whether this further commitment is an epistemic advantage or not will depend on the epistemic status of that variety of theism. However that may be, given the recent discussion of strong versus weak explanation, it would seem that the cosmological argument does not satisfy the criteria for *being a proof*: it fails to show that God exists.

A CONCLUDING REFLECTION ON THE COSMOLOGICAL ARGUMENT

If our argument to this point is correct, the cosmological argument is not a proof. Nevertheless, it is not certain that some other version of the argument might not yet constitute a proof. But even if it does not constitute a proof, this is not to say that the argument is utterly without philosophical interest; for one thing, it provides a way of construing and expressing at least part of the relationship between God and the world as classical monotheism conceives it. That relationship is conceived in terms of the world depending on God for its existence, rather than the converse: there is a one-way, asymmetrical dependence relation between God and the world, in which the world is dependent. Furthermore, the cosmological argument understands this dependence relationship not as merely accidental, but as somehow deriving from the nature of God and of the world. And in addition, such notions as "necessary existential independence" and "strong rationality" provide one way of articulating what it is about God and the world from which this one-way dependence derives. But the cosmological argument does not bring in the notion of the creation of the world as a free creative action, or, strictly speaking, of divine *agency* at all (although, cast along the lines considered above, it *is* compatible with this notion). By contrast, the notion of agency is central to the teleological argument—another of the traditional arguments that might succeed where the cosmological argument fails.

THE TELEOLOGICAL ARGUMENT

An explanation consists of an *explicans,* which does the explaining, and an *explicandum,* which is what is to be explained. An explanation is de facto ultimate if its *explicans* is not the *explicandum* of another explanation, and necessarily ultimate if it is logically impossible that its *explicans* be the *explicandum* of another explanation. A *type* of explanation is ultimate if there is at least one explanation that is ultimate and that is also of that type.

One type of explanation, then, is *teleological*: a teleological explanation explains a phenomenon by reference to the intentional actions of an intelligent agent.[16] An action **A** by Ralph at time **t** is *basic* if there is no other action Ralph has to perform at time **t** in order to perform **A**; an end **E** that Ralph has is *ultimate* if there is no other end that Ralph has in terms of which Ralph would justify having **E**. Another type of explanation is *mechanistic*[17]: a mechanistic explanation explains a phenomenon by reference to physical events and a theory that relates physical events to one another by means of lawlike statements. Phenomena so explained will be themselves first provided with a physical description. A physical event is ultimate if its occurrence is referred to in the explicans of an ultimate mechanistic explanation.

One version of the teleological argument runs as follows: (1) Necessarily, mechanistic and teleological explanations are irreducibly different and exhaustive. (2) Necessarily, it is rationally preferable that there be only one type of ultimate explanation for all phenomena. (3) Necessarily, for any phenomenon **x**, if **x** is mechanistically explicable, then it is also teleologically explicable, although the converse of this is not necessarily true. (4) Some phenomena are teleologically explicable. Thus, from premises (3) and (4), it follows that (5) it is not possible to have only one type of ultimate explanation if there are ultimate mechanistic explanations. But then, from premises (2) and (5), it also follows that (6) it is rationally preferable that there be no ultimate mechanistic explanations—that is to say, it is preferable that no ultimate explanation be mechanistic. And, given premises (1) and (6), it follows that (7) it is rationally preferable that all ultimate explanations be teleological. Given that (8) necessarily, there are explanations of some phenomena, and (9) necessarily, if there are explanations, then some explanations will be ultimate, it follows that (10) it is rationally preferable that there be ultimate explanations that are teleological, and indeed there are such explanations.

FROM ULTIMATE TELEOLOGICAL EXPLANATIONS TO GOD

Even if the argument is correct to this point, it does not follow that God exists; at best, it follows only that any series of explanations

16. One might object that there are teleological explanations in, say, biology that do not fit this characterization; perhaps this is so, but nevertheless, the characterization offered here seems to be most relevant to the teleological argument.

17. I am using the word *mechanistic* in a sense that does not require its being part of a "mechanical" world view.

terminates in the basic actions of agents who perform those actions for ends that they hold as intrinsic values, and that only in that rather modest sense are the explanations ultimate. It is not highly plausible that a human agent will be involved in an explanation that is ultimate in the sense that its *explicans* is not (let alone cannot be) the *explicandum* of a further explanation. Clearly, the argument must go further if even the portion of it presented so far is to be plausible. Let us consider, then, the following continuation: (11) necessarily, it is rationally preferable that some one ultimate explanation be *finally ultimate*—that is, ultimate in the sense that its *explicans is not, and cannot be,* the *explicandum* of some further explanation. (12) Among teleological explanations, only a theistic explanation is finally ultimate. It follows that (13) it is rationally preferable to accept a theistic explanation.

The rationale behind (12) is something like this: if we refer to some end **E** that Ruth has, even if there is no other end by which she justifies having **E**, it is at least possible that there is some physical state **A** such that **A** *obtains* explains her having **E**; but if it is the case that God has some end **E** such that there is no other end by which he justifies **E**, then there is no further explanation (physical or otherwise) of the fact that he has **E**. This, in turn, will explain God's acting in such a way as to realize **E**.

THE MECHANISTIC COUNTERARGUMENT

Obviously, there is an argument analogous to the teleological argument just presented that we might call the mechanistic argument. The first two premises of the mechanistic argument are the same as those of the teleological argument: (1) Necessarily, mechanistic and teleological explanations are irreducibly different and exhaustive, and (2) necessarily, it is rationally preferable that there be only one type of ultimate explanation. But premise (3) is replaced by (3') necessarily, for any phenomenon **x**, if **x** is teleologically explicable, **x** is mechanistically explicable, but not conversely, and premise (4) is replaced by (4') some phenomena are mechanistically explicable. From premises (3') and (4'), we can conclude that (5') it is not possible to have only one type of ultimate explanation if there are ultimate teleological explanations.[18]

18. The argument might require only (3'') necessarily, for any phenomenon **x**, if **x** is teleologically explicable, **x** is mechanistically explicable, *and conversely,* and (5'') it is possible to have only one type of ultimate explanation if there are ultimate mechanistic explanations. Present purposes do not require us to investigate this complication.

If theism is false, then presumably (3') is true; if theism is true, then presumably (3) is true. It is hard to see how, exactly, we could decide between (3) and (3') without deciding about the truth of theism. So one problem with this version of the teleological argument seems to be that we cannot know that (3) is true or that (3') is false without knowing that theism is true.

In any case, the counterargument continues as follows: (6') It is rationally preferable that there be no ultimate teleological explanations—that is, it is preferable that no ultimate explanation be teleological. Given premises (1) and (6'), it follows that (7') it is rationally preferable that all ultimate explanations be mechanistic. Given premises (8) and (9) of the teleological argument—that necessarily, there are explanations of some phenomena, and necessarily, if there are explanations, then some explanations will be ultimate, we can conclude that (10') it is rationally preferable that there be ultimate explanations that are mechanistic.

The argument concludes as follows: (11') Necessarily, it is rationally preferable that some one (perhaps very complex) ultimate explanation be de facto ultimate—that is, ultimate in the sense that its *explicans* occurs in a science that cannot be reduced to another and that it is not the *explicandum* of some further explanation within that science. (12') Among mechanistic explanations, only a physicalistic explanation the *explicans* of which refers to the primitive entities of a basic science is de facto ultimate. So it follows that (13') it is rationally preferable to accept a de facto ultimate physicalistic explanation. If this conclusion is correct, it will not be rationally preferable to accept a theistic explanation.

The difference between premises (11) to (13) of the teleological argument and premises (11') to (13') of the mechanistic argument parallels the disagreement between *sufficient* and *weak* explanation in the context of the cosmological argument. Obviously, we could still argue about what sort of explanation is requisite with regard to the accessibility of the universe to scientific research; it is not clear that the possibility of science requires a universe that is *strongly rational.*

A SECOND VERSION OF THE TELEOLOGICAL ARGUMENT

A different variety of the teleological argument concerns relative probabilities in the following manner: (1) The physical environment of our earth serves as the setting for the physical and moral development of moral agents. (2) It is more probable that the first premise is true if theism is true than if theism is false. So it follows that (3) relative to the situation described in the first premise, theism is more probably true than false.[19]

Once the sort of argument represented in premises (1) to (3) comes to mind, a more complex sort of argument suggests itself, in terms of the following propositions: (F1) the earth supports sentient life. (F2) The earth provides the environment for moral agents. (F3) There are moral and religious saints. (F4) A great many people believe in God. (F5) There are places of extraordinary beauty. (F6) The world is orderly in a sense that makes science and common sense possible. (F7) Various persons, who have lived at various times and places, have had numinous experiences. On the basis of these propositions, we might formulate the following argument: (1) The set of facts assembled in propositions (F1) to (F7) will more probably obtain if theism is true than if theism is false. (2) The set of facts assembled in propositions (F1) to (F7) does obtain. So it follows that (3) relative to propositions (F1) to (F7), theism is more probably true than false. We might also note, however, that this is compatible with theism being *overall* (i.e., relative to our *total* data) more probably false than true.

A REPLY TO THE SECOND VERSION

Consider another set of facts: (F'1) The earth supports poisonous snakes and annoying insects; (F'2) the earth provides the environment for persons who are criminally insane or tragically retarded; (F'3) there are morally depraved persons and religious frauds; (F'4) a great many persons have never been exposed to monotheism; (F'5) there are places of extraordinary ugliness; (F'6) the ultimate laws of physics may be random; (F'7) various persons, who have lived at various times and places, have failed to have numinous experiences. Suppose, for the sake of the argument, that (F'1–F'7) can be explained or set into a theistic context such that the following is true: (4) Relative to (F'1–F'7), that theism is false is not more probable than that theism is true. If (4) is not true, (1–3) will do very little relative to providing any grounds, of a teleological or any

19. Given premise (2), this argument also might be construed as a version of the moral argument, but nothing of philosophical importance depends on which way it is viewed.

other sort, for accepting theism, because there will be a significant set of facts which cannot be explained or set in a theistic context in such a way that they do not render it more probable that theism is false than it is that theism is true.

Even if (4) is true, (1–3) may do very little on theism's behalf. Suppose that the Cleveland Cavaliers beat the Boston Celtics in a National Basketball Association game; relative to the data this game provides, the Cavaliers have a better chance at winning the NBA championship than the Celtics have. Relative to their overall records, the reverse is true. If one has seen only one rhinoceros, and it was albino, then relative to one's sensory evidence, it is probable that every rhinoceros is albino; the proposition *Every rhinoceros is albino* is not much accredited thereby.

The idea that one can assign probabilities along the lines suggested by (1–3) has attracted some philosophers. If, relative to (F1), theism is more likely true than false, it is hard to see why *Vast (in fact, most) portions of the universe support no sentient life at all* does not have the reverse import. That is, consider: (Fa) Vast (in fact, most) portions of the universe support no sentient life at all. Then consider this argument: (1a) If the fact (Fa) reports obtains, then theism is more likely false than true; (2a) the fact (Fa) reports obtains; so (3a) theism is more likely false than true. Or consider this argument: (1b) If the facts reported by (F1) and (Fa) obtain, theism is not more probably true than false; (2b) the facts reported by (F1) and (Fa) do obtain; so: (3b) theism is not more probably true than false.[20]

To say that *Relative to a fact* **F**, *theism is more probable than not,* presumably, is to say that *If theism is true, it is more probable than not that* **F** *will obtain* and *If theism is false, it is not more probable than not that* **F** *will obtain.* If *The earth supports sentient life* favors theism, then *If theism is true, it is more probable than not that the earth supports sentient life.* But then why should it not be true that, in the same sense, *Mars does not support sentient life* favors atheism? Perhaps the idea is that theism only favors *there being sentient life,* and is neutral to how much there is. But then why can't atheism be neutral to whether there is sentient life (it could allow a little of it, as an "accident"), but favors there not being a lot of it?

20. The (1b–3b) argument supposes that the fact (F1) reports counts as much for theism as the fact (Fa) reports counts against it.

Consider, then, the set of facts: (Fa) Vast portions of the universe support no sentient life at all; (Fb) a great many persons, without appearing to be wicked or intellectually dishonest, embrace religious views incompatible with theism; (Fc) the history of monotheistic religion contains some most discouraging chapters; (Fd) without apparent wickedness or intellectual dishonesty, some brilliant minds have reflected about the question as to whether there is any evidence that God exists, and have concluded negatively; (Fe) evolutionary theory appears well confirmed and presents a rather chaotic picture of the development of biological events on earth; (Ff) the documents regarded as revelatory by the monotheistic religions (e.g., the Bible) are interpreted, by people who claim to accept them as revelation, in very diverse ways; (Fg) monotheism is split into varieties, and its varieties are split into still more subvarieties.

Consider, then, this argument. (i) The set of facts reported by (Fa–Fg) will more probably obtain if theism is false than if theism is true; (ii) the set of facts supported by (Fa–Fg) obtains, (iii) theism is more probably false than true.

One can explain the facts that (Fa–Fg) report if one is a theist; one can explain the facts that (F1–F7) report if one is an atheist. That the (Fa–Fg) set of facts obtain does not refute theism; that the (F1–F7) set of facts obtain does not refute atheism. Theism does *not* entail that the (Fa–Fg) set does *not* obtain, nor does atheism entail that the (F1–F7) set does not. It is hard to see that the considerations of the kind mentioned above decide much of anything one way or the other. The theist can appeal to the sort of considerations noted on his behalf, and the atheist can appeal to the sort of considerations noted on his behalf, without its being clear that one probabilistic case is superior to the other.

It should be noted that the facts appealed to in the probabilistic statement of the teleological argument were not those which theism (or atheism) *entails* will obtain. But a nagging doubt remains as to how one establishes what *is* probable, given the truth of theism, or probable, given the truth of atheism, where this is sharply distinguished from what theism, or atheism, entails. It cannot be a matter of what theism, plus our "background information," or of what atheism, plus our "background information," entails.[21] It cannot

21. Where, roughly, "background information" is that set of propositions, essential neither to theism nor atheism, that are known or reasonably believed.

be a matter of what *surprises*, or *would surprise*, a theist (or an atheist) should it obtain. Perhaps it is what theism (or atheism), plus our total information, makes probable. But how is that established?

Even waiving the doubts the last query reflects, it seems clear that probabilistic arguments of rather equal weight can be mounted by both theist and atheist. If this is so, then of course the variety of the teleological argument under discussion fails to be a proof.

A CONCLUDING REFLECTION ON THE TELEOLOGICAL ARGUMENT

The teleological argument in both its more and less sophisticated versions seems not to be a proof.[22] But it is also true that the concepts crucial to the argument provide at least one way of understanding part of the relation between God and the world as conceived by classical monotheism. For God to create the world is for God to perform an intentional action[23]—to exercise his power and knowledge to effect his purpose (thereby providing part of the background for the notion that human agency is an imitation of the divine). The core concepts, then, of the cosmological and teleological arguments provide at least one way of articulating the relation between God and the world, Creator and creation.

A COSMOLOGICO-TELEOLOGICAL ARGUMENT[24]

It was noted earlier that there are logically contingent beings—beings whose nonexistence is not logically impossible—and that the fact of their existence cannot be entailed (and so explained) by the assumption that a logically necessary being exists, although it might be explained by the actions or activities of such a being. These actions or activities, however, must themselves be logically contingent—that is to say, it must be logically possible that their

22. For example: (1) Artifacts (e.g., automobiles) and natural objects (e.g., carrots) manifest a similar orderliness; (2) orderliness in artifacts is produced by an intelligent agent; (3) probably, the orderliness in natural objects is produced by an intelligent agent; (4) orderliness in natural objects (a) is not produced by human agents, and (b) is at least as well explained by one as by many agents; so (5) there is a nonhuman, intelligent agent.

23. Or, perhaps a *continuous* action of sustaining the world in existence, and/or a *series* of creative actions.

24. This section, perhaps, is rather more abstract than others in this chapter, and the reader may wish to continue on to the section "The Ontological Argument."

agent not perform them—or the existence of allegedly logically contingent beings would again be rendered logically necessary.

One response to this would be to deny that there are any contingent propositions or beings. But if we have any very firm grasp on the notions of logical necessity and logical contingency, it seems quite clear that *Hatfield House exists alongside a magnificent garden* and *Detroit is the largest city in Michigan* are logically contingent propositions, and that it is not logically necessary that there ever have been a Hatfield House or a Detroit. Further, monotheism of an orthodox Christian (or Jewish, or Islamic) sort contains a doctrine of creation, which is inconsistent with everything that exists being logically necessary. A logically necessary being would *always* exist, and *could never fail* to exist; it could neither be created nor destroyed, even by omnipotence.

A fully successful cosmological argument would establish that either (a) a logically necessary being (which might, but need not, be omnicompetent) exists, or (b) an omnicompetent necessarily existentially independent being that is logically contingent exists. If (b) is true, then there are *only* contingent beings.[25] But even if either (a) or (b) is true, it does not follow from the existence of a necessarily existentially independent being alone that there are dependent contingent beings: some activity or action on the part of that being is necessary.

If (a) is true, this activity or action cannot be logically necessary; it must be possible that it not occur, because otherwise the existence of contingent beings would follow from the necessary truths that God exists and that he creates (that is, if we assume, for convenience of expression, that the necessary being is in fact God). But then the things "created" would not be contingent, but necessary (and so would not be created things after all). So if (a) is true, and there are contingent beings, then God's creative activity must be logically contingent and hence explicable (provided the perspective of the proponent of the cosmological argument regarding strong explanation and strong rationality is correct). The theist's position requires that God's creative activity be explained teleologically rather than mechanistically. This requires that the teleological argument be successful—that the ultimate explanation of there

25. Unless there are *abstract* necessary beings, which need not concern us at this point.

being something rather than nothing comes in terms of the intentional actions of an intelligent agent. The theistic position also requires that this action be done for morally good and sufficient reasons, which would not be guaranteed by an argument that proved only that the world was caused by an intelligent agent acting intentionally.

If (b) is true, then (the omnicompetence of the necessarily existential being having been established *ex hypothesi*) a teleological conclusion can be drawn without reference to the teleological argument, and an omnicompetent being can be assumed to act intentionally only from morally sufficient reasons: an ultimate teleological explanation is already included in (b).

Thus one might consistently accept both the cosmological argument and the proposition that there are logically contingent beings by holding that the existence of logically contingent and existentially dependent beings is to be explained by (i) the logically contingent activity of a logically necessary being, or (ii) the (conditionally) logically necessary activity of a logically contingent but necessarily existentially independent being, or (iii) the logically contingent activity of a logically contingent but necessarily existentially independent being. Further, the (a) branch of the cosmological argument *requires* a successful statement of the teleological argument in order to relate *A necessary being exists* to *God exists*, and the (b) branch already includes the materials for a teleological argument.

THE ONTOLOGICAL ARGUMENT

The ontological argument suggests that *God does not exist* is a contradiction, and hence that *God exists* is a necessary truth. It seems clear that negative existential propositions can be proved "by reflection alone"—as, for instance, the proposition *There are no objects that are both perfectly spherical and perfectly cubical.* It would also seem to be the case that some affirmative existential propositions are provable—as, for instance, the proposition *There is a prime number greater than seven.* Furthermore, it does not seem absurd to suggest that there may be some necessarily true affirmative existential propositions concerning areas other than mathematics and items other than numbers.

A FIRST VERSION OF THE ONTOLOGICAL ARGUMENT

One version of the argument goes as follows. "God," by definition, means "that being (if any) than whom no greater can be conceived." Given this definition as background, the argument proceeds as a *reductio*; it starts out with a proposition which is the denial of what one wants to prove, and (if it succeeds) shows that this proposition is false. Thus: (1) *God exists in the understanding only.* For **x** to "exist in the understanding only" amounts to something like this: that someone can think of **x** though **x** does not exist. Unicorns, then, "exist only in the understanding." The idea, of course, is to show that God does not exist in the understanding alone. Still, since persons are able to think about, or have a concept of, God, it is the case that: (2) *God exists in the understanding.* But (3) *To exist both in the understanding and in reality is better or greater than to exist in the understanding alone.* So: (4) *If (1) is true, then a being can be conceived which is greater than God (namely, one which exists in both the understanding and reality).* But (5) *No being can be conceived which is greater than God.* So (6) *God does not exist in the understanding alone.* And since (7) *If God does not exist in the understanding alone, God exists in reality,* it follows (from (6) and (7)) that (8) *God exists in reality.*

This version of the ontological argument is puzzling. What is one to make of (3), which, in effect, says: For any **x**, **x** is greater if someone has a concept of it and it exists than it is if someone has a concept of it and it does not exist?

ANSELM'S PROLOGUE

There is a prologue to Anselm's version of the ontological argument which can be put in some such fashion as this. Some words in our language are plainly nonreferential; "or," "but," "if-then," for example, are not words used to refer to any actual or possible items. Other words are referential, in that they have referential success or else referential failure[26]: "swan," "albatross," "unicorn," and "elf" are among them. Without trying to go beyond this roughhewn distinction, one can put the prologue's first premise as: (i) if one understands referential word **W** at **t**, then there is in one's mind at

26. Strictly, such success or failure occurs only as such terms are used in sentences whose truth value is determined by whether things exist to which these terms refer.

t some mental phenomenon **M** in virtue of which one understands **W** (one's understanding **W** involves one's having **M**); (ii) one understands the word "God"; so, from (i) and (ii), it follows that: (iii) there is some mental phenomenon (something in one's mind) in virtue of which one understands "God." But (iv) if there exists something in one's understanding in virtue of which one understands "God," then God exists in one's understanding (which is *not* to say: one understands that God exists). So: (v) God exists in one's understanding. One obvious restriction on (i) would be to require that it be logically possible that the term in question have referential success; this would rule out "round square," for example. Another, less obvious, restriction on (i) would be to rule out such referring terms as "the number one higher than any ever specifically thought of by the one whose idea this is," or, perhaps, to distinguish between the sort of mental phenomenon required in such cases as the last one and the sort required for understanding "swan." In any case, the idea seems to be that "God" has ambiguity of reference of some sort—to a mental phenomenon (whose existence makes *God exists in the understanding* true) and to the creator of heaven and earth (whose existence makes *God exists in reality* true). Apparently, this leads to talk of God existing only one way, or only the other, or in both ways, but means that having a concept of God is one thing, and God's existing is another.

If God does not exist, this suggests that there is nothing whatever that he is greater than. If God does not exist, and someone has a concept of God, this does not give God a greatness that he previously lacked. If God exists, he maximizes greatness in himself, so to speak; he does not become greater when some human being forms a concept of him. Presumably the ontological argument is not intended to deny this. One basic problem for one who wishes to offer the argument is to state (3) so it does not deny any of this—does not involve comparing a nonexistent God with an existent one—and is true, or else to replace (3) by some claim that is true and will serve the overall purposes of the argument.

THE PROLOGUE REJECTED

The difference between the words "swan" and "elf" is not that the former word can be used to refer to *two* sorts of entities (one a mental phenomenon in the mind of anyone who understands the word "swan," the other a kind of feathered mammal) and the latter word can be used only to refer to *one* sort of entity (the mental phenomenon in the mind of anyone who understands the word "elf"); rather the former word refers to *one* sort of entity, and the latter to *none*. The version of the ontological argument presented above cannot be cogent if it requires us to think of the word "God" as having two sorts or referent, one mental, one not, or if it were to ask us to suppose that the entity that results from the combination of the mental phenomenon in anyone's mind who understands the word "God" *plus* the creator of heaven and earth is greater than just the mental entity alone, for there is no such combined entity. The argument will certainly be better off if it does not require that there be some mental phenomenon present in the mind of anyone who understands a referential word, for that analysis of what it is to understand, or to have concepts, is hardly unchallengeable; a natural theology that did not require it would be more plausible as a result.

(3), then, is puzzling. It is not clear how one is to understand it; insofar as it bids one compare a thing which exists with that very thing's nonexistence, it (for the reasons noted) is not very encouraging. If we read it as *If one has a concept of* **x** *and of* **y**, *and* **x** *exists but* **y** *does not, then* **x** *is greater than* **y**, what little grasp one has on the concept of greatness, if it suggests anything, suggests that if **x** exists and **y** does not, **x** is greater than **y** even if one has a concept of **y** but none of **x**—that a thing's greatness is not affected, one way or the other, by one's having a concept of that thing.

THE FIRST VERSION REJECTED

If, then, one puts the argument along the lines so far suggested, it reads: (1') One has a concept of God. (2') For God to be such that God exists and one has a concept of him is greater on God's part than for God not to exist and one to have a concept of him. (3') If it is the case that God does not exist and one has a concept of God, then one can conceive a being greater than God (namely one which exists and satisfies the concept of God, or, perhaps, one which both satisfies *any* concept, and exists). (4') One cannot conceive of a greater being than God. So (5') It is not the case both that one has a concept of God and God does not exist. So (from (1') and (5')) It is not the case that God does not exist. Hence (6') God exists.

There seems to be no reason not to put the (1'–6') argument more straightforwardly; the reference to one having a concept of

God seems mere window dressing, and the argument to amount to something like: (i) God is that being than whom no greater can be conceived. (ii) If God does not exist, and a peanut does, then the peanut is greater than God. (iii) If a peanut is greater than God, then it can be conceived as being greater than God. (iv) No peanut can be conceived as being greater than God. Now (v) There are peanuts, and none of them is greater than God. Hence (vi) God exists. One question the critic will want to ask is: What entitles one to take the definition to amount to more than this—that *If God exists, then no being exists which is greater than he* is a necessary truth? If this is what (i) means, then (iv) is false; if a peanut exists, and God does not, then the peanut is greater and can be conceived as such. At least, this is so if one takes existence to enhance, or be a necessary condition of, greatness, and it seems that the ontological arguer has this sort of thing in mind.

ANOTHER STATEMENT OF THE ARGUMENT

This "balder" statement of the ontological argument might be replaced by one balder still; (a) God = (def.) a being having all perfections. (b) Necessary existence is a perfection. So: (c) God has necessary existence. Since (c) is identical to "*God does not exist*" *is a contradiction,* this yields the conclusion the ontological arguer desires.

THE NOTION OF A PERFECTION AND ITS PROBLEMS

One standard puzzle regarding the ontological argument concerns some such premise as *Existence is a perfection* or *Necessary existence is a perfection,* where perfections are properties of some sort or other. Leibniz offered perhaps as full and clear a definition of "perfection" as any. Suppose that, for some property **A**, there is a degree **N** of *being* **A** such that it is logically impossible that anything be **A** to a degree greater than **N**. Then **A** has a *logical upper limit.* Omniscience, it seems, is the logical upper limit of knowledge, and omnipotence of power. *Necessary existence* might then be viewed as the *logical upper limit* of existence, even though existence seems to allow only the "degrees" *logically contingent* and *logically necessary.* Properties having no such limit are not perfections. Again, if a property is a perfection, it is one which it is better to have than to lack—better, presumably, for anything whatever, or for anything whatever that *can* have it, or the like. So part, anyway, of what it is for a property **A** to be a perfection is for **A** to have a logical upper limit and be better to possess than not. Finally, **A** must be a positive, and not a negative, property; perhaps what this amounts to is that **x** *is* **A** ascribes, rather than denies, a property to **x**, as **x** *knows* **P** ascribes something to **x** and **x** *is ignorant of* **P** denies of **x** what the former ascribes to **x**. Still, this hardly makes the notion lucid. Has (or is) being pure red a logical upper limit? Perhaps it is not a property it is better to have than to lack, even if it also is not better to lack than have. Or perhaps it is better for some things to have it, and others not, and this is what prevents it from being a perfection. Is *being omnibenevolent* the logical upper limit of *being a loving being*? Presumably, it is logically impossible that there be some proposition which is not known by an omniscient being; not even if he is omnipotent can an omniscient being create a proposition an omniscient being does not know to be true (if it is true) or false (if it is false). But presumably an omnipotent being can create one more rational being than it has so far created, and if he is omnibenevolent, he will love this new creature as well as loving all the other rational creatures previously created. Or, if one views propositions as eternal abstract objects (and so uncreatable), it is logically impossible that there be a proposition whose truth value is unknown by an omniscient being, but possible that an omniscient, omnipotent being create new rational creatures which, if he is omnibenevolent, he will love as he has loved old ones.

Perhaps *being all-loving* is a perfection, and **x** has this property if (i) **x** loves every person there is, at every time, and (ii) were there more persons than there are, then, relative to loving, **x** would be related to them as **x** is to the persons there are. But this is not for *being all-loving* to have a logical upper limit, in the sense in which it would appear that *being omnipotent* and *being omniscient* do have logical upper limits. It seems clear that the notion of *being a perfection,* or *being perfect,* or *being great,* is not a lucid notion. It is not clear what it includes; it is not clear that it includes all, or includes only, what the ontological argument requires that it include, if the ontological argument is to succeed. Nor is it clear that this deficiency is reparable.

A VERSION OF THE ARGUMENT NOT REQUIRING THE NOTION OF A PERFECTION

Another version of the argument runs as follows. Let **G** = *God exists* and **N** = *Necessarily, God exists,* and **NN** = *Necessarily, God* *does not exist.* Then: (1) **G** or not-**G**. (2) If **G**, then **N**. (3) If not-**G**, then **NN**. (4) **N** or **NN** (5) **NN** is true if and only if **G** is a contradiction. (6) **G** is not a contradiction. (7) **NN** is false. So: (8) **N**.

(1) is a necessary truth. (4) follows from (1–3).[27] (5) is a necessary truth, and (6) seems true, though it has been challenged. (7) follows from (5) and (6), and (8) from (4) and (7). The argument succeeds, then, provided (2) and (3) are true. (2) says that if *God exists* is true, then it is a necessary truth; (3) says that if God exists is false, then it is a necessary falsehood. Neither (2) nor (3) is obviously true; if *God exists* is logically contingent and true, or is logically contingent and false, both (2) and (3) are false. If (2) is true, then so is (3) (and conversely), for if (2) is true then *God exists* is a modal proposition—a proposition which, if false, is a contradiction and, if true, is necessarily so; but then (3) is also true.

THE ARGUMENT REJECTED

The argument is not yet a proof; (2) may be false. One can argue for (2) in the following manner. (2) is a hypothetical statement—it has the form *if* **P** *then* **Q**. One can prove a hypothetical proposition by *assuming* **P** and then deriving **Q** from **P** by using only propositions known to be true. So the first step will be: (2a) G. Then we add: (2b) Necessarily, if God exists, then God is everlasting. Suppose one can derive (2c) Necessarily, God is everlasting, from (2a) and (2b). (2b) entails: (2d) Necessarily, for any time **t**, God exists at **t**. But (2e) *Necessarily, for any time* **t**, *God exists at* **t** entails *Necessarily, God exists.* So, from (2d) and (2e), it follows that: (2f) Necessarily, God exists. Since (2f) is the consequent of (2), if the derivation is proper, then the consequent of (2) has been derived from the antecedent of (2); (2) will have been proved.

Nonetheless, the derivation is not proper; the supposition that (2c) follows from (2a) and (2b) is false. The form of the *(2a) and (2b), so (2c)* inference is: **P**; *Necessarily (if* **P** *then* **Q**); *so Necessarily,* **Q**. Notoriously, this form of argumentation is invalid. Consider this argument: (i) *There are five fingers on the human hand; (ii) Necessarily, five is greater than four; so: (iii) Necessarily, there are more than four*

27. It is not clear that (4) is a necessary truth; if *God exists* is logically contingent, (4) is false, and it is not clear that *God exists* is not logically contingent.

fingers on the human hand. Now (i) and (ii) are true; if (iii) is true, it is logically impossible that God have created persons with four-fingered hands and that is false. So (iii) is false. Since (i) and (ii) are true, (iii) cannot follow from (i) and (ii). So the derivation is not proper. Hence the derivation does not provide a justification of (2).

A MORE COMPLEX VERSION OF THE ONTOLOGICAL ARGUMENT[28]

A more complex version of the ontological argument runs along these lines. Consider the claims (A) God exists in reality; (B) God cannot be thought not to exist in reality; (C) God cannot not exist in reality (i.e., God cannot fail to exist in reality). If (A–C) are true, then presumably the conclusion of the ontological argument is true. An argument that showed that (A–C) were true would properly count as a successful variety of the ontological argument.

Let "God" be defined as above. Then consider these claims: (1) If God exists in the mind alone, then God does not exist in reality. (2) If God does not exist in reality, then God can fail to exist in reality. (3) If God can fail to exist in reality, God can be thought not to exist in reality.[29] (4) If God can be thought not to exist in reality, then God can be thought to have a beginning and an end. (5) If God can be thought to exist in reality, then God can be thought not to have a beginning or an end. (6) If God can be thought to have a beginning and an end, and God can be thought not to have a beginning and an end, then God can be thought to be greater.[30]

28. While at least as plausible as the previous version of the ontological argument, this version has been less discussed. The discussion of the argument is itself somewhat complex, and the reader may wish to skip over to the section "A 'Possible Worlds' Statement of the Ontological Argument."

29. Reading "can" as "it is logically possible that," understanding "X exists in realitv" as "X exists," and understanding "X exists in the understanding alone" as "X does not exist, but someone has a concept of X," (1–3) seem to be true.

30. (7) is true, provided the concept of God, as defined above, is not inconsistent. Regarding (5), presumably "God can be thought not to have a beginning or an end" means "consistent with the definition offered earlier, a concept of God can be formed according to which *if* X *is God, then* X *has neither beginning nor end,* or *if* X *is God, then* X *exists in reality and* X *has neither beginning nor end,* is true, and if that concept can be formed, it can be formed whether God exists in reality or not"; but since God's existing in reality would not be a barrier to the possibility of forming that concept, and since it can be formed, (5) is true.

The idea behind (6) seems to be that *existing and not being able to have a beginning or an ending* is better than such states as *existing and being able to have (but also not to have) a beginning and being able to have (but also not to have) an end* or *existing and being able to have a beginning and an end* or *existing and being able to have a beginning* or *existing and being able to have an end.* The suggestion is that the *concepts* of these states of affairs are to be ranked in a hierarchy corresponding to the hierarchy of the states of affairs; thus a being to which the concept *existing and not being able to have a beginning or an end* applies is greater than one to which *exists, and is able to have (but also able not to have) a beginning and able to have (but also able not to have) an end,* and so on. Perhaps one can put the point behind (6) in this way: suppose we have the concept **C** of a being which is all-knowing, all-powerful, and all-good, and are wondering whether **C1** *is not capable of having beginning or end,* or **C2** *has neither beginning nor end,* or **C3** *is capable of having a beginning or end,* or **C4** *has both beginning and end,* should be used to complete **C**; perhaps (6)'s point is that **C1** rounds out **C** in the most elegant fashion.

To (1–6), the argument adds: (7) God can be thought to exist in reality, (8) It is false that God can be thought to be greater than he is, and (9) If God exists in the mind alone, and God can be thought to exist in reality, then God can be thought to be greater than he is. The claim is that (1–9) are true, and entail (A–C).

(1–9) do entail (A–C). (7–9), for example, entail (A) God exists in reality, provided we assume that *It is false that* **X** *exists in the mind alone* is identical to **X** *exists in reality,* for (9), in effect, says *If God exists in the mind alone, and (7) is true, then (8) is false.* That (8) is true entails that either God does not exist in the mind alone or (7) is false; this, plus (7), entails that God does not exist in the mind alone. But (9) involves familiar problems about comparing a thing with its own nonexistence.

Proposition (C) God cannot not exist in reality, entails proposition (A), so if (1–9) contains a proof of (C), it also includes a proof of (A). But (B) God cannot be thought not to exist in reality, entails (C), and it is hard to see how (C) will be established without inferring it from (B) or something much like (B). Does (1–9) establish (B)? Premise (3) reads: If God can fail to exist in reality, then God can be thought not to exist in reality.

(B) is identical to the denial of (3)'s consequent; if (1–9) contains a proof of (B), (3) will probably be essential to that proof.

(3)'s converse is: If God cannot be thought not to exist in reality, God cannot fail to exist in reality; since this is true, (3) is true. But this, by itself, does not show that (1–9) provides a proof of (B).

THE MORE COMPLEX ARGUMENT REJECTED

Unfortunately, it seems clear that the argument will involve claims to the effect that a being is greater if it cannot have a beginning and an end than if it can, and so God cannot have a beginning and an end. It will continue to the effect that if God can be thought not to exist, then he can be thought to have a beginning and an end, and thus conclude that God cannot be thought not to exist. Presumably, this line of reasoning will require that (4) be true; (4) says that if God can be thought not to exist in reality, God can be thought to have a beginning and an end, and that is false. It seems true that *Necessarily, if God exists then he has neither beginning nor end*; one can grant that proposition and be an atheist. Thus God can be thought not to exist in reality even if he cannot be thought to have beginning or end; one can accept both *If God exists, then God is everlasting* and *God does not exist* without inconsistency, unless *God does not exist* itself is a contradiction—which is what the argument is supposed to prove. Since (4) is both essential to deriving (B) from (1–9), and false, this version of the ontological argument fails.

A "POSSIBLE WORLDS" STATEMENT OF THE ONTOLOGICAL ARGUMENT

Leibniz suggested an equivalence between **P** *is a necessary truth* and **P** *is true in all possible worlds,* and between **P** *is a contradiction* and **P** *is false in all possible worlds.* This way of looking at logically necessary truths and falsehoods obviously is connected with the notion of a logically possible world. Let us call what makes a proposition expressed by a declarative sentence true, if it is true, a *state of affairs*; what makes My *pen is black* true is the state of affairs of my pen's being black.[31] Then one can develop the notion of a possible world

31. One might say that the state of affairs that makes My *pen is black* true is a state of affairs that *obtains,* and the state of affairs that would make My *pen is green* true, were it true, is a state of affairs that does *not* obtain. Both these states of affairs are possible, and possibly obtain, though only one does obtain. Since there is nothing that could occur or obtain that would make My *pen is not a pen* (or any contradictory proposition) true, no states of affairs, obtaining or nonobtaining, are related to it as possible states of affairs are related to My *pen is black* and My *pen is green.*

along these lines. State of affairs **A** *includes* state of affairs **B** if and only if **A** *obtains* entails **B** *obtains*, and **A** *precludes* **B** if and only if **A** *obtains* entails **B** *does not obtain.* Then a state of affairs is *maximal* if it either includes, or else precludes, every other state of affairs. Then a *possible world* is a maximal state of affairs. A *logically necessary being* is one which exists in all possible worlds; a *logically contingent being* will exist only in some.

As noted above, the ontological argument endeavors to show that *God does not exist* is a contradiction, or that *God exists* is a necessary truth, or that under any logically possible conditions it is true that God exists. Still another way of putting its conclusion is by saying that *God exists in all possible worlds*; then since the actual world is one of the possible ones, God exists in the actual world.

Assume that a being can "exist" in more than one possible world. As noted, a necessary being exists in all possible worlds, a contingent being only in some. Let a being's *excellence* in a given world **W** depend on the properties it has in **W**; if **A** and **B** exist in worlds **W1** and **W2**, and in **W1** **A** is more intelligent, stronger, more attractive, of better character, and similarly for all other excellence-relevant features, than **B**, whereas in **W2** **B** has the advantage in all of these ways over **A**, then **A**'s excellence is greater than **B**'s in **W1** but B's excellence is greater than **A**'s in **W2**. A being's *greatness* will be a function of its excellence in all the worlds in which it exists. A being which is all-knowing, all-powerful, and all-good in **W1** will have *maximal excellence* in **W1**; *maximal greatness* will belong only to a being which has *maximal excellence* in every world in which it exists, and which exists in every possible world.

Given these definitions, developed by Plantinga, one can state various "possible worlds" versions of the ontological argument. (One way of taking Anselm's definition of "God," given a possible worlds perspective, is "Necessarily, God has maximal greatness.") One of the simpler versions of the ontological argument, the "possible worlds" version, goes as follows. Since each premise is intended to express a necessary truth, the word "Necessarily" will be understood at the beginning of each premise. While fairly simple, this version nonetheless seems to bring out the most essential features of this sort of argument. Let "world" be understood as "possible world," and let "MG" be short for "'maximal greatness." Then: (1) If **x** has MG in any world, it has MG in every world. (2) It is logically possible that God has MG in at least one world. (3) If it is logically possible that God has MG in at least one world, then God does have MG in at least one world. So (from (2) and (3)): (4) God has MG in at least one world. Thus, from (1) and (4), it follows that: (5) God has MG in every world. But: (6) If God has MG in every world, then God exists in every world. And: (7) If **x** exists in every world, then it is a necessary truth that **x** exists. So: (8) It is a necessary truth that God exists (from (5-7)).

The first premise of the ontological argument, the "possible worlds" version, claims that if **x** has MG in any world, then **x** has MG in every world. Select some arbitrarily chosen possible world **W**; what is it to have MG in **W**? If **x** has MG in **W**, then of course **x** has maximal excellence in **W**. But **x**, again in **W**, also has this more complex property: *for any world* **W'** *such that* **W'** *is not identical to* **W**, **w** *has maximal excellence in* **W'**. One might call this complex property that **x** enjoys in **W** something like *other-world-maximality*. So if **x** has MG in **W**, then **x** enjoys *maximal-excellence-in-***W** and *other-world-maximality-in-***W**. And given that **x** has these properties in **W**, for any world **W*** it will be the case that **x** enjoys *maximal-excellence-in-***W*** and *other-world-maximality-in-***W***, though what worlds are "other" in **W*** will not be quite the same worlds that are "other" in **W'**. So if **x** has *maximal-excellence-and-other-world-maximality* in any world, **x** has it in every. But to have MG in a world is to have *maximal-excellence-and-other-world-maximality* in that world. So to have MG in any world is to have it in every; premise (1) is true.

The truth of (3) follows from what it is to be a possible world; (7) expresses a "possible worlds" understanding of logical necessity. As noted, (4) follows from (2) and (3); (5) follows from (1) and (4); (8) follows from (5) and (7). Thus the interesting premise is (2). (2) is true unless the proposition *God has* MG is logically contradictory. Since it at least *seems* not to be contradictory, (2) at least *seems* true.

A "POSSIBLE WORLDS" DISONTOLOGICAL ARGUMENT

A *disontological* argument has as conclusion *It is logically impossible that God exist* or *Necessarily, God does not exist*. A disontological argument, constructed from "possible worlds" materials and made analogous to the ontological argument just presented, goes as follows. Again, each premise is intended to be necessarily true, "world" is short for "possible world," and "MG" does duty for "maximal greatness." Then: (1) If **x** lacks MG in any world, it lacks MG in every world. (2) It is logically possible that God lack MG in at least one world. (3) If it is logically possible that God lack MG in at least one world, then God does lack MG in at least one world. So, from (2) and (3): (4) God lacks MG in at least one world. Thus, from (1) and (4): (5) God lacks MG in every world.

Here, of course, we cannot go on as before; it will not do to claim that: If God lacks MG in every world, then he exists in every world. After all, every human being lacks MG in every world, both in those in which they exist and in those in which they do not. But it does not follow that any human person has logically necessary existence, or exists in all possible worlds. The most promising way to continue, presumably, is along some such lines as these: (6) In any world in which God exists, God has MG. Then, from (5) and (6): (7) God does not exist in any world. But (8) If **x** exists in no world, then **x** *does not exist* is logically necessary. Hence, from (7) and (8): (9) *God does not exist* is logically necessary. Premise (6), of course, accepts a "possible worlds" analysis of Anselm's remarks about God being that being than which no greater can be conceived.

Once again, premise (1) is true by virtue of the meaning of "maximal greatness." Like the property *being blue in every possible world*, the property *possessing maximal greatness in every possible world* is an every-world or else a no-world affair. Again, (3) is true, given the way in which "possible world" is defined, and (8) expresses a "possible worlds" understanding of logical necessity. (2) and (3) entail (4); (1) and (4) entail (5); (5) and (6) entail (7); (7) and (8) entail (9). As noted, (6) expresses the same analysis of the concept of God as was used in the "possible worlds" version of the ontological argument presented above; if one accepts that analysis, one cannot in consistency reject (6). So the premise of interest is (2).

Premise (2) is true only if the proposition *God has* MG is logically contradictory. It at least *seems* not to be contradictory. So premise (2) of the disontological argument at least *seems* to be false.

AN ASSESSMENT OF THE "POSSIBLE WORLDS" VERSIONS OF THE ONTOLOGICAL AND DISONTOLOGICAL ARGUMENTS

A proposition is either *necessarily true*, *necessarily false*, or else *logically contingent* (whether true or false). Along the lines of the arguments just presented, this amounts to a proposition being either *true in all possible worlds*, or *true in no possible worlds and so false in all*, or *true in at least one and false in at least one.*[32] Necessary truth, necessary falsehood, and logical contingency provide the logical *modalities*. (*Being possibly true* is identical to *being necessarily true or else logically contingent*.) A proposition has just one such modality, and whatever modality it has, it has necessarily; a proposition's modality cannot change.[33]

The proposition *God has* MG is either true in all possible worlds, or else it is true in none; so it is either a logically necessary truth or else a contradiction.

Many theists do not hold that *God exists* is a necessary truth; either they hold that it is true but logically contingent, or they simply hold that it is true and have no views at all (and perhaps have not thought much about) what its modality might be. Further, so far as I can see, it is a perfectly respectable theism which holds that *God exists* is true but logically contingent—which holds, say, that *Necessarily, God has maximal excellence* in the sense that *If God exists, then he has maximal excellence*, but that *(Necessarily) God has* MG is false. For such a theist, God presumably will be not only omnipotent, omniscient, and omnibenevolent, but also ontologically independent, Creator, Providence, and Savior. But while he will have these features, he will not—on this conception—be a logically necessary being.

According to the ontological arguer of the sort described here, since *God exists* is logically necessary (and necessarily so), the view that *God exists* is logically contingent (and necessarily so) is not merely *false*; it is *necessarily false* or contradictory. On this view "*God exists*" *is logically contingent* is a contradiction.

According to the type of theist described in the preceding paragraph but one, since the proposition *God exists* is logically contingent and true, and since a proposition possesses its modality with logical necessity, it is the case that "*God exists*" *is necessarily true* is itself necessarily false or logically contradictory.

The "possible worlds" disontological arguer could contend that *God has maximal excellence* is logically contradictory—that *being om-*

32. This provides the "possible worlds" account of logical modality.

33. The view is that every proposition has a modality which it has necessarily: Cp→N(Cp), Np→N(Np), and N(not-p)→ N(N(not-p)), where C="it is contingent that" and N="it is necessary that."

nipotent or *being omniscient* or *being omnibenevolent* is an incoherent notion, or that it is impossible that all three concepts describe any one being. But he need not. He may hold that *God has maximal excellence (in the actual world)* is perfectly consistent—that it is logically contingent and might have been true. What he cannot allow is that *God has* MG might be true. God might have had maximal excellence in our world; he may have it in some nonactual possible world. But he could not have had it in *all* possible worlds. But how could we tell that this is so (or that it is not)?

Suppose my shirt is blue. Couldn't my shirt exist in all possible worlds? And couldn't it (or something anyway) be blue in all possible worlds? One way to argue that the answer to these questions is negative would be to rehearse the notions that together make up the concept of a possible world, or resort to legitimate metaphors about how such worlds are "constructed." But in the end, however useful a "possible worlds" model may be, when one wants to know whether *My shirt exists in all possible worlds* or *In all possible worlds, something is blue*[34] is true, the question is whether *My shirt exists* is a necessary truth, and whether *Something is blue* is a necessary truth—i.e., whether the denials of these propositions are contradictory. And of course the answer is negative.

Analogously, if one wants to know whether *God has* MG is true, the question is whether *God exists and has maximal excellence* is a necessary truth. And since *If God exists then he has maximal excellence* is very plausibly viewed as a necessary truth, the question plausibly reduces to whether *God exists* is a necessary truth. If it is true (and so necessarily true) that God has MG, then *God exists* is itself a necessary truth. But that *God exists* is itself a necessary truth is not so obvious—even to many theists—that one who doubted that *God exists* is a necessary truth would be irrational to argue that (i) that *God exists* is not clearly a necessary truth, and since (ii) *God has* MG entails *"God exists" is a necessary truth*, it follows that (iii) it is not clear that *God has* MG is true. One who so argued would allow doubts about *Necessarily, God exists* to infect one's epistemic attitude toward *God has* MG, and nothing in this seems to me epistemically improper. Nor need one who so argued base any of her doubts on hesitations about theism generally, or in all of its varieties.

34. Whether "something" is read as "some one item" or as "some item or other."

The ontological arguer supposes that *God has* MG is true. If it is true, it is necessarily true; and if it is true, then *Necessarily, if God exists, then God has* MG also is true. So the ontological arguer must accept this latter claim too. The disontological arguer also requires *Necessarily, if God exists, then God has* MG. As noted, this proposition occurs as an essential premise in the disontological argument.

Two things seem especially relevant here. One is that the properties orthodox monotheism ascribes to God—in particular, those included in *omnicompetence* or *maximal excellence*—are not such that God's possessing them entails his possessing *logically necessary existence.* The other is that while *God has logically necessary existence* does not seem contradictory, it also does not seem that *God has logically contingent existence* is contradictory. On the doctrine that a proposition possesses its modality with necessity, one of these propositions *is* logically contradictory; either (i) it is logically contradictory that *God has logically necessary existence,* or (ii) it is logically contradictory that *God has logically contingent existence.* If (i) is true, it is necessarily true that *God has logically contingent existence, or it is logically necessary that God does not exist*; if (ii) is true, it is true that *God has logically necessary existence or it is logically contradictory that God exist.*

Premise (2) of the "possible worlds" version of the ontological argument presupposes that (i) is true and (ii) is false. Thus, if (ii) is true, premise (2) of the ontological argument is false. Nothing in the "possible worlds" version of the ontological argument, so far as I can see, establishes that we should accept (i) rather than (ii). That one accepts *God exists* does *not* militate in favor of (i) over (ii), or of (ii) over (i). Even after the ontological argument, (ii) remains at least equiplausible with (i). Hence—where (2), again, is the second premise of the ontological argument—*not-(2)* is equiplausible with (2). Thus the "possible worlds" version of the ontological argument is not a proof.

THE MORAL ARGUMENT

Perhaps, where the previous arguments fail, the moral argument may succeed. Kant's varieties of such arguments—perhaps torn from the strictures of his epistemology—have been influential in this regard, and suggest certain relevant themes. One way of putting the moral argument begins with some such notion as this: it is wrong that a person be worthy of happiness, and not receive it; the "highest good" would include, or perhaps be comprised by, every person receiving just that amount of happiness which their morally relevant conduct has deserved. In a world in which moral propositions are true, the "highest good" will be realized; in our world, moral propositions are true. So, in our world, the "highest good" will be realized. But the chances that each person's happiness fit hand-in-glove with that which she deserves, without omnicompetence being involved, must be astoundingly small. So there is an omnibenevolent, omnipotent, omniscient being whose justice is manifested in his proportioning worthiness of happiness to happiness in every case.

This line of reasoning has more problems than premises. Is omnibenevolence strictly required if one is to proportion happiness to worthiness thereof? is omnipotence? is omniscience? More basically, what is one to make of the notion that a good person is *worthy* of happiness? Presumably, one might speak of something like *moral happiness,* meaning the satisfaction one rightly takes in the state of affairs in which a person (oneself or another) does what is right. But then one who *does* what is right presumably has access to moral happiness without the requirement that omnicompetence be involved, save as omnicompetence may be involved in creating and sustaining the world anyway. But if happiness means something along the lines of *physical happiness,* meaning that things (morally and otherwise) go as one (insofar as one is rational and moral) wishes (or would wish), what reason is there to think that even (i) *Insofar as one is morally good, one deserves (ought to receive) physical happiness* is true, let alone (ii) *Insofar as one is morally good, one will receive physical happiness,* which the argument, at some point prior to the conclusion, will require? Perhaps virtue is just its own reward, and that is the end of it; the "highest good" would just be every person doing what is right, period. Or perhaps (i) is true, but (ii) is false. Even if (i) is true, and known to be true, why believe that (ii) is true?

A different sort of theme arises if one argues that one's moral obligation is to be morally perfect. Once one has sinned, one cannot any longer be perfect, but the obligation to be perfect remains. The best one can hope for, once one has chosen or acted wrongly, is that one shall ever after *approach* moral perfection, always more closely, as one chooses rightly. Only if this hope lies before one is one fully rational in being moral; since one is fully rational in being moral, this prospect does lie before one. So one must be immortal. But not just *any* immortality will do; an afterlife in which one could not choose rightly, or had no freedom of choice, or faced no morally significant alternatives, or the like, would not do, and an omnicompetent moral ruler is postulated to guarantee that in the afterlife one continues to exist in a world in which moral agency is possible.

This line of reasoning, too, is filled with problems. Must a moral ruler be omnicompetent in order to carry out his assigned tasks? Might one be justified if one sinned in order to assure one's immortality? More basically, is any good reason given for supposing that persons are immortal? Suppose Ralph, at time **t**, who has made a few moral choices, all freely and rightly, now makes his first wrong choice. Then (the idea is) he cannot be, or become, morally perfect. Either this inference is correct, or it is not. Suppose it is. Then if he cannot be, or become, morally perfect, he is not obligated to be, or become, morally perfect; what he cannot do, he cannot be obligated to do. What he is obligated to do is to be, or become, as good as he can. This obligation will remain with him, even should he make a second moral mistake, and a third, and a thousandth. But then no argument to immortality can be launched from an obligation to be, or become, morally perfect.

Suppose the inference is incorrect; Ralph still can be morally perfect, or can become so. Presumably this will be the case if we reject the quantitative model that seems to be assumed by the argument.[35] Instead, being morally perfect will be understood along some such lines as these: one is morally perfect at time **t** if and only if (whether one has ever done wrong or not) at **t** it is true of one that one will do what is right in each actual choice or action done at **t**, and would do what is right, no matter what morally relevant choices or actions one were to face at **t**. Or, perhaps, one would want to require that this sort of thing is true of one *at* **t** *and any time after* **t** *at which one existed* if one is to be morally perfect at **t**. On this account, human moral perfection will be rare indeed, but it will not be rendered unavailable to Ralph simply because Ralph once falls from the straight and narrow path of virtue. But then, on this account of moral perfection, even if one has a duty to be, or become, morally perfect it does not follow that one is immortal.

35. A necessary, and sufficient, condition of one being morally perfect is that every morally relevant choice or action that one makes is made rightly, and that one does make such choices and perform such actions.

A VERSION OF THE MORAL ARGUMENT

The question arises, then, as to whether one can derive, from these or other themes, something that seriously can be called an argument. Suppose Ralph discovers that he can save his son's life only by contributing a kidney to him; the kidney must be healthy, of course, and the problem Ralph faces is that he has one healthy kidney and one bad one. If he contributes the kidney, Ralph runs grave risk of condemning himself to death, since his other, bad, kidney will probably burst if it is left alone in the ecology of Ralph's body. Under the circumstances, it probably will be said, Ralph's giving his kidney is *supererogation*; it is above and beyond the call of duty if he does this.

Suppose further, however, that only Ralph's son has the ability to discover the cure for some dread disease, and is on the verge of doing so, provided of course that he lives in good health (which he will do only if Ralph gives him one of Ralph's kidneys). Then, perhaps, it will be Ralph's *duty* to give the kidney, even at high price to himself. The core idea of the development of an *argument* from this sort of case—and there are many types of real cases corresponding to our simple hypothetical example—involves its being somehow *irrational* for Ralph to do his duty even though it is *always rational* to do one's duty.

If the argument is to the effect that Ralph is imprudent (and in *that* sense irrational) to give a healthy kidney to his son, this may be true, but it is hard to see how this gives rise to an argument of any cogency. The argument would go along some such lines as these: (1) It is sometimes *prudentially irrational* to act in a way that is morally right. (2) Necessarily, it is always rational to act in a waythat is morally right. (3) Necessarily, if it is rational to act in a particular way, it is not also irrational (prudentially or otherwise) to act in that way. Thus, from (3), it will follow that (4): (1) and (2) cannot both be true. But: (5) Necessarily, if two propositions **P** and **Q** are incompatible, and **P** is a necessary truth, then **Q** is false. So, from (1), (2), and (5), we get: (6) (1) is false. Then the remainder of the argument will follow some such line as the following. (1) appears to be true; indeed (1) is true, unless it is the case that Ralph will not give up his life if he gives his son a healthy kidney. Ralph almost certainly will give up his life *in this world* if he gives the kidney; so (almost certainly?) Ralph in fact will survive death. But not just any sort of survival of death will render Ralph other than prudentially irrational to give his kidney away, and an omnicompetent deity must be postulated to make sure Ralph's doing his duty is properly rewarded and does not exact a sacrifice it is not reasonable to ask of him.

THIS VERSION REJECTED

The general idea behind this argument can be expressed in some such terms as these: (the capacity of) reason has various applications, some moral, some theoretical, some prudential, and (in a rational universe) these applications can never conflict. Prudential reasoning calculates what is to our advantage; moral reasoning reflects concerning our duties. What it will be to our advantage to do, then, will never conflict with what it is our duty to do; any apparent conflict is such that it will be reasonable to remove it by assuming (what is thereby shown to be likely true) whatever proposition or propositions there may be whose truth will remove the conflict. There always will be such a proposition or propositions, and in cases in which various one-or-more membered sets of such propositions will remove the conflict (and one knows this, and knows as well which they are), one is entitled to take it that the disjunctive proposition which results from their combination is true. When there is only one such set, one is justified in believing that set.

In most, if not all, cases, one can find various sets which fit the expressed criteria. For example, one might hold that Ralph's son will survive death, and in his afterlife continue doing scientific work, discover the cure for which he was working and send the message back to various mediums who would then share it with the medical community, who would rejoice in the knowledge thereby conveyed. This set of propositions has not much to recommend it, but it does satisfy the condition that if it is true, the clash between prudence and duty is avoided. Ingenuity could suggest a host of other sets that met the same condition.

More basically, why suppose that one's interests and one's duty cannot conflict? If one supposes that one's duty overrides one's interests, one has no dilemma; this involves rejecting the assumption that one application of reason never leads to different conclusions than that of another, including never leading to the conclusion that one sort of action both is, and is not, the appropriate one (on different criteria of appropriateness). Then one can simply hold that some applications or reason—for example, valid reasoning from some sorts of premises—is more weighty, so to say, than some others. Either prudence is not a moral virtue, or it is one which ranks lower than the virtue of doing one's duty. So much for the alleged conflict, and hence for the alleged need to deal with the conflict by positing speculative propositions.

ANOTHER VERSION OF THE MORAL ARGUMENT

There is another way, however, of stating the argument: (1) Each person has inherent value. (2) Sometimes, it is a person's duty to sacrifice his or her life for the sake of others. (3) If a person's death is the end of the existence of that person, then when a person sacrifices his or her life, a person brings to an end something of inherent value. (4) It is never a person's duty to bring to an end something of inherent value. So: (5) A person's death is not the end of the existence of that person.

The perspective this argument reflects is one which rejects the commensurability thesis; the value resident in being a person is not, like the pleasure of eating ice cream and the joy of completing a task, to be tossed into the sum of satisfactions awaiting utilitarian calculation. Less plausibily, it assumes that tragedy—at least, tragedy of a certain magnitude—does not occur. But suppose that the tragedy of the cessation of existence of persons does occur. Then, perhaps, there are conflicts of duties—conflicts in terms of saving one person's life over another's, or of either losing one's own life or not saving another's. Perhaps, in a theistic world—a world created and governed by an omnicompetent deity—such conflicts will not be ultimate; perhaps the (1–5) argument considered above should be expanded along some such lines as these: (1) Each person has inherent value. (2) Sometimes, it is a person's duty to sacrifice his or her life for the sake of others. (3) If a person's death is the end of the existence of that person, then when a person sacrifices his or her life, a person brings an end to something of inherent value. (4) It is never a person's duty to bring an end to something of inherent value, which would be an ultimate tragedy. (4a) One always can perform one's duties without causing an ultimate tragedy, and that this is so is no accident. (4b) Only in a world governed by an omnicompetent deity is it other than an accident that one always can perform one's duties without causing an ultimate tragedy.

So: (5) The death of a person is not the end of that person, and (5a) the world is governed by an omnicompetent deity.

THE MORAL ARGUMENT REJECTED

But obviously one can reply to this argument exactly as before: there may be conflicts of genuine duties and ultimately tragic moral choices to be made. At least some versions of theism hold that ultimate tragedies may never occur, even if we scrupulously attend to our duties. Perhaps if theism is false there is no such guarantee, and in fact there will be conflicts of duties such that carrying out either duty will involve ultimate tragedies. But unless we have evidence that theism (and in particular, theism of a variety that rules out ultimate tragedy) is true, we have no reason to think such conflicts do not occur. Unless we know (independent of knowing that theism is true) that there are no ultimate tragedies, we lack knowledge of a premise crucial to the argument, and so the argument is not a proof.

It seems to be generally true that moral arguments will exploit some such strategy as that involved in the expanded version of the argument under consideration. They will argue that (i) everyone has (or at least some persons sometimes have) a certain duty **D**. (ii) It is always reasonable to carry out a duty. (iii) It is reasonable that one carry out **D** only if condition **C** holds. So, it follows that (iv) if **C** holds, then the proposition *Persons survive death* or *Persons are immortal* and/or *God exists* or *The world is governed by an omnicompetent Deity* is true. Similar issues seem to be involved with other varieties of the argument as with those discussed here; if so, it follows that the varieties of the moral argument will fail to be proofs.

THE SIGNIFICANCE OF THE "PROOFS"

It has been argued that certain versions among the more plausible of the arguments for monotheism fail to be proofs. I do not know (and I suspect no one knows) whether certain crucial steps in these arguments are true; they may be true, and the arguments may be sound and valid, but unless they are known to be sound and valid, they do not comprise proofs in the requisite sense: they do not extend our knowledge. Unless these steps are better known to us than that God exists (and I do not find them so), they do not increase our epistemic security regarding the conclusion of the arguments in which they appear.

One or more of the arguments is sometimes said to have epistemic relevance of a different sort. They are said to render their conclusion reasonable to believe, and so to absolve those who embrace their conclusion of any charge of being irrational in so doing. This will be so, at best, only for those who accept that conclusion on the grounds of those arguments. That it is reasonable, given **r** to believe that **P** is true will not render one's belief that **P** is true reasonable if cognition of **r** plays no role in one's having the belief. It may well be that it is reasonable to accept (but also reasonable to reject) the crucial steps, and so reasonable to believe (but also reasonable not to believe) that God exists, in the light of one or more of the arguments we have considered. If so, those who do so believe (but also those who do not) do not believe (or fail to believe) unreasonably, and so are not culpable of violating the axioms, whatever exactly they may be, of the ethics of belief. But this fact, if it is one, puts us in no better position than we were before with regard to the question of whether God exists.

THE POSITIVE ROLE OF THE CENTRAL CONCEPTS OF THE ARGUMENTS

We might wonder whether there is any more positive result that might be derived from the discussion of the alleged proofs than what has emerged so far. At least a *further* result seems available: let us suppose that one were to ask what ways there might be of expressing a coherent monotheism, and in particular of expressing it so that it related to such things as the fact that there are existentially dependent contingent beings (whereas there need not have been), that there is order in the universe of a sort so as to make common sense and science possible (whereas there need not have been), and the like; the considerations that give rise to the arguments we have been considering are immensely relevant to answering such questions. Monotheism conceives of God as a being who does not depend for his existence on anything else; perhaps the best way to express the notion of God as Creator includes its not even being possible that he be dependent (that is to say, ascribing necessary existential independence to him). For monotheism, at least some of God's actions are conceived of as providing the *explicans* of an ultimate teleological explanation; in particular, his actions regarding there being dependent contingent creatures, rational-moral agents, and comprehensible natural order (as well as natural beauty) are viewed in this way.

Such considerations are not irrelevant to a rational assessment of monotheism. It is essential to understanding a conceptual system that one know what propositions it entails. The sorts of features of the world that the premises of the classical monotheistic arguments draw to our attention are pervasive and significant ones. It would be a defect in any general conceptual scheme if it were to ignore or deny them. Any such system is plausible only to the degree that it either renders them explicable, or explains why they need no such explication and are instead only to be used in explaining other, less pervasive or basic phenomena.

The cosmological argument endeavors to show that the world (that is to say, "the set of all beings that are not necessarily existentially independent") depends on a being that is necessarily existentially independent. The teleological argument endeavors to show that the sort of order that our universe manifests is only explicable (or is best explained) by reference to a nonhuman intelligent agent's basic actions that realize that agent's ultimate ends—and that such reference must involve an ultimate teleological, and hence a theistic, explanation.[36]

Obviously not every version of these arguments has been considered here; only representative formulations with representative limitations have been considered. Perhaps the most significant thing about there being such arguments is not that they serve as proofs, but that they point out that theism (in some of its formulations, at any rate) can explain and integrate a variety of facts—that there is something rather than nothing, or that there are contingent beings; that the universe manifests the sort of order that makes common sense and science possible; and that there are moral agents and moral duties.[37] Given theism, these are not "surds." The same, of course, is true of other perspectives, but were such facts inexplicable within a theistic perspective, theism's epistemic virtue would be small indeed. In fact, they are not.

36. It may be, however, that the notion of a logically necessary being has little or no explanatory value, save as it is linked to the notion of necessary existential independence.

37. This theme will be explored more fully in Chapter 7.

SUGGESTIONS FOR FURTHER READING

1. General

Charlesworth, Maxwell John. *Philosophy of Religion: The Historical Approaches.* London: Macmillan, 1972.

An analysis of a variety of ways in which the connections between philosophy and theology have been conceived.

Plantinga, Alvin. *God and Other Minds: A Study of the Justification of Belief in God.* Ithaca, NY: Cornell University Press, 1967.

An empathetic and critical assessment of various theistic arguments.

Purtill, Richard. *Reason to Believe.* Grand Rapids, MI: Eerdmans, 1974.

An excellent introductory work.

Ross, James F. *Philosophical Theology.* Indianapolis: Bobbs-Merrill, 1969.

Ross discusses various theistic arguments, considering their medieval sources and contemporary significance.

Swinburne, Richard. *The Coherence of Theism.* London: Oxford University Press, 1977.

______. *The Existence of God.* London: Oxford University Press, 1979.

______. *Faith and Reason.* London: Oxford University Press, 1981.

Swinburne takes up issues of the internal coherence of theism, the theistic proofs, and the nature of faith in this stimulating trilogy.

Yandell, Keith E. "Some Arguments for the Existence of God" and "Religion and Morality." In *Basic Issues in the Philosophy of Religion.* Boston: Allyn and Bacon, 1971.

______. Rev. of *Proslogion II and III: A Third Interpretation of Anselm's Argument,* by Richard LaCroix. *The Journal of Value Inquiry,* 8 (Summer 1974): 143-57.

2. The Cosmological Argument

Craig, William. *The Cosmological Argument from Plato to Leibniz.* New York: Barnes & Noble, 1980.

______. *The Kalam Cosmological Argument.* New York: Barnes & Noble, 1980.

Edwards, Paul. "The Cosmological Argument." In *The Cosmological Argument,* edited by Donald R. Burill. Garden City, NY: Doubleday-Anchor, 1967.

Edwards defends the "weak" rationality side of the cosmological dispute. Taylor (see below) defends the "strong" rationality side.

Farrer, Austin. *Finite and Infinite.* Westminster: Dacre Press, 1943.

Mascall, E. L. *He Who Is.* New York: Longmans, Green, 1954.

Rowe, William. *The Cosmological Argument.* Princeton: Princeton University Press, 1975.

Rowe provides a splendid analysis of the classic formulations of the cosmological argument: Aquinas's *Summa Theologica* and Samuel Clarke's *Discourse Concerning the Being and Attributes of God.*

Taylor, Richard. *Metaphysics.* Englewood Cliffs, NJ: Prentice-Hall, 1963. Pp. 91ff.

3. The Teleological Argument

Bertocci, Peter. *Introduction to the Philosophy of Religion.* New York: Prentice-Hall, 1951.

Butler, Joseph. *Bishop Butler's Analogy of Religion.* New York: Harper, 1852.

Hume, David. *Dialogues Concerning Natural Religion.* Indianapolis: Bobbs-Merrill, 1947.

Hume presents the classic traditional critique of the teleological argument.

Paley, William. *Natural Theology.* London: Rayer, 1817.

The classic traditional presentation of the teleological argument.

Swinburne, Richard. *The Existence of God.* London: Oxford University Press, 1979.

The most thorough recent defense of the teleological argument.

Tennant, R. R. *Philosophical Theology.* Cambridge: Cambridge University Press, 1928-30.

This two-volume work presents the classic post-Hume version of the teleological argument.

4. The Ontological Argument

LaCroix, Richard R. *Proslogion II and III: A Third Interpretation of Anselm's Argument.* London: E. J. Brill, 1972.

An excellent discussion of Anselm's classic traditional presentation of the ontological argument in his *Proslogion.*

Plantinga, Alvin. *God, Freedom and Evil.* New York: Harper & Row, 1974.

______. *The Nature of Necessity*. Oxford: Clarendon Press, 1974.

Perhaps the richest contemporary defense of the ontological argument.

Plantinga, Alvin, ed. *The Ontological Argument from St. Anselm to Contemporary Philosophers.* Garden City, NY: Doubleday-Anchor, 1965.

5. The Moral Argument

Beck, Lewis White. *A Commentary on Kant's "Critique of Practical Reason."* Chicago: University of Chicago Press, 1960.

England, Frederick Ernest. *Kant's Conception of God.* London: Allen & Unwin, 1929.

Kant, Immanuel. *Critique of Practical Reason.* Chicago: University of Chicago Press, 1949.

The standard traditional statement of the moral argument.

Rashdall, Hastings. *Philosophy and Religion.* New York: Scribner's, 1910.

Sorley, W. R. *Moral Values and the Idea of God.* 3d ed. Cambridge: Cambridge University Press, 1935.

Taylor, A. E. *The Faith of a Moralist.* London: Macmillan, 1930.

Wood, Allen W. *Kant's Rational Theology.* Ithaca, NY: Cornell University Press, 1978.

PART TWO
THE NONCOGNITIVIST CHALLENGE TO THEISM

ANALYTICAL TABLE OF CONTENTS TO CHAPTER 3

literal union between them, (ii) being veridical, and (iii) involving "direct" contact with God. 114

11. Even "direct" contact with God involves concepts, however, and so it is not immune from error; furthermore, attempts to argue from analogy to allegedly incorrigible perceptual experiences end in results quite different from those hoped for. 115
12. We can offer a characterization of what it is to have a concept without using a form of the abstraction theory. 118
13. "Passive," or noninferential experience is not immune from error; since the attempt to justify divine ineffability by appeal to mystical experience succeeds only if it is the case that "direct" experiences are conceptless and immune from error, this attempt is not successful. 119
14. We might suppose that God is ineffable not in himself, but merely relative to all the languages we do (or shall) have, but even this supposition is intrinsically inconsistent and thus self-defeating. 121
15. In any case, if we were able to demonstrate that God is ineffable, this would only serve to bring an end to theology and theological ethics. 124
16. Therefore, no genuine loss is involved in abandoning the claim that God is ineffable; in the final analysis the ineffability thesis does not constitute a rational barrier to the claim that theism is "cognitively significant" (i.e., that it is either true or false). 125

CHAPTER 3
IS GOD INEFFABLE?

The varieties of scepticism are only one challenge to the view that religious traditions in general, and Christianity in particular, make truth-claims or in essential part are comprised of conceptual systems—organized, and, at least in intent, coherent sets of propositions. This challenge is discussed in Chapter Four. Another challenge has its source in one or another of the claims that objects of religious discourse are ineffable or inexpressible or aconceptual or the like.[1]

TWO SOURCES OF THE CLAIM THAT GOD IS INEFFABLE

In contrast to trees and tortoises, God cannot be seen, felt, smelled, or tasted. If he is heard, it will not be because he has spoken with a larynx and lips: he has neither. He is Creator, and so not part of the creation; he is Lord of nature and history, and so not part of the network of natural processes or the succession of historical events; he is radically different from anything else. It is sometimes thought that if we concentrate on creation, we have one consideration that suggests divine ineffability, and that if we focus on the Creator, we have another. Language, it is suggested, was created to refer to ordinary physical objects—cattle and shrubs, dogs and rocks, and the like. Constructed for mundane purposes, it allegedly cannot serve to describe God; made on earth, it cannot breathe in Heaven. God, it is suggested, transcends our puny abilities of reference and

1. One motivation for this is the view that God is so unlike human beings as to be "wholly other"—so radically different from humans as allegedly to share no properties with them. In part, then, talk of ineffability is motivated from within theistic (and other) religious traditions.

description; being infinite, he is utterly beyond our finite human thoughts. Thus, given the origin and function of language and the uniqueness of God's divine nature, it has been suggested that he is ineffable. The purpose of this chapter is to examine this suggestion: what does it mean to say that God is ineffable, and what are the implications of such a view?

THE MEANING OF "INEFFABLE"

An item is ineffable only if it cannot be expressed in language. Ineffability has no degrees; strictly speaking, it is logically impossible that one thing be more (or less) ineffable than another, just as it is logically impossible that one thing be more (or less) perfect than another. One can give a sense to such language, however; to say that one thing is more perfect than another passes as a way of saying that the former item more closely approximates some standard or ideal of perfection than does the latter. Similarly, to say that one thing is more ineffable than another might pass as a way of saying that one thing is harder to describe, more difficult to express, more elusive, than another. But no credibility would thereby be given to the claim that anything, literally speaking, is ineffable. That it is harder to describe one thing than another does not entail that there is something indescribable any more than the fact that one positive integer is higher than another entails that some integer is the highest of all. It is often enough the case that a proponent of the claim that some particular item is literally ineffable will, upon criticism, shift from this claim to the quite different claim that the item is hard to describe, only to return to the original claim once the critique is no longer pressed. But this is to evade a matter of crucial significance: that some things are harder to describe than others is scarcely a matter for serious debate, but whether there are items that are literally ineffable is a question of considerably greater philosophical interest.

Such locutions as *that book is inexpressible, the pain is unspeakable, my joy is unutterable,* and the like, do not ascribe literal ineffability to a book, or pain, or joy. The same is true of such locutions as *God's love is unspeakable, the peace of God passes all understanding, the Atonement involved inexpressible sacrifice,* and the like: they need not be understood to suggest that God's love, or the peace that he gives, or Christ's atoning sacrifice is ineffable; instead, they can be seen as involving merely hyperbolic or poetic language, against which no protest need be entered.

The claim that something is ineffable is a strong claim: it says that something is inexpressible, uncapturable in language, aconceptual, equidistant from all concepts, something about which nothing true—or false—can be said. We might well ask why someone would be motivated to make such claims, what reasons might be offered for them, and, in particular, what might motivate someone to defend the *ineffability thesis*—that is to say, the claim *God is ineffable.*

INEFFABILITY AND DIVINE INFINITY

That God is ineffable is sometimes taken to follow from the fact that he is infinite. Whether this entailment does hold depends on what we understand *infinity* to mean in a proposition such as *God is infinite.* Sometimes **X** *is infinite* is taken to entail *There are an infinite number of truths about* **X**, but this would seem to be true of every item that exists. If we understand the smallest badger in Wisconsin to be of size **n**, for instance, then we can safely assume that it is smaller than anything that is **n + 1**, and smaller than anything that is **n + 2**, and so on. Indeed, there seem to be an indefinite if not infinite number of truths about very modest, finite items, nor is it clear why the alleged fact that there are an infinite number of truths about God should be thought religiously important. The consequence sometimes drawn is that, since there are an infinite number of truths about God, he cannot be exhaustively known. But by the same token, there is an inexhaustible fund of knowledge about my smallest toe—it is smaller than the smallest badger in Wisconsin, and is some determinate number of centimeters from that creature, and is larger than a pin, and so on. The sheer number of propositions true of something seems no sane measure of that thing's relative significance, nor does it require that the item be ineffable; indeed, it is incompatible with the item's alleged ineffability.

Monotheism has characteristically taken God's *infinity* to be a matter of his *omniscience, omnipotence, omnibenevolence,* and perhaps his *aseity* (i.e., his *ontological independence*). Since God's *omnipresence* is a matter of *being able to act anywhere at any time,* it adds nothing to his omnipotence, and so is typically not taken to be a significant feature of his infinity (although the importance of a sense of proximity to divine aid has led some to include it as a separate item on lists of divine attributes). But if the proposition *God is omnipotent, omniscient, omnibenevolent, and ontologically independent* is true, then of course *God is ineffable* is false, for we have found a means of describing him.

INEFFABILITY AND DIFFERENCE IN LEVEL OF BEING

Some people conceive of God as being different in kind, on a *different level of being,* from us. The notion of a level of being is itself not altogether clear, but the rough idea is that if **A** is organizationally more complex or has more complex capacities than **B**, then **A** is on a higher level than **B**. Part of the force of talk about levels of being involves the use of description. For instance, we might describe rocks, plants, and animals in terms of an ascending series of levels based on the differences in complexity and capacity involved in being *material,* being *material and living,* and being *material and living and sentient.* If we view human beings as *material, living, sentient, and rational,* we might expand our list of the levels to the following: *rocks, plants, animals, humans.* If we view God as *immaterial,* and hold that *being immaterial* is better than *being material* (perhaps on the ground that an immaterial being can produce a material one but not conversely), and if we hold that God is living, sentient, and rational, we might expand our list still further, to the following: *rocks, plants, animals, humans, God.*[2] Crude as they are, perhaps these remarks give some notion of what has been meant by *levels of being*.

Some people have defended the contention that God is ineffable by arguing that the difference in level of being between a human being and God renders the latter cognitively impenetrable to the former. The suggestion is that no being existing at level **n** can comprehend one that exists at level **n + 1**. A discouraging feature of this suggestion, however, is that it seems to be quite clearly inconsistent with its conclusion: in order to establish that God has the higher level of being that the suggestion assigns to him, it must be supposed that he has effable divine attributes (omnipotence, omniscience, etc.). This much is necessary to substantiate the view that nondivine beings belong to a natural hierarchy that reaches its peak in God. Then it is supposed to follow that

2. As these remarks about the superiority of immateriality suggest, the force of talk about levels of being is *evaluative* as well as *descriptive.* We might suppose, for instance, that if **A** and **B** inhabit adjoining levels, **B**'s level being higher, then **B** is more valuable than **A**, and **B**'s departure from existence would be more lamentable than **A**'s.

God is simply incomprehensible to all beings beneath him in this hierarchy. But if that were the case—if God were indeed ineffable—then it would not be possible to ascribe any attributes to him, divine or otherwise, and without the ascription of divine attributes to substantiate the doctrine of a natural hierarchy, the argument would no longer present any basis for accepting the ineffability of God. Thus a natural hierarchy doctrine does not entail the ineffability thesis in any convincing manner; and a natural hierarchy doctrine without this entailment is of no present concern.

EFFABILITY

An item is *effable* if one or more concepts apply to it. The notion of a concept applying to an item perhaps bears some scrutiny. An apple is effable since the concept of color applies to it. The concept of God, on the other hand, would seem to preclude his being red, or green, or any other color. Does, then, the concept *color* "apply to" God? If this means "Is God some one or more determinate colors?", the monotheistic answer is negative. But "God has no color properties" is a sentence whose subject term is "God" and which contains "color" in its predicate. Further, given monotheism, presumably it is true. One might distinguish, then, between the propositions *God is omnipotent* and *God is chartreuse.* Given monotheism, *God is omnipotent* is true; thus the concept of omnipotence *describes* God, and so of course *applies* to him. Given monotheism, presumably *God is chartreuse* is false, inasmuch as the concept of *not* being chartreuse describes, and so applies to, God.

Our way of putting matters regarding their opposites suggests that the concept of being chartreuse *applies* to God, but does not *describe* him (the same thing being true of the concept of not being omnipotent). The idea is that for any item **x**, and for any concept **C** and its opposite **not-C**, both **C** and **not-C** will apply to **x**, but only one of them will describe **x**. This way of putting the matter has various advantages: it is clear, for instance, and it precludes the need to discern any pseudo-propositions that have no truth value whatsoever, by presenting a simple true/false alternative. We might, for instance, consider the following continuum (if continuum it is): *(1) God is omnipotent, (2) God is chartreuse, (3) God is identical to the number 14*; if we assume monotheism to be true (and if we read the three propositions categorically, or as having existential import), then (1) is true and propositions (2) and (3) are false; if monotheism is false, then all three propositions are false.[3] Furthermore, on this proposal the propositions *God is not identical to the number 14* and *God is not chartreuse* (or, if one prefers, *If God exists, then he is not identical to the number 14* and *If God exists, then he is not chartreuse*) are true, whereas if the concepts *being identical to the number 14* and *being chartreuse* do not apply to God, then these propositions are not true—or false either (after all, if the denial of a proposition is meaningless, the proposition itself can hardly be true).

There seems, then, to be much to recommend the view that for any concept **C** and item **x**, exactly one of the pair *being* **C** and *being* **not-C** describes **x**, and both *being* **C** and *not being* **C** apply to **x**. It implies that in order for something to be ineffable, it must be true not only that it cannot be described by any concept, but also that no concept at all will apply to it. This perspective is not universally shared, however. It has been argued, for instance, that each object has its essence, or essential properties, and that given this, there are other properties an object cannot have. A standard example concerns a man, a wall, and the capacity of sight. A man, by nature, is a seeing being; if a man lacks sight, his nature is to that degree defective. A wall, by nature, is not a seeing being; if a wall lacks the capacity for sight, its lack does not constitute a defect. Given these facts, the conclusion is drawn that *having sight* and *not having sight* simply do not apply to walls; neither *The wall has sight* nor *The wall has no sight* has truth value. Of course, this conclusion does not *follow* from the facts cited; it is perfectly compatible with those facts that the proposition *The wall has no sight* is true and the proposition *The wall has sight* is false.[4] Thus, despite

3. If (1–3) are read conditionally, or as having no existential import, (1) is true, and (2) and (3) are false.

4. Even if we suppose that walls have some set **A** of essential properties such that **X** *has* **A** entails **X** *has no sight,* this is compatible with **X** *is a wall and has sight* being a contradiction, and hence false. A different way of putting the point would be to say that there are some properties that an item does not happen to have, but might have (e.g., a wall that is white might have been brown), and other properties that an item just cannot have (e.g., a wall cannot become an aviator or have a high I. Q.), and this distinction is not marked out by (nor is it compatible with) the simple, straightforward proposal comprising **C**, **not-C**, and **x**. The simplest reply

the fact that it is not universally accepted, the simple, straightforward proposal seems highly plausible and gives us one clear way of understanding the notions of a concept's applying to and describing an item, and of a concept's applying to an item which it does not describe; every concept, then, applies to, and either describes or else does not describe, anything. Of course, rejecting the proposal would be very far from embracing some variety of the ineffability thesis.[5]

THE INCOHERENCE OF THE UNREVISED INEFFABILITY THESIS

In any case, it is contradictory to claim that there is something to which no concepts apply, or some item of which nothing is true; to claim such a thing regarding some item is to apply concepts to it, and assert a proposition to be true of it. For the ineffability thesis regarding some item to be stated coherently, then, it must be only some considerable subset of concepts which fail to apply to it; at most it must be said to be ineffable relative to *some range* of concepts rather than relative to all concepts whatever. There seems to be considerable tendency to trivialize this important criticism, and to regard it simply as a consequence of an inconvenience that unfortunately attaches to claims, namely that they must appear in language if they are to make an appearance in the forum of public thought. But suppose one merely thinks to oneself to the effect that something is ineffable; once again the thesis entertained, strictly speaking, is inconsistent. The relative publicity or privacy of the claim—the question of whether one recites it to an audience or merely reflects on it in one's study—is irrelevant to its logical status.

The locution *being effable* expresses a concept which either describes the moon, or anything else, or does not; if it does not, the concept *being ineffable* applies. But anything which a concept, including that expressed by *being ineffable*, describes is such that it is

---

is to note that either the distinction in question is one of logic, or it is not. If it is, then *The wall has become an aviator* is necessarily false, whereas *The wall is brown* is contingently false—and this is quite compatible with the proposal. If the distinction is not one of logic, then *The wall has a high I. Q.* is false, and its being false will require an extralogical explanation (which need not be incompatible with the proposal).

5. On this account, roughly, one has the concept of **x** if and only if one knows what is the case if and only if there are **x**'s; this is discussed below.

not ineffable after all; the same applies to anything to which any concept, including that expressed by *being ineffable*, applies.

EXPRESSIBILITY AND REFERENCE

That we can express a concept does not entail that it applies to anything. Consider, for example, the concepts expressed by *does not have logically compatible properties, is not self-identical, has no properties at all*, and *does not exist.* No item that enjoys existence is described by any of these concepts. So that *being ineffable* expresses a concept does not entail that the concept in question describes or refers to anything at all.

THE INCOHERENCE OF THE INEFFABILITY THESIS, STRICTLY INTERPRETED

Without some restriction being made on it—that is, in its pure and pristine state—the thesis that something is ineffable simply is contradictory, and so false. To put the objection in different language: if some proposition is true of some item, then concepts—namely, those expressed by the sentence that expresses this proposition—apply to this item. The truth of *God is ineffable* requires what it forbids—it is true only if those concepts which in their interrelationships comprise the proposition in question apply to God, in flagrant violation of the proposition's content. So one needs a characterization of ineffability which is not logically inconsistent but captures as much as possible of the stringency of our first characterization.

A REVISION OF THE INEFFABILITY THESIS

Perhaps this will do: some properties are possessed by whatever exists; call these *existence-entailed* properties.[6]

6. Some theologians have denied that God exists, appealing to the alleged fact that **X** *exists* entails **X** *has spatial properties* and **X** *has temporal properties*, whereas, they hold, God has properties of neither sort. But then, since the view in question is hardly expressed by simply saying *God does not exist*, one holding this view must invent some new word to do the work "exists" previously did, but without having the alleged entailments; thus *God subsists*, or the like, replaces *God exists*, and one could talk about *existence-or-subsistence-entailed properties.* But it seems to me not contradictory to hold, with Plato, that Forms exist, Forms being conceived as abstract, nonspatial entities which exist independent of thought and which in somewhat complex, if not obscure, ways provide the conditions under which one can think truly. If the notion of being an eternal, or atemporal, being

One existence-entailed property, I take it, is simply *having properties*; for example, *God exists but has no properties* is inconsistent. *Having only compatible properties, being material or immaterial*, and *being contingent or necessary* are existence-entailed properties. If something exists, then the concept of having such properties describes, and hence applies to, it. Perhaps, then, the way to put (a revised version of) the ineffability thesis, relative to monotheism, is something like this: *God is ineffable** = (def.) *Only existence-entailed concepts, plus the concept of being ineffable*, applies to God*.

One problem with this suggestion is that nothing can be such that it *only* has existence-entailed properties; nothing can have only such properties as *having only logically compatible properties* and *having properties* and *being self-identical*, or only such properties plus being *ineffable**. Anything that exists requires specific properties beyond such thin abstractions as these; for things to have these properties is for them to have other "thicker" properties by virtue of which they enjoy these "thin" ones, and that this is so is a necessary truth. But then of course the (presently available or in principle constructible) concepts of these "thicker" properties apply to the item to which allegedly only existence-entailed concepts apply. So once again we fail to have a coherent way of putting (even a revised version of) the ineffability claim.

Put in other language, the existence-entailed concepts are indeterminate relative to other properties; *being self-identical* is indeterminate relative to, say, *being a self-identical elephant* or *being a self-identical door*; *having properties* is indeterminate relative to, say, *having cognitive properties*, which in turn is indeterminate relative to, say, *being omniscient* or *having an I.Q. of 87*. But for any indeterminate property **A, X** *has* **A** entails **X** *has some property* **B** *which is determinate relative to* **A**. Some properties—say, *being pure red* or *being exactly seven feet tall*—are as determinate as a property can get; these are *maximally determinate*. For any indeterminate property **A, X** *has* **A** entails **X** *has some maximally determinate property* **C** *which is determinate relative to* **A**. But no maximally determinate property is an existence-

---

is not incoherent, then *An eternal being exists* is coherent. Otherwise put, substituting *God subsists*, or the like, for *God exists* seems to be neither necessary nor profitable. Whatever existence-entailed properties there are, then, will belong to a monotheistic deity as much as to any other being. If God is conceived as *everlasting*, *God exists* will entail *God has temporal properties*.

entailed property. So if God has existence-entailed properties, he also has other properties, and if the concepts of existence-entailed properties (so much as) apply to (let alone describe) God, then there are concepts of properties which are not existence-entailed that also apply to God (half of which would describe him).[7]

INEFFABILITY AND THE ORIGIN OF CONCEPTS

One view that could be, and probably first was, adopted without monotheism or ineffability in mind, is the thesis that *Nothing is in the intellect which was not first in the senses* or that *Every concept is abstracted from sensory experience or else is completely definable by means of those which were*. The idea is that the sensory biography of a person will include, for example, his or her seeing various things that are red in color but different in shape—a red square, a red circle, a red triangle, say—and, noticing the same color in each, he or she will form an idea of redness. Similarly, sensory biographies will contain items with the same shape but different colors—a red circle, a green circle, a blue circle, say—and one so blessed will be able to form the concept of circularity. If one has the ideas of redness, greenness, and blueness, then one has the materials for forming the concept *color*;[8] if one has the ideas of circularity, roundness, and squareness,

7. One might object to this that it is logically possible that **B** be a property that is determinate relative to **A**, that it be logically possible to form a concept of **A**, but yet it may not be logically possible to form a concept of **B**. The objection is rather abstract, and perhaps an example will help to make clear what is being said. The suggestion is that, for example, while *being pure red* is determinate relative to *being colored*, and it is logically possible to form the concept of being colored, it does not follow that it is logically possible to form the concept of being pure red. One plausible reply is that if it is logically possible that something have a property, it is logically possible that a concept of its having that property, and a concept of that property, be formed, and that this is so is a necessary truth. Another is that if (1) *The property of being pure red is determinate relative to the property of being colored* is true, it seems possible to know that it is true. That **P** be true but not knowable will be the case, if ever, only if either **P** or **P** *is true* entail **P** *cannot be known to be true*; but (1) seems to have no such entailment. So presumably if (1) is true, it is possible to know that (1) is true. If it is possible to know that (1) is true, of course it is possible to know that *being red* is determinate relative to *being colored.* It is not possible to know this without having the concept of being pure red. So if (1) is true, it is possible to have the concept of being pure red. Thus if a proposition of the form *Property* **B** *is determinate relative to property* **A** is true (and can be known to be true), then it follows that it is possible to form a concept of property **B**.

8. *Forming an idea of a color* often means both *being able to frame an image which was that color* and *using the same word to designate the color of items which are that color.*

then one has the materials for framing the concept *shape.* Given the concepts *color* and *shape*, perhaps plus others of this sort, one can form the concept *property.* Thus an account can be given from this perspective of how rather abstract concepts can be framed.

Given this view, we noted, for one to have a concept of **x** is for one to be able to form an image of an **x**, pick out **x**'s from non-**x**'s, and (unless the concept of **x** is primitive) to define "**x**" in terms of words which express primitive concepts. Roughly stated, the idea was that *every* concept, or at least *every* concept by means of which *reference* is possible, has an origin of the sort just recited, and that the range of reference any concept could have was to be severely restricted by the sort of origin it had.

One way of articulating this line of reasoning goes as follows. Suppose that we somehow "just have," or in connection with our gaining the use of other concepts "just acquire," the concepts of logic. The concepts of logic will include those expressed by such terms as quantifiers (all, some, none), inference terms (hence, so, therefore), connectives (and, or, if . . . then), negation (not), and modalities (necessary, contingent, possible, impossible, consistent, contradictory), perhaps among others. Adopt *the principle of acquaintance,* which says that *For any concept* C *such that one has* C *and such that* C *is descriptive, either one has experienced an item to which* C *applies or one can define* C *in terms only of the concepts of logic plus concepts which are descriptive of items that one has experienced*. Add *the narrow empiricist claim* that *All experience is perceptual (either sensory, or else introspective*); the gist of this claim is that what we experience is what we see, or hear, or taste, or smell, or touch, or are introspectively aware of (e.g., pain, fear, hope, or wonder). Then presumably every descriptive concept we have will be either the concept of an object of perception or definable only in terms of such concepts plus the concepts of logic; or, perhaps, every descriptive concept we have will be the concept of an object of perception, or the concept of an observable property of a perceptual object, or definable only in terms of such concepts plus the concepts of logic.

It is true that if this account of things is correct concerning some person, then that person's conceptual furnishings will be comparatively meager: he or she will be completely befuddled by such propositions as *It is morally wrong to torture children for pleasure* and *Oxford is a beautiful city* and *God created heaven and earth,* for it seems most implausible that the concepts expressed by *is morally wrong* and *is beautiful* and *God* are themselves concepts of perceptual objects (or of the observable properties of perceptual objects), or are definable in terms only of concepts of perceptual objects (or of the observable properties of perceptual objects) and the concepts of logic. The same seems true of concepts expressed by phrases such as *is atomic, is a black hole, expresses a concept, causes tooth decay,* and *threatens world peace.* Unless either logic or introspection involves considerably more than it is typically understood to involve, it would seem that few if any persons are in fact limited to those concepts that the principle of acquaintance and the narrow empiricist claim would allow. Indeed, given only such concepts as these theses would allow, it is hard to see how the theses themselves could be formulated; concepts such as *perceptual, sensory, introspective, descriptive, experience,* and *concept* seem unlikely prospects for being either themselves concepts of perceptual objects (or of observable properties of perceptual objects) or for being definable in terms only of these sorts of concepts in concert with the concepts of logic.

Two separable themes combine in the theory just rehearsed. One theme concerns the *nature* of concepts, suggesting that they are analyzable or definable in terms of the primitive or indefinable words of a language (other than those of logic and mathematics, perhaps), which denote items with which one has had direct perceptual acquaintance (the derivative word being accessible to definition without remainder by use of only the primitive words). This thesis seems simply false regarding a great many of the concepts we actually have, including those required for expressing the theory as a whole, and its theme about the nature of concepts in particular. The second theme concerns the *origin* of (primitive) concepts (other than those of logic and mathematics, perhaps), suggesting that they are elicited by sensory experiences or, in more contemporary language, that they are learned on occasions in which one is perceptually in the presence of the items to which the concepts apply. By itself, this sets no limits on the nature of concepts; to paraphrase Kant, even if all our concepts are elicited by objects of perception, that fact does not entail that they only apply to such objects—the theme regarding the origin of concepts does not entail that concerning their nature.

Keeping this second theme in mind, let us suppose that Ralph is aware of some of his own capacities—say, of his ability to do such things as tie his shoes and speak his name, and of his knowledge that gold is heavier than cotton and that Newton's theories preceded Einstein's. Ralph might reflect that it would be nice to be able to have the entire history of philosophy at his intellectual fingertips, or indeed to have all knowledge as his province. He might reflect that some such account as *if it is logically possible that* **P** *be known, then* **S** *knows that* **P** perhaps captures the sense of **S** *is omniscient,* and that if he had all knowledge as his province he would satisfy and be described by that concept; he might also reflect upon the fact that he need not be omniscient to realize that he is not omniscient, and that this realization requires his possessing the concept of omniscience. Analogous reflection might yield the conclusion that something like *if* **P** *is not a contradiction, and it is not contradictory that* **P** *be made true by* **S**, *then* **S** *can make* **P** *true* perhaps captures the sense of **S** *is omnipotent.* In any case, it seems possible to develop very complex and abstract concepts from very modest conceptual beginnings; the theme concerning the origin of our concepts seems to provide no significant support for the notion that God, or any other being, or indeed anything at all is ineffable.

INEFFABILITY AND MYSTICAL EXPERIENCE

One potent source of the notion that God is ineffable is the contention that God is the object of mystical experience, which is itself ineffable; presumably the assumption is that all experience of God is mystical and that no knowledge of God is available save that allegedly provided by, or in, mystical experience. But what, exactly, is the connection supposed to be between mystical experience and the ineffability of God?

UNITY AND DISTINCTNESS IN MYSTICAL EXPERIENCES

When mystical experience, and hence God, is alleged to be ineffable, often an ontological thesis and an epistemological thesis are involved. The ontological thesis is to the effect that in mystical experience, the person whose experience it is literally becomes one with God. The "language of union" that mystics often use is not always understood in this fashion; it is often understood to involve a close relationship, an agreement of mind and unity of purpose. Indeed, for a human being to become literally one with God would seem to be scarcely acceptable from a theistic perspective inasmuch as it is tantamount to sheer blasphemy. A theist who offers the character of mystical experience as evidence of divine ineffability cannot consistently interpret that experience as one in which the mystic becomes identical with the Creator of heaven and earth. There is also the question of whether any sense can be given to the claim that a human being literally becomes one with God such that it is possible for the claim to be true; the union is usually taken to last only so long as the experience does, but that does not make the claim that it occurred any less problematic—indeed, it requires the truth of not only *Ralph became God at time* **t1** but also *God became Ralph at* **t1**. Perhaps the proposition *Ralph (for a while yesterday) became a lime gumdrop* can be understood, but not so as to be true; the proposition *Ralph (for a while yesterday) became God* seems not different in this regard.

Insofar as mystical experience is to be taken as evidence for divine ineffability, then, perhaps the ontological claim is best understood to be suggesting that in mystical experience, God, while remaining God, enters into a very close relationship with the mystic, who remains himself or herself.

MYSTICAL EXPERIENCE AND VERIDICALITY

Anyone basing an inference to divine ineffability on the nature of mystical experience presumably must hold at least some mystical experiences to be veridical (i.e., to be genuine experiences of God), and that claim can be, and has often been, challenged. We might in one sense deal with this difficulty by phrasing the argument in terms of a hypothetical proposition—such as *If mystical experience is veridical, then God is ineffable*—and then shifting the inquiry to a consideration of whether such a premise, if true, would support the conclusion.

"DIRECT CONTACT" OR UNMEDIATED KNOWLEDGE

If the ontological claim must concern a unity of close contact, so to say, rather than a literal unity between God and mystic, what will the epistemological claim be? Part of the idea is that the contact is direct, or immediate, that it involves no mediation of any sort. It also assumes that the contact is cognitive (or at least that it includes a cognitive element), involving knowledge of God. Still another assumption is that direct knowledge cannot involve mistakes—that immediacy eliminates the possibility of error—on the grounds that direct acquaintance with an object of knowledge is passive (the object impressing its nature on the mind, as it were), and immediate contact precludes interpretation and so eliminates error. The suggestion is then made that knowledge involving concepts always involves interpretation and thereby includes the possibility of mistakes, so that it must always be mediate and indirect. Thus, the knowledge involved in mystical experience cannot involve any concepts, and, being aconceptual, it must be ineffable, since where concepts are absent, language cannot enter.

This line of reasoning involves various assumptions, perhaps all, and certainly some, of which will not bear up under examination. Perhaps the most important concerns the nature of concepts, which are seen somehow as intermediaries, or, better, inferences, which get between the knower and the known, or the perceiver and the perceived, or the experience and the experienced.[9]

This notion by itself is richly problematic and highly dubious. Regarding perception, it raises the question as to how, if in perception one is directly acquainted with concepts (which are *ideas* or *images*) and only indirectly acquainted with objects, one can ever know that there *are* objects with which to be acquainted; perhaps ideas are but ambassadors without countries to represent. Or, picking up on the noninferential/inferential way of putting the contrast rather than the direct/indirect, if one must infer from one's (immediate acquaintance with) ideas to (one's mediated acquaintance with) objects, how is the inference to go? Presumably, it will contain some such premise as *Ralph now has idea/image* A and some such conclusion as *Ralph now perceives object* O; but some further premise is needed. Presumably, it will be something like *Whenever anyone has (an idea like) idea* A, *one perceives (an object like)* O; but this proposition is no necessary truth, and since one can never get at an object directly to compare it with its alleged representative idea or image, it cannot be inductively confirmed by arguing *This object is accurately represented by its idea in this case in which certain conditions are met, so probably there is an object accurately represented by an idea*

9. Or they are viewed as necessary and inevitable intermediaries in the case of sensory perceptions—as being ideas or images which *represent* physical objects, and the ideas or images are what we directly and noninferentially are aware of, whereas physical objects are only indirectly and inferentially perceived—but as unnecessary and unwelcome intruders in those "intellectually purer" experiences in which the object of knowledge is not a physical object, nor an object of any sensory modality or possessed of any observable qualities, but something of a different, nonsensory nature.

whenever these conditions are met; even this weak justification is not available. So the result seems to be skepticism about the existence of objects, or else an idealism which denies that there are objects and restricts its perceptual ontology merely to ideas or images.

If the latter route is taken, a certain irony easily arises. Among those attracted to this route have been some who accepted *the principle of transparency,* which states that, regarding such purely personally private and transient entities as those ideas and images into which, on the theory under discussion, objects degenerate, it is the case that they have the properties they appear to have, and appear to have the properties they have, and thus are epistemically transparent to their owners. No error about them is possible. But then it is easy to deny that ideas or images are concepts, and to insist instead that these are themselves the constituents of perception about which no error is possible and concerning which our acquaintance is passive and requires no concepts, concepts being required only for those cases (such as knowledge of other minds, or of God) in which our knowledge extends beyond our own immediate sensory and introspective consciousness. In sum, then: the account of perception included in the argument from mystical experience to divine ineffability is highly dubious; apparently, it leads to skepticism (quite contrary to its intent).[10]

How essential is this reference to a particular theory of perception in this account? It provides a contrast between the allegedly more "intellectual and spiritual" knowledge of God (which involves no use of concepts) and the allegedly more "perceptual and material" knowledge of objects.[11] Further, it arises from, or is tantamount to, the *theory* of concepts which *is* essential to the argument, concepts being ideas or images that occur in perception. Thus to drop the account of perception is to drop an essential link in the argument.

Perhaps it is worth noting that if one accepts the view of the origin of concepts that is expressed by the slogans *whatever is in the intellect is first in the senses* or *all concepts are abstracted from sensory*

10. Or to idealism (also quite contrary to its intent), which easily and plausibly leads to a perspective for which concepts are required in the very cases involving knowledge of items which are not among the objects or components of one's private, momentary, immediate awareness, as will any knowledge of God.

11. As noted, one who accepts *the principle of transparency* regarding private images and states is likely to reverse the claim as to where concepts are required.

experience, and adds the thesis that the future use of our concepts is limited to the sorts of occasions on which they arose, but also wishes to allow ethical, metaphysical, or theological knowledge (or for that matter, knowledge in the natural or social sciences), one must suppose that there is knowledge which does not involve the use of concepts. This way of putting things is made necessary by the (inadequate) theory of concepts with which one began, plus the admission that there is knowledge of more than the existence and observable properties of perceptual objects. The question of the origin of concepts—of how we come to have them—has at least large psychological and experimental components; it cannot be decided purely by examples, reflection, and argument. The question of the nature of concepts is a different matter; no excursus into psychology or experiment is required to determine whether, say, the concept of a table is definable without remainder into concepts of observable properties plus the "is of class membership."[12] Whether the answer is negative or positive, presumably, is to be decided by examples, reflection, and argument.

WHAT IT IS TO HAVE A CONCEPT

Suppose, then, one offers the following characterization of what it is to have a concept: *Ralph has the concept of an* **x** *if and only if Ralph knows what is true if and only if there are* **x**'*s.*[13] Ralph has the concept of a pen if and only if Ralph knows such things as *There are pens if and only if there are writing instruments which contain, or are dipped into and then retain, ink and There are pens if and only if there are writing instruments which, while in use, usually are held in one hand*. There will be degrees to which one has a concept (or: has a concept *clearly*) which will be functions how fully one knows what is true if and only if there are things which the concept describes. Further, a concept need not be a perceptual concept, or a concept of a perceptible (sensory or introspective) object, property, or state, for while one will have the concept of an ostrich if and only if one

12. Plus, perhaps, the "is of identity"; the answer seems to be negative, in that the "is of predication" is required, and so the concept of a substance, or property bearer.

13. This is a characterization, not a complete analysis. A complete analysis would have to face such questions as "*How much* of what is true if and only if there are **x**'s must Ralph know in order to have the concept of an **x**?" Of course there are degrees of clarity in having concepts, and perhaps there is no single, perfectly general answer to this question.

knows what is true if and only if there are ostriches, one also has the concept of God if and only if one knows what is true if and only if there is a God. It is impossible that there be a perfectly spherical cube—not a cube embedded in a sphere or a sphere embedded in a cube, but an object perfectly and only spherical and also perfectly and only cubical—in that a cube must have, whereas a sphere must lack, corners. To have the concept of a perfectly spherical cube will be to know that **x** is a perfectly spherical cube if and only if **x** both has and lacks corners; so to have the concept of a perfectly spherical cube—at any rate, to have a clear concept of such—is to know that there can be no such thing, to know that the concept of a perfectly spherical cube cannot describe anything. Similarly, one who has the concept of *prime number which is higher than 142*—at any rate, who has a clear concept thereof—will know that there are numbers this concept describes. There is, then, a modest characterization of what it is to have a concept which does the same sort of duty as an account of what a concept is, and which allows us to have concepts of cows and cucumbers, but also of duties, persons, theories, and God. So the claim cannot be made that no relevant treatment of concepts is available which allows that persons have a concept of God.

INFERENCE AND POSSIBILITY OF ERROR

Another element in the argument from mystical experience to divine ineffability is also dubious: the assumption is made that if perception or some other cognitive experience is "passive," then the information obtained in or from the experience cannot contain error (*passivity* in this context being a matter of *not including inference* or *involving no intermediary*). In such an experience, the suggestion is that we are acquainted with the item about which we form our opinions or receive our information. But why should we assume that *passivity* would, in the relevant sense, render an experience immune to error? Why should we assume that in cases of direct acquaintance we will experience the things we are acquainted with exactly as they are? By definition *inference* is precluded, but is mistaken inference the only possible source of error? What about *misperception*? The assumption is that misperception or experiential mistake is impossible (i.e., that things are always precisely as they seem to be), but why make that assumption?

In the case of such private and typically fleeting images and states of which some philosophers have thought *the transparency thesis* true—such as pains, afterimages, daydream images, and the like—various sorts of mistakes are possible, though perhaps not likely. One *might*, for instance, mistake a persistent afterimage for a physical object, or in a state of profound confusion, one might be unable to distinguish daydreams from reality. The transparency thesis will be plausible only regarding such properties as the color and shape of items of direct acquaintance.[14] An afterimage cannot *seem* to be orange if it is not, since according to the transparency thesis the essence of such an item resides in its being perceived, and thus it must be exactly as it appears.

Critics of the view that the transparency thesis applies even to such things as private images have traditionally invoked the example of (the image of) the speckled hen: If one has an image of a speckled hen, can one be mistaken as to how many speckles it boasts? The query underscores the difficulty of deciding exactly what will count as an "observable property." However we answer the speckled hen question, the fact remains that it is possible to be wrong about the duration, the cause, the order, the classification, and in general the nonobservable properties of the objects of private perceptions. In these respects, error is altogether a possibility.

Of course, the case of the mystic is alleged to be different; it is not a private object—a mental image or state, or the like—that the mystic is said to be aware of, but a being distinct from himself or herself. Further, the experience is allegedly one of "intellectual" or "spiritual" and "nonperceptual" acquaintance, though of course not one involving the use of nonperceptual concepts—that would render it effable; in this respect, too, it differs from private perceptual experience, or awareness of mind-dependent images and states.

A consequence of this difference, however, is that what is probably the strongest consideration in favor of the claim that for some not-easy-to-specify range of properties, we cannot be mistaken about whether certain sorts of items have them, is not available to the mystic—namely that the existence of the item in question depends on its being an object of awareness, and to be aware of it is to be aware of it as possessing observable properties, and that, as a result,

14. Stating the range of properties to which the transparency thesis applies, or can with plausibility be said to apply, is not an easy matter, but roughly it is to apply to "observable properties" or whatever analogues to these can attach to private items.

what distinguishes it from other mind-dependent objects is that it is perceived as having (and so has) the set of observable properties that it has, and not some other. It is neither a necessary truth (nor true at all) that God depends for his existence on being experienced, nor that God is distinguished from other beings only by virtue of being experienced to have the properties he (therefore) has. If the transparency thesis is true of any objects of experience at all, and regarding any set of properties at all, it is true of the perceptual properties of mind-dependent items; insofar as mystical experience is viewed as involving an awareness of nonperceptual properties of a mind-independent being, it differs in relevant ways from the sort of experience of which it is maximally plausible to regard the transparency thesis as true. There seems to be no good reason to think that having a mystical experience precludes the possibility of one's being mistaken even about those properties that God, from within the experience (so to speak), seems to have. In any case, passivity or lack of inference or absence of intermediaries, in the case of experience of the existence and properties of things which, if they exist, exist and have their properties independently of their being experienced, does not preclude the possibility of error on the part of one who experiences such items.

Thus it seems that the argument from mystical experience to the ineffability claim fails, both due to its reliance on a mistaken theory of concepts and its assumption that experiential immediacy precludes error, even in the case of experiencing mind-independent objects. For this theory, and this assumption, are crucial to the view that mystical experience, if veridical, provides grounds for the ineffability claim.

INEFFABILITY RELATIVE TO A LANGUAGE

By way of retreating to a more modest thesis, one might suggest ineffability is relative to some language or other; perhaps *being red* is ineffable relative to a language containing only terms of arithmetical theory, or *being conscious* ineffable relative to a language containing only the terms of physics—if it is possible to have a language containing only such terms. Then *God is ineffable* is incomplete, analogous to *An elephant is a big*; the former leaves us asking "Ineffable with respect to *what language*?" as the latter leaves us asking "A big what—animal, mammal, object, or . . .?"

Ineffability of this sort is less imposing and less interesting than the sort of ineffability we have been considering. Previously, ineffability was assumed somehow to follow from God's nature; the way to put such ineffability along present lines would be to say that God is ineffable relative to all languages whatever, actual or possible, whereas the point of introducing ineffability relative to a language seems to be lost if we say this. The point seems to be that as color properties may be ineffable relative to a purely mathematical vocabulary, so God may be ineffable relative to some set of languages (not to all possible languages, since he could speak or write his autobiography, if he chose to)—perhaps he is ineffable relative to all the languages we happen to have, or ever shall have. Part of the idea seems to be to have something like genuine ineffability and yet to escape the sorts of objection that have been raised. Perhaps, then, everything is ineffable relative to some language or other. Or perhaps some concepts—say, those of elementary number theory or of basic logic—are such as to be presupposed by, or at least implicitly embedded in, all languages whatever, so that a realist about numbers or logical connections would view some abstract items—numbers, or propositions, or states of affairs—as effable relative to all languages, and nothing is ineffable relative to all. Then only some things would be ineffable relative to some or most languages.

Consider, then, the suggestion that God is ineffable relative to some, but not all, languages. He shares this distinction with snakes, swans, human beings, and walking sticks. Strengthen, then, the suggestion so that God is ineffable relative to all the languages we possess. What are we to make of this suggestion?

That we discover that something exists which was hitherto beyond our ken does not entail that the new item is, or was, ineffable, even relative to the language we have. Suppose someone discovers, in an obscure swamp, a creature with the legs and tail of a tri-color collie and the body and head of an alligator; this *allidog*, as we might call it, was not ineffable yesterday but effable today. Always describable, it is actually described only once it is discovered, and its description is a new composite of old concepts. That things exist whose existence as yet is unknown is of no consequence by itself for the ineffability thesis.

Suppose we were to combine all of the descriptive and referential resources of all presently available natural and artificial languages into one language **L**. Then we can express the most recently proposed variety of divine ineffability as follows: *God is ineffable* *relative to* **L**. This seems more informative than it is. Consider the difference between (i) **X** is the number one higher than any number that any human being has ever specifically thought of, and (ii) There is some number, call it **X**, which is one higher than any number any human being has explicitly thought of. Now (i) is what logicians call an "open sentence"; in it, **X** is a place-holder or variable, and (i) is not true or false, but becomes so only once one replaces **X** by a term specifying some determinate number. Thus (ia) *Seven is the number one higher than any number any human being has ever specifically thought of* is a *closed* sentence, being constructed by replacing "**X**" by "*seven*"; (ia) is false, whereas (i) has no truth value at all. A relevant feature of (i) is this: if one pays attention to what one is doing in replacing "**X**" by a term designating some specific number—if one *thinks* of the number designated by a term one substitutes for "**X**"—then the result of one's efforts will be false. In (ii), by contrast, **X** functions much as a name, not as a variable, and (ii) is not an open, but a closed, sentence; indeed, (ii) is true. But of course we do not know what number **X** is, though we know it is a number, one much higher than seven.

Now consider: (iii) God is ineffable relative to **L**, and (iv) There is something, call it *God*, which is ineffable relative to **L**. The word "*God*" can function as a description (say, "the omnicompetent creator") or as a name (comparable to "*Jahweh*"); its role as a name or description is fixed by, and dependent on, the theological tradition in which it occurs. Thus, as description or as name, the word "*God*" functions so as to describe, or else name, an effable being. But then (iii) is false. It says that God—the creator, or the one worshiped by King David, or Jehovah, or Jahweh (or the like)—is ineffable; and that is not so. This point is independent of the question as to whether God exists or not; even if the word "God," like the word "unicorn," fails to refer, it (so to say) can try and fail only if the word "God" expresses a concept, or only if *If God exists, then he is effable* is true. So (iii) is false.

Given this discouraging result regarding (iii), one might embrace (iv). In (iv), "God" does not serve to express either the description "the omnicompetent Creator" or the tradition-dependent name (comparable to Jahweh); it simply refers to that alleged item, whatever it may be, which is not effable in **L**. If there is such an item, its religious interest might be paltry; or the news of its existence might be tragic. There is no reason to think that this is, or is not, so.

This, then, seems to be the result of supposing that it is coherent to say that something is ineffable relative to L. The result is not that God—that being, so to speak, about whose existence monotheists and atheists disagree—is said to be ineffable; rather, something or other is said to have this dubious distinction, though this fact may be disguised by using a familiar word in a new way to express something quite different than what it did before—indeed, by turning it into a variable, with no sense of its own.

In fact, it is by no means sure that *Something is ineffable relative to* L is coherent. For one thing, this something is at least capturable by those concepts involved in the claim in question. For another, presumably this something is such that existence-entailed concepts apply to it. So one needs some way of saying what sort of concepts, or class of concepts, does not apply to this alleged item. This is but to say that here, too, familiar difficulties arise with regard to this version of the ineffability thesis, and presumably pursuing them will lead to familiar results.

SOME LIMITATIONS INEFFABILITY WOULD IMPOSE

It is curious that ineffability has been attractive to anyone interested in establishing, among other things, the existence of God. An "ineffable claim" cannot be false, or be proved false; but then it cannot be true, or be proved true, either: the notion of an "ineffable claim" or an "aconceptual thesis" or a "contentless proposition" is a contradiction in terms. There can be no such thing, any more than there can be perfectly cubical spheres or genuine contradictions that are true; an ineffable theory, or system, or hypothesis, or theology, or the like, is logically impossible.

SOME CONSEQUENCES OF DIVINE INEFFABILITY

If we were to suppose, despite the fact that it is logically impossible, that the proposition *God is ineffable* were true, then certain conclusions follow: for one, the proposition *God exists* would be neither true nor false; it would assert nothing at all, for to think otherwise would be to suppose that concepts—at least that of *existence*—apply to God. Another conclusion would be that, save for existence-entailed concepts (if they are permitted), the contention that God is ineffable would entail that he was equidistant from all concepts—that any given description of God would be as accurate or inaccurate, as reliable or unreliable, as any other: although the propositions *God is all-good, God created the world,* and *God is just* are viewed by Judeo-Christian monotheism as truths, given the claim that God is ineffable, their contradictions would be just as close to (or as far from) the truth as they are. Such propositions as *God delights in the torture of the innocent* or *Only cannibals receive God's favor* would represent God as accurately as any other claim would, or could, including the claim *God loves all persons.* No view that has these consequences can be construed as a defense of theism. Furthermore, if God were indeed ineffable (or ineffable save for existence-entailed concepts), then we would be justified in supposing that no standard of behavior was any more religiously or theistically appropriate than any other: it would presumably be as appropriate to sacrifice children as to construct facilities for their care, or to curse God as to praise him.

In sum, then, divine ineffability is incompatible with there being any theology, any account of the properties and actions of God. The simple consequence of divine ineffability is that Christian (or any monotheistic) theology and ethics (which in turn provide the point and content of institutions and practices) become "cognitively meaningless"—neither true nor false. Similarly, we can conclude that if Christian (or any monotheistic) theology or ethics can be shown to be either true or false, then the claim that God is ineffable must be false.

CONCLUSION

The notion of divine ineffability seems altogether indefensible. Its consequences are no more encouraging than its content or its grounds. Whatever its causes—misinterpretation of the doctrine of the incomprehensibility of God, reverence without reason, a misinterpretation of biblical texts, the various doctrines discussed above, or a combination of these (and perhaps other) sources—it seems philosophically, theologically, and religiously disastrous, and hence provides no genuine barrier to holding that there are religious conceptual systems, Christianity among them.

SUGGESTIONS FOR FURTHER READING

Hopkins, Jasper. *Concise Introduction to the Philosophy of Nicholas of Cusa.* Minneapolis: University of Minnesota Press, 1980.

_____. *Nicholas of Cusa on God as Not-Other: A Translation and an Appraisal of De Li Non Aliud*. Minneaplis: University of Minnesota Press, 1979.

Mascall, Eric L. *Words and Images*. New York: Ronald Press, 1957.

Mitchell, Basil. *The Justification of Religious Belief*. New York: Macmillan, 1973.

Penelhum, Terrence. *Problems of Religious Knowledge*. New York: Macmillan, 1971.

Ramsey, Ian. *Religious Language*. London: SCM Press, 1957.

Plantinga, Alvin. *Does God Have a Nature?* Milwaukee: Marquette University Press, 1980.

Wolfson, Harry Austryn. *Studies in the History and Philosophy of Religion*. Cambridge, MA: Harvard University Press, 1973, 1977. 2 vols.

Yandell, Keith E. "On Windowless Experiences." *Christian Scholar's Review*, 4 (1975), 311–18.

_____. "Some Varieties of Ineffability." *International Journal for the Philosophy of Religion*, 4 (1975), 167–79.

_____. "The Ineffability Theme." *International Journal for the Philosophy of Religion*, 10 (1979), 209–31.

ANALYTICAL TABLE OF CONTENTS TO CHAPTER 4

CHAPTER 4
DO RELIGIOUS CLAIMS HAVE TRUTH VALUE?

To all appearances religious traditions include claims about God, humanity, nature, and morality. To accept a religious tradition involves accepting its doctrines as truths. Occasionally, proponents of a religious tradition will disavow the notion that their tradition has any doctrines, but upon examination we will typically find that they are actually claiming that their tradition has clear truths, whereas all other traditions have mere doctrines.

The doctrines, tenets, or claims of a tradition shape its institutions and practices, its rites and rituals, and its code of conduct or commended life-style. Christianity is a creedal religion; one finds various statements of its doctrinal content, perhaps the most famous and widely accepted of which is the Apostles' Creed. But noncreedal religions also have authoritative texts that contain standard patterns of doctrine that are normative within their tradition. Thus both creedal and noncreedal religious traditions at least seem to be cognitive, to contain propositions that are either true or false.

Nonetheless, many philosophers have been loath to talk about "religious knowledge,"[1] perhaps supposing that there is no such thing because religion is a noncognitive affair, or that whatever cognitive factors play a role in religious matters go beyond the bounds of knowledge into the realm of faith or hope or superstition. One reason for this is the pervasive influence of a particular view

1. Indeed, considerably more radically, some have refused to countenance even religious *belief*, at least in any straightforward sense of "belief," and this refusal is considered here in some detail.

of what knowledge, and its epistemic cousin reasonable belief, amount to—a view called *foundationalism.* There are several varieties of foundationalism, and no one formulation will serve to describe it adequately. The discussion here concerns what some now call "strong" foundationalism. This view was called forth as a response to scepticism and joins scepticism in making certain basic epistemic assumptions which, if nothing else, greatly simplify the epistemological alternatives by reducing them to two: foundationalism or scepticism. Along with these assumptions goes a certain conception of "the ethics of belief," if such there be. Since the basic interest of the present enterprise is in the question as to whether, and if so how, religious doctrines and conceptual systems can be rationally assessed, it seems appropriate to consider foundationalism, scepticism, and (briefly) their associated ethic of belief.

FOUNDATIONALISM

One kind of certainty precludes mistakes. Whatever precludes mistakes about important matters is of great value. So one kind of certainty is of great value.

This reasoning expresses the normative element in a foundational view about knowledge. One tenet of this view is that knowledge requires *epistemic* certainty—the sort of certainty we have about a proposition when we believe it to be true and cannot be mistaken in so believing. *Epistemic* certainty can be defined in contrast to *psychological* certainty, or sheer stable conviction: one can be *psychologically*, but not epistemically, certain that a false proposition is true—that one's head is made of glass, for instance, or that the world was created by a pheasant—whereas it is not possible for us to be *epistemically* certain of such a thing. We might say that epistemic certainty is *justified* psychological certainty.

The proposition *Knowledge requires epistemic certainty* is one tenet of a foundational view of knowledge, and the proposition *Reasonable belief requires knowledge* is another.[2] According to foundationalism, it is reasonable to believe what we know to be true, and it is reasonable to believe what we can justify by appeal to what we know, but it is not reasonable to believe anything else. The term *founda-*

2. This perspective describes what some contemporary proponents of "weak" foundationalism might wish to call "old-fashioned" or "Cartesian" foundationalism; "weak" foundationalism is similar in some ways to what we will call *confirmationism* at a later point in this chapter.

tionalism comes by way of an architectural analogy: it is assumed that some propositions are initially known to us, that we have epistemic certainty about them; these constitute the foundation of our knowledge. Other propositions, which we justify by appeal to these foundational propositions, constitute the superstructure of our system of knowledge. In order to assess the foundational view of knowledge, it will be necessary that we give further consideration to two of its essential elements: *epistemic certainty* and *justification by appeal to foundational propositions.*

EPISTEMIC CERTAINTY

It is tempting to say that (1) Ralph has *epistemic certainty* with regard to a proposition **P** if it is logically impossible both for Ralph to believe that **P** is true and for **P** to be false. It is tempting because on this account Ralph cannot believe falsely. But consider Goldbach's Conjecture:[3] *Every even number greater than two is the sum of two primes*; presumably if this proposition is true, then it is necessarily true—which is to say that if it is true and Ralph believes it, then Ralph cannot believe mistakenly. This will be so for any necessary truth. But if Ralph does not know that it is true, he also will not know that he cannot mistakenly believe it. Further, even if it is true, Ralph might nevertheless suppose it to be false.

According to this characterization of epistemic certainty, the ground of certainty lies altogether on the side of the proposition that is necessarily true; it will be true whether Ralph believes it or not. The connection, then, between certainty and truth is *external.* This comes out most clearly when we note that Ralph may *falsely* believe that a proposition is a necessary truth. If, for instance, he believes that $2 + 2 = 4$ and $5 + 3 = 8$ are necessary truths, and he also believes that it follows from these that $2 + 5 + 3 = 12$ on the mistaken ground that when an even number appears more than once in a sum its appearances beyond the first are redundant, then presumably he will mistakenly believe that $2 + 5 + 3 = 12$ is a necessary truth. In sum, if the proposition **P** *is a necessary truth* is true, then the proposition *Ralph cannot believe that* **P** *is true and be mistaken in so believing* will also be true, but the proposition *Ralph*

3. Or Fermat's Last Theorem, which says that *There are no four numbers x, y, z, and n, all greater than o, such that* $x^{n+2} + y^{n+2} = 2^{n+2}$. Neither the Conjecture nor the Theorem has been proved.

believes that **P** *is a necessary truth* does not entail the proposition **P** *is a necessary truth.*

A foundationalist who is bothered by the purely external relation between the ground of certainty and belief in the first characterization of epistemic certainty might offer a different characterization as follows: *(2) Ralph has epistemic certainty regarding proposition* **P** if his belief that **P** is true serves to make **P** true, and if **P** would not be true if he did not believe it. We might then speak of a case in which Ralph's belief that **P**, and only that, rendered **P** true as in a case in which belief that **P** is true and **P**'s being true have a purely *internal* relationship. There will not be many (if any) *first-order* first-person beliefs (i.e., beliefs about oneself that are not beliefs about one's beliefs), and none that are not first-person beliefs, that are accessible to epistemic certainty according to this characterization. Ralph's belief that he exists, or that he has beliefs, or that he is capable of having beliefs, or that he is conscious, can presumably be true whether or not he believes them, and even if he neither believes nor disbelieves them, so they will not fit the criteria for our second characterization of epistemic certainty.

If Ralph believes that flying is a perfectly safe mode of travel, then, and then alone, will his *second-order* belief that he believes that he thinks air travel is safe be true. But one can be mistaken about what beliefs one has; Ralph can believe that he believes that flying is perfectly safe, and upon having it pointed out that he travels some other way whenever possible, that he cannot sleep the night before those flights he is forced to take, and that he always takes a powerful sedative upon reaching his seat on a plane, he can come to see that he was mistaken after all about his having had that belief. The range, then, of this characterization of epistemic certainty seems distressingly small, if not entirely vacuous.[4]

We might then propose a third characterization of epistemic certainty as follows: (3) epistemic certainty regarding proposition **P** if *Ralph believes that* **P** *is true* entails **P** *is true,* whether **P** was true

4. It will be if (i) for any first-order belief, one can be mistaken about whether one has it, (ii) the truth of second-order beliefs depends on whether one has the corresponding first-order ones, so (iii) one's knowledge of what second-order beliefs one has depends on one's knowledge of one's first-order beliefs, or if (iv) what beliefs one has depends on what dispositions one has, and (v) one cannot infallibly know what dispositions one has. For epistemic certainty always is intended to rule out the possibility of error.

otherwise or not. Thus if Ralph believes that he exists, is conscious, has at least one belief, or is capable of believing something, then his having the belief will entail that the belief is true. Perhaps the same goes for Ralph's belief that he has a headache, or feels dizzy, or feels nauseous, or is in pain. In such cases it seems that the belief that something is so entails that it is so. The scope of this characterization of epistemic certainty is not nil, but it is nevertheless quite restricted, and one might be forgiven for thinking that nothing very substantial can be built on such foundations as fall within that scope.

One might formulate the notion of epistemic certainty as follows: Ralph has epistemic certainty with regard to a proposition **P** if and only if he has one of the three characterizations of epistemic certainty we have just outlined with regard to **P**. Can such claims as *I exist* and *I see a brown desk* come within the scope of such epistemic certainty? Within severe limits, *I exist* can. It is logically impossible for me to believe falsely that I exist; *At time* **t**, *I believe that I exist* entails *At* **t**, *I exist.* It does not entail *At a moment before* **t**, *I existed* or *At a moment after* **t**, *I will exist,* and so does not entail *I, who cannot falsely believe that I exist, am an enduring being.* One might argue that to have beliefs at all necessarily is to possess capacities or dispositional properties and that only an enduring item can have such properties, or that to have beliefs at all is necessarily to be a member of a community of language users. I am inclined to think the former of these arguments more promising than the latter, but if a foundationalist accepts either line of reasoning, the result will not be to increase the knowledge that falls under epistemic certainty, but to call into severe question whether we can know that we have any beliefs at all, since it is by no means epistemically certain that we have capacities or dispositional properties or that we belong to a community. Insofar as foundationalists can know that belief is possible, they must assume that it is private, episodic, and nondispositional.

A proposition such as *I see a brown desk* cannot come within the scope of epistemic certainty. *Perhaps* I cannot be wrong about whether it seems to me that there is a desk; nonetheless, *I seem to see a desk now* does not entail *I see a desk now* or *There is a desk now.* To generalize, claims that are true only if some physical object or other (or some mind other than my own) exists do not fall within the scope of epistemic certainty, nor, of course, do propositions that presuppose such claims. It seems unlikely that *God exists* or *God created the world* or *God is just* falls within that scope, or that they are propositions with respect to which any of the three characterizations of epistemic certainty that we have considered applies.

JUSTIFICATION BY APPEAL TO FOUNDATIONAL PROPOSITIONS

Having considered the notion of epistemic certainty, it is time to investigate the other essential element of the foundational view of knowledge: *justification by appeal to foundational propositions.* The simplest, clearest sense of justification is expressed by the phrase "is entailed by." A proposition **P** is justified by a (one-or-more-membered) set **S** of foundational propositions if and only if **S** *but* **not-P** is a contradiction—that is to say, if and only if it is logically impossible that **S** be true and **P** be false: foundationalist justification is a matter of being entailed by foundational or epistemically certain propositions. Other varieties of justification might be suggested; for example, **P** is justified by **S** if and only if **S** makes **P** more probable than **not-P**. But this strategy will require that we argue along lines such as the following: (1) **S**; (2) if **S**, then probably **P**; so (3) probably **P**. In fact, it is hard, if not impossible, to discover instances of propositions of the sort for which (2) provides the schema which either come within the scope of epistemic certainty or follow from propositions that do. For example, neither *If I exist now, probably I existed a moment ago* nor *If it seems to me that I see a desk, probably there is a desk that I see* is epistemically certain or follows from propositions that are. Neither proposition is necessarily true, and neither is such that my believing it makes it true, and neither is such that its being true follows from my believing it.

FOUNDATIONALISM AND CHRISTIAN BELIEF

If foundationalism is true, then the justification of Christian belief must be foundationalist. Beginning with propositions regarding which we have epistemic certainty, one will be expected to derive the propositions of Christian theology, or else belief that those propositions are true will not be reasonable. The prospects of such a task are not encouraging, however. It is not clear that there are any propositions that fall within the range of anyone's epistemic certainty from which the propositions of Christian theology (or Marxist ideology, or humanistic religion, for that matter) follow; it is not clear that *any* perspective with much content follows from this very restricted set of propositions. In fact, it is not clear that the demands of foundationalist justification are met even if God's existence can be proved by arguments of the sort Thomas Aquinas apparently sought.

Aquinas required that the premises of arguments for the existence of God be *self-evident* or else *evident to the senses.* Self-evident propositions, perhaps, include only necessary truths, or those necessary truths simple enough to be easily accessible to us, such as those expressed in the propositions *There is no highest positive integer* and *If a proposition is contradictory, then it is false.* Propositions evident to the senses are those one literally can perceive to be true, such as *Some objects are larger than others* or *Some things move in relation to other things.* But the propositions alleged to be evident to the senses, however epistemically secure they may be, do not meet foundationalist standards. If we consider the particular cases that confirm a statement such as *Some objects are larger than others*—the proposition *My hand is larger than my pen* is one such example—then we can see that no such proposition will meet foundationalist standards, since no such proposition is a necessary truth or else such that our believing it to be true makes it true or entails its truth. But unless some such proposition comes within the scope of epistemic certainty, how can *Some objects are larger than others* come within that scope? One might simply assume that a proposition such as *Either my hand is larger than my pen, or my pen is larger than my hand* entails *Some objects are larger than others*—and it does, so long as we assume that the proposition *My hand and pen exist* is true, but the problem remains that the latter proposition does not come within the scope of anyone's epistemic certainty. Further, it is *logically possible* (i.e., not a contradiction) that my hand and pen are of equal size and that the denial of *that* proposition comes within the scope of no one's epistemic certainty. So propositions that are evident to the senses, even if we seem to know them securely enough to believe anything that follows from them, cannot serve as foundational propositions, and since each of Aquinas's arguments essentially contains at least one proposition of this sort, we can conclude that they do not constitute proofs by foundationalist standards, even if they are otherwise impeccable. This underlines the stringency of foundationalist strictures.

If foundationalism is true, then religious doctrines—including those of Christian theology—cannot be known, or reasonably believed, since they do not follow from claims about which we can have epistemic certainty. Foundationalists who wish to contend that Christian doctrines have no "truth value" (i.e., are neither true nor false) will argue in two stages: in the first place they will claim that Christian doctrines are not entailed by foundationalist propositions, that they do not follow from propositions that fall within the scope of epistemic certainty; in the second place they will claim that only what is entailed by foundationalist propositions can have truth value. A rationale for this contention can be provided if we accept two further claims: (i) if a proposition has truth value, we can tell what that value is (i.e., if a proposition is true or false, we can tell which it is); and (ii) we can tell what the truth value of a nonfoundational proposition is only if it or its contradictory follows from foundational propositions: if it follows from foundational propositions it is true, and if its contradictory follows from foundational propositions its contradictory is true (and so it is false).[5]

DIFFICULTIES OF FOUNDATIONALISM

Foundationalism has come upon hard times. As was the case with the elusive Verification Principle of logical positivism, the tenets of foundationalism have been powerfully criticized. Among the more important criticisms are the following. First and foremost, *Knowledge requires epistemic certainty* and, especially, *Reasonable belief requires knowledge,* are not themselves propositions which fall within the scope of anyone's epistemic certainty.[6] If foundationalism is true, then we do not know that foundationalism is true, nor are we reasonable in accepting it. Second, that I know or reasonably believe that my hand is larger than my pen, and of course a great

5. Since a proposition (roughly) is what is asserted by one who uses a declarative sentence standardly, it is necessarily true that a proposition is true, or else false; thus (i), strictly, should be stated along such lines as "if a sentence (whose standard use) is alleged to express a proposition really does express one, then the truth value of that alleged proposition must be discoverable," and analogously for (ii). Thus (i) and (ii) are stated elliptically for convenience.

6. Neither do propositions (i) or (ii) in the preceding paragraph, so a consistent foundationalist cannot accept them either. So the foundationalist argument against theological propositions having truth value fails. Of course one might claim that (i) and (ii) are just self-evident, but the denials of (i) or (ii) do not appear to be contradictory and philosophers sharply disagree about whether (i) and (ii) are true, so they are poor candidates for being self-evident.

many other propositions, is much more plausible and less challenge-able than is foundationalism. *Energy is conserved, Lincoln was once President of the U.S., and Torture for pleasure is wrong,* given foundationalism, are neither known nor reasonably believed. Since foundationalism is in epistemic competition with what seem to be eminently reasonable beliefs, it is highly implausible. Third, as is clear from the second point, foundationalism's price is high; the range of propositions anyone knows to be true will be very restricted—so much so that none of the natural or social sciences, and none of the humanities, in whole or in significant part, will be included. Such propositions as *I am married, I have parents,* and *There are trees* are in the same boat. Thus, upon reflection, both the plausibility and the attractiveness of foundationalism suffer enormous attrition. There seems to be no good reason (foundationalist or otherwise) to accept foundationalism; and no good reason to suppose that Christian theology either receives foundationalist justification or else is neither known nor reasonably believed to be true.

SCEPTICISM AND FOUNDATIONALISM

The lifeblood of foundationalism is the fear of scepticism. Foundationalism has its positive promise—epistemic certainty includes psychological certainty, and while there do not seem to be any propositions with regard to which we have epistemic certainty which also provide solutions to problems over which humans anguish, *if* there were such propositions, and we knew it, this would be important. Nonetheless, the actual performance of systems constructed with foundationalist intentions and allegedly within foundationalist strictures has not been encouraging in this regard. One might unkindly suggest that if certainty could have degrees, the epistemic certainty of a proposition often would be inversely proportional to its importance.

A great part of foundationalism's influence, then, is probably traceable to a perspective that can be characterized as follows: *foundationalism or scepticism; not scepticism; so foundationalism.* Scepticism need not be universal in its scope; a sceptic about religion need not be one about science, and a sceptic about science need not be one about religion, for example. But the scepticism to which foundationalism sometimes seemed the only alternative is universal.

SIMPLE SCEPTICISM

How, exactly, is scepticism to be stated? One might distinguish between a sort of scepticism which maintained *In fact, no one knows anything* and one which held *No one can know anything*; on the former, but not the latter, ignorance may be remediable. But no one could know the truth of either view, for either the view in question is false (and so can't be known for that reason) or is true (and can't be known compatibly with its truth). It seems implausible that scepticism of either sort should long retain the allegiance or the interest of any intelligent person, for no sceptic can claim to know or to reasonably believe either view without inconsistency. Scepticism's roots, surely, are deeper than these remarks reveal.

SCEPTICISM BASED ON FOUNDATIONALISM

Scepticism of a rather forceful sort could be mounted on foundationalist premises. Define a proposition as *epistemically interesting* if its truth or falsity requires the existence of physical objects, a mind other than one's own, or God.[7] Accept the basic tenets of foundationalism: *Knowledge requires epistemic certainty* and *Rational belief requires knowledge.* Hold that one knows only those propositions which fall within the scope of epistemic certainty, and what they entail. Then note that no epistemically interesting proposition either falls within the scope of epistemic certainty or is entailed by those which do. The result is that not a single epistemically interesting proposition is known to be true. While not a perfectly general scepticism, the result is unrestricted enough to merit the adjective "sceptical." In this light foundationalism and scepticism appear as common heads of a single hydra, and whatever reasons one has to be reserved about the truth of foundationalism, insofar as they concern the basic foundationalist tenets, also will be reasons to be reserved about a scepticism of this sort.

RELATIVISM

Scepticism has epistemic cousins in the varieties of relativism. One variety of relativism holds that truth is relative to persons; if I

7. Strictly, where the "truth conditions" of a proposition are what must exist if the proposition is to be true, an epistemically interesting proposition is one the truth conditions of which include the existence of a physical object, a mind other than one's own, or God, or the contradictory of any such proposition.

believe that **P**, then **P** is true for me. In one sense of "true for me," to say that something is true for me is simply to say that I believe it. Then *If I believe that* **P**, *then* **P** *is true for me* becomes *If I believe that* **P**, *then I believe that* **P**; which, while true, is neither interesting nor a form of relativism. So "true for me" apparently means something else; perhaps it is a fancy way of just saying "true." Then the claim is that if I believe that **P**, then **P** is true. But this claim is absurd; I cannot make myself a millionaire merely by coming to believe that I am or cause pigs to fly by coming to believe they fly. Further, it is easily refuted—anyone can refute it simply by disbelieving it.

Another variety makes truth relative to a society; if **P** is believed in society **S**, then **P** is true in **S**. "Believed in **S**" presumably means "believed by everyone in **S**" (or "believed by the majority of persons in **S**") or the like. Either way, the view has curious consequences. Consider the proposition *Iron always floats in water.* On the view in question, if everyone in a society believes this, iron will always float on water, though if one person reverses his or her opinion on the matter (or if the majority reverses its opinion) iron will change its behavior in water. If one can change people's minds by bribing them, one can change the behavior of iron in water simply by bribing persons, without those persons having to do anything save change their minds. Further, it seems unlikely that anyone could persuade, say, the majority of U. S. citizens that whatever the majority of U. S. citizens believe is true simply because they believe it, or is made true by their believing it, or that "is true (in the U. S.)"—as opposed to "is *regarded as* true in the U. S."—just means "is believed by the majority of U. S. citizens." That view seems one likely *not* to be held by the majority of U. S. citizens. So, on its own terms, it is false.

On the face of things, and at their depths, these views are false; they are also rather silly. They are epistemic cousins of radical scepticism, however, in that their gist is to the effect that there really is no truth of the matter about anything; and in that respect they are incoherent. But they nonetheless suggest some of scepticism's deeper roots, and that (along with their continued popular influence) is our reason for considering them here.

COMPLEX SCEPTICISM

Perhaps the following account locates those roots. To some extent, each individual has his or her own view of the world. Persons living at the same time in the same society usually will share a common perspective; the views of the world held by two such persons will overlap in many subtle ways. Persons living at diverse times, and/or in different cultures, will view the world differently; the views of the world held by two such persons may not overlap very much. It may be difficult to map any significant portion of the view of one onto that of the other. The basic concepts of individuals or particulars within (and partly constitutive of) one view may be highly different from the basic concepts of individuals or particulars within (and partly constitutive of) the other, and the same may be true for basic concepts of relationships between individuals. So, at least, goes stage one of this story.

Stage two goes like this. The various concepts of a conceptual system get their meaning from their role within the system as a whole. Two systems of concepts, with no concepts in common, are thus two systems of meaning, with no meanings in common. Such systems are incommensurable; thus they bear no logical relationships to one another, and so cannot be consistent or inconsistent with one another. Thus ends stage two.

Stage three completes the story. Questions of truth arise only *within* and not *between* conceptual systems or views of the world. While there are procedures for deciding between alternative propositions which are formulated within a single conceptual perspective, there are (and, worse, *can be*) no procedures for deciding between competing conceptual systems. Nor is there any way of observing or otherwise obtaining access to the world in a way that is independent of reliance on one or another system of concepts; but (the assumption is) only such independence would provide us with the opportunity of checking whether a system represented the world accurately. Thus ends the story.

That the result at which the third stage arrives is sceptical may not be obvious; after all, it allows that there be procedures for establishing the truth of one among competing hypotheses formulated within a single view. Nonetheless, since it is alleged that there is no way of showing that one conceptual system or world view in any way is rationally superior to another, or closer to the truth than another, or the like, then even if one could choose which view of the world one would hold, the choice would be rationally arbitrary. Nonarbitrary choices between hypotheses (it is alleged) are possible only within some conceptual system such that if one could choose, or had to choose, between it and some other conceptual system, no rational grounds are (or could be) available to guide one's choice. This result seems deeply sceptical; more sophisticated than the varieties of scepticism examined earlier, complex scepticism entails that no one worldview is more rational to hold, or closer to true, than another. That, surely, is a variety of scepticism?

The reluctance of those who hold the view just described to call it, or its consequences, sceptical rests on a feature of the view that we have mentioned but not emphasized.[8] Let **A** and **B** be world views; according to the view in question, **A** and **B** are incommensurable. No term, and no proposition, in **A** translates into a term, or proposition, in **B**, and conversely. No logical relationship—entailment, consistency, contradiction, contrariety, or any other—holds between propositions within **A** and propositions within **B**, nor between **A** and **B** themselves. So proponents of **A** are held not to *disagree* with proponents of **B**. Since there is no dispute between proponents of **A** and proponents of **B**—since **A** and **B** are not competing views, though they also are not consistent with one another (but not because they are inconsistent)—there can be no task that is properly called "deciding between **A** and **B**" or "deciding whether **A** represents the world better than **B** does." A simple sceptic would say this task cannot be performed, but would not deny that the task can be described. On the view under discussion, it cannot even be described—at any rate, not in coherent terms. But, of course, a task that cannot even be described in coherent terms also cannot be performed; assessment of competing views of the world is as impossible on this view as it is on sceptical (or on more standardly sceptical) views. One thing that makes complex scepticism different is its assurance that nothing is lost because such assessment is impossible; it cannot be a loss that something which has no coherent description has not been achieved. Otherwise put, nothing that is, or might be, lacks a coherent description; on the view in question, there is no coherent description of the sort of comparative-assessment-of-world views which the nonsceptic sought; so there is no loss (even to the nonsceptic) in its not being found.

The net result of this view for Christian theology is plain—it is, and can be, no better or worse a view of what there is than any

8. Whether what I have called "complex scepticism" is regarded as a variety, or a successor, of scepticism will make no difference to the overall argument of the chapter.

other view, religious or nonreligious. Nor is it related, say, to atheism or Theravada Buddhism in the ways it seems to be—for example, by being in many ways logically incompatible with these perspectives. (That, in fact, is one feature of the view that many find attractive.)

Perhaps our discussion has made tolerably clear the sort of roots, as well as consequences, possessed by a more sophisticated scepticism (or, if one prefers, successor to scepticism). How does the view fare when it is assessed? It is not a view of the world—at least it has not been cast here in those terms, but rather along the lines of a view about views of the world to the effect that they are incommensurable and necessarily inaccessible to assessment. So it does not entail that it cannot be rationally appraised, nor even if it did entail this would it follow that it could not be assessed.

COMPLEX SCEPTICISM AND DIFFERENCES ABOUT WORLD VIEWS

Stage one seems simply to involve claims about how diverse various conceptual systems are. In order to know that the world views of a Stone Age hunter and a contemporary university president were profoundly diverse in a way in which the world views of a contemporary university president and his strongest critic among the alumni were not, one obviously would require information about the views under discussion. There seems to be, and presumably is, a great deal of information about the views of things held in different cultures at different periods—information which reveals considerable diversity of opinion about what there is, and about how what there is fits together. This information, by itself, provides no support for scepticism or its sophisticated successor. Often, persons in the same culture hold the same views regarding God, humanity, nature, and morality. Often, persons in different cultures hold different views regarding God, humanity, nature, and morality. Sometimes, persons in the same culture hold different views regarding God, humanity, nature, and morality. Sometimes, persons in different cultures hold the same views regarding God, humanity, nature, morality. There are *degrees* of differences and similarities in these views. None of this even tends to show that complex scepticism is correct. The presence of disagreement shows that the parties differ as to where the truth lies; it does not show that there is no truth of the matter or that the truth of the matter cannot be found.[9]

Assuming (what seems likely) that many of these cross-cultural reports are reliable, it is possible to compare "our" view of the world with that of others. Of course, there is a great variety of perspectives in our own culture—varieties of atheism and theism, for example, supplemented by a small variety of Eastern religions and a large variety of popularizations and imitations of Eastern religions. Either understanding a complex culture such as our own or comparing different cultures requires comprehending various perspectives, many of which, in intent at least, are universal in the sense of explaining everything whatever[10] save that which the view in question takes to be primitive or given or ultimate. Such understanding, then, seems to require the comprehension, by a single mind, of quite a variety of world views, or outlines of same, each of which (on the sort of scepticism, or successor-of-scepticism, under review) is incommensurable relative to the others.

That various world views are comprehensible by a single person seems obvious. The history of Western philosophy contains numerous quite incompatible conceptual systems, developed within different cultural contexts; this history has been often written and more often read, frequently with apparently high degrees of comprehension. The same holds for Eastern philosophy. Various writers have produced comparative histories of philosophy, introducing yet more diversity of world view and cultural perspective, and the authors and readers of such works apparently understand what is said. One finds similar problems raised, similar solutions offered, parallel criticisms made, in apparently independent Eastern and Western cultural and intellectual contexts. Similarly, any of the many intellectual disciplines which trace their roots to Aristotle transcends our culture to comprehend portions of others. Indeed, could one not comprehend distinct varieties of cultures and understand quite

9. If one accepts the claims made in this paragraph, one cannot go on to *define* "culture" in terms of groups holding different world views. To do that would make it logically necessary that members of different cultures hold different world views, and logically impossible that members of the same culture hold different world views.

10. At least in very general, and perhaps programmatic, terms.

distinct world views,[11] one could not so much as grasp the data which comprises the first stage of the argument for complex scepticism. Similar comments apply to discussions of religious traditions, which traditions often are complexly intertwined with philosophical themes and theses.

THE DIFFICULTY OF BEING INCOMMENSURABLE

Two views are incommensurable if and only if they bear no logical or epistemic relations to one another. Views **A** and **B**, of whatever sort, apparently can have any of various logical relationships to one another. Consider some examples. If both can be true, they are *logically consistent* with one another. If the truth of either entails the falsity of the other, they are *logically inconsistent.* If both can be false but both cannot be true, they are *logically contrary.*

Further, views **A** and **B** apparently can have any of various epistemic relationships with one another. Consider some examples. Perhaps **A**'s being true is evidence for **B**'s being true. Perhaps **A**'s being false is evidence that **B** is false. Or, perhaps, **A**'s being false is evidence that **B** is true. Or, perhaps, the truth or falsity of one is no evidence at all regarding the truth or falsity of the other.

To know that views **A** and **B** are incommensurable, one must be able, so to say, to hold both in mind and not merely to be unable to relate them but also to see that they cannot be related. *Mathematics is reducible to logic* and *Atlanta is in Georgia* are not incommensurable, for they are logically compatible. Perhaps no two propositions **P** and **Q** are incommensurable, since (whatever propositions **P** and **Q** are) **P** and *If* **P** *then* **Q** will entail **Q**.

It is entire conceptual systems which are said to be incommensurable. Perhaps explicitly considering this suggestion will yield a more promising prospect than does consideration of the view that single propositions are incommensurate. Let an existence-explanation be an explanation of the fact that some particular thing, or sort of thing, or anything at all, exists. A general existence explanation will be an explanation (or series of explanations) such that whatever exists either is explained by it or else is referred to in the system's most basic *explicans*; the latter sort of entity will be primitive

11. No doubt it is not perfectly clear how "understanding distinct varieties of cultures" and "understanding quite distinct world views" are related, but if there is no relation, then complex scepticism is without even apparent empirical basis, at least along the lines discussed here.

or given or ultimate for the system in question. A general existence explanation will be, or will be part of, a world view. Thus a view that says that everything whatever is comprised of indivisible material particles or is itself such a particle, and explains the existence of present particles (singly or in combinations) by reference only to the existence of particles (singly or in combinations) in the past, plus laws or descriptions of how particles always or usually behave, is a general existence explanation. So is a view that says that everything whatever is a mind, or a mental state, and explains the present existence of minds, and/or their states, by reference only to the existence of minds and their states in the past, plus laws or descriptions of how minds always or usually behave. These views (materialism and idealism) are contraries—both can be false, but both cannot be true. For example, both are false if mind-body dualism is true. Mind-body dualism holds that *being a mind* and *being a body* are kind-defining properties, and that nothing can belong to both of the kinds that they define. On another view, called the mind-brain identity theory, *material object* and *mind* refer to the same type of thing. It holds that whenever a sentence of the form *Mind* **x** *is in mental state (or has mental property)* **P** is true, a corresponding sentence of the form *Material object* **y** *is in physical state (or has physical property)* **Q** is true though not conversely since there are bodies which are not identical to minds. On this account each sentence is true although the sort of language in which the one is expressed is such that no translation from it into the language in which the other is expressed is possible. Even so, on this view, both the propositions which express the material explanation and the propositions which express the mental explanation are true. Since to say that a system of explanation is true is only to say that the propositions that comprise it are true, the mind-brain identity theory holds that each view is true (and so is compatible with the other).[12]

Note, then, that whether materialism and idealism are contrary or complementary, they at any rate are not incommensurable. This would remain true even were there to be various institutions and rites associated with them—for example, a *celebration of there being particles* which involved ritual dances which followed the physicists' patterns for particle interaction and were participated in by those

12. How the alleged identities of reference or extension, and correspondence of propositions, are to be established is another matter, but our present task is not in assessing the views just described.

who accepted the particle explanation, and a *festival of mental rejoicing* at which poems in praise of cognitive capabilities were recited by and to those who accepted the mental explanation. (Mind-brain identity theorists might attend both sorts of festivities.)

In fact, it seems clear that the views just briefly outlined are related in such a way that none of them, strictly speaking, is incommensurable with the others.[13] The identity theory seems closer to materialism than to the other alternatives mentioned. Perhaps the identity theory just is materialism, cast—in intent if not in fact—in such a manner as to render it impervious to the objections which blighted traditional, "old-fashioned" materialism. If so, then materialism and identity theory are hardly incommensurable. If mind-body dualism is true, materialism and identity theory and idealism are false; if idealism is true, the other three alternatives are false. Of course, these four views may not be the only possible ones; that is neither here nor there for present purposes. What is relevant here is that these (very briefly described) general views simply are not incommensurable. Nor, of course, will any of the detailed, fleshed-out views (philosophical, scientific, religious, or common-sensical) which fit within one or another of these general views. The truth value of one is not completely unrelated or simply irrelevant to the truth value of the others, as incommensurability would require.

It seems that the view, called mathematical realism, that numbers are abstract objects existing independent of human thought, and its competitors (e.g., that *the number two* refers only to pairs of things which are not themselves numbers) is independent of mind-body dualism, and its competitors, in the sense that one could consistently hold either of them and reject the other. But if mathematical realism is true, materialism is false, so one competitor to dualism is false. If mathematical realism is true, idealism also is false, so another competitor of dualism is removed.[14]

The point of these remarks is not to investigate dualism and its

13. Mind-body dualism, of course, will have its own sort or sorts of explanation of the present existence of minds and bodies, and the identity theory its own sort of explanation of what it thinks there currently is. But we need not pursue this here.

14. But then one can rephrase materialism, and idealism, by adding to each the qualification "except numbers" or "except abstract objects." Materialism, then, will claim that all nonabstract, or concrete, objects are material; a rephrased idealism, then, will claim that all nonabstract, or concrete, objects are mental.

competitors for their own sake; it is simply to note that views which appear to be incommensurable (in this case, anyway) in fact are not, but that rather they do bear logical and epistemic relationships to one another. What is true for mind-body dualism and mathematical realism—themselves parts of world views—is true of different views of God, or of humanity, or of nature, or of morality; they, too, have logical and epistemic connections. So they, too, are not incommensurable.

Apparently, then, for two world views to be incommensurable, they would have to be about different things, and not about the same thing at all—perhaps simply about different worlds altogether. Since there actually is, and by necessity can be only, at most one world or universe, that this be so would seem to require a very radical sort of perspective, one on which, for example, two views "about God" are not really two views about God, for that would be for both views to involve claims about the same topic. Or, perhaps, if it occurs as part of a system of belief, one's belief that something exists will have to be sufficient for existence, but only for or to oneself and not for or to another (however this is to be conceived). One could create unicorns and leprechauns by merely believing in them, and the existence of cows and alligators would depend on one's assent; one could never falsely believe that something existed. In its way, this view returns to the "true" means "true to me" theme, and shares that theme's incoherence. Neither the "different worlds" nor the "no existential belief is false" lines promise any coherent account of a perspective on which distinct conceptual systems are incommensurable.

Two conclusions arise from this discussion. One is this: that general views **A** and **B** share no concepts (insofar as this is possible) does not entail that **A** and **B** are incommensurable. By hypothesis, the materialist explanation and idealist hypotheses mentioned above share no substantial, determinate concepts; yet, as we saw, they are not therefore incommensurable.[15] The other conclusion is this: general conceptual systems, roughly speaking, are about the same world;

15. Nor is it clear that two general conceptual systems *can* completely fail to share concepts. For example, presumably they will share some of the concepts expressed by our logical connectives (and, or, if . . . then, but, etc.), negation, quantifiers (all, some, none), and inference-terms (so, hence, then, entails, implies, therefore, etc.). Perhaps, as Kant suggests, they will also share determinate concepts that fall under the basic categories of *substance, quality, cause, and event.*

in this sense, they have a common subject matter. Whether competing or complementary, they will fail to be incommensurable. Conceptual systems are about a reality external to themselves; the language that expresses them is inherently referential. In this respect, the locution "language game" is misleading as a characterization of a conceptual system, for while there are rules for language and (usually) rules for games, games generally have nothing in them that refers beyond the game whereas languages contain devices for reference. Rules are imperatival; a language, and in particular a language rich enough to express a general conceptual system, cannot be purely (or even mainly) imperatival. Rather, it is assertive, rich in propositional content, and so prolific in its capacity for expressing truths and falsehoods.

THE SUGGESTION THAT CONCEPTUAL SYSTEMS CANNOT BE RATIONALLY ASSESSED

All of this, however, does not touch the most important contention that can be brought forth on behalf of scepticism, or scepticism's successor—the contention that there is no way of rationally assessing conceptual systems, even if we grant that they are commensurable and that different general conceptual systems, which endeavor to deal with the same data, are logical contradictories or else logical contraries and so are *competing* accounts of what there is. It is not merely that there is no mechanical decision procedure whose rigid application always yields rigorously derived results—after all, this sort of procedure is rarely available even within conceptual frameworks—but there is no set of nonmechanical rational procedures whose application requires creativity and insight which will show that some conceptual frameworks are better candidates for truth than others. The contention, even the suspicion, that this is so is a powerful root of scepticism or its successor, and the contention, even the suspicion, that though it may be false regarding scientific theories, nonetheless it is true regarding religious traditions is a powerful root of scepticism regarding the possibility of there being actual religious claims—propositions essential to religious traditions which are either true or false. No amount of criticism of one or another variety of scepticism regarding some or all of what is alleged to be known, or reasonably believed, is of much philosophical value unless this contention is discussed and grounds offered for its dismissal.[16]

FOUNDATIONALISM AND SUSPENSION OF BELIEF

It is often assumed that in the absence of epistemic certainty we can suspend judgment. It would not be pointless to distinguish between propositions with regard to which one had epistemic certainty, or else propositions which followed from these, calling these *foundationally justified propositions,* and those *foundationally unjustified propositions* which satisfy neither of these conditions, even if we could not suspend judgment with regard to all propositions we knew to be foundationally unjustified. The distinction still would mark an important difference in the epistemic status of our beliefs, though (sometimes, anyway) not one relevant to whether or not they *were* our beliefs. Nonetheless, the foundationalist is likely, plausibly, to think there is more point to the distinction if one can suspend judgment with regard to any and all foundationally unjustified propositions; from a foundationalist perspective, this would make it possible to escape risk of error. Some (but not all) sceptics have thought such suspension of judgment possible; David Hume, for example, was adamant that it is impossible in some cases.

FOUNDATIONALISM AND THE ETHICS OF BELIEF

Consider two propositions: (1) *Suspension of judgment is possible with regard to all propositions which are not foundationally justified*; (2) *One ought to suspend judgment with regard to all propositions which are not foundationally justified.* It seems plainly inconsistent to hold that (1) is false but that (2) is true, although one might well enough hold that (1) is true but (2) false. Suppose that both (1) and (2) are true, and that (3) *No epistemically interesting proposition is foundationally justified*—that is, that every proposition which is true or false only if there is a physical object, a mind other than one's own, or if God exists, is foundationally unjustified. Then, if one is a theist, one holds a belief one ought not to hold; the belief that God exists is a belief one ought to refrain from, given (2) and (3). Presumably, an atheist is in the same inelegant ethical position, since presumably

16. Hence the importance of arguments of the sort offered in Chapters 1 and 8, and the potential positive role of the "proofs" discussed in Chapter 2.

God does not exist is also foundationally unjustified; only the agnostic does his epistemic duty regarding theistic belief, if (2) and (3) are true.

One ought to suspend judgment with regard to all propositions which are not foundationally justified expresses the basic principle of one conception of the ethics of belief. One could deny that there are any "ethics of belief," holding (say) that while actions which significantly affect persons are right, or else wrong, beliefs can be neither; along the lines of this suggestion, one can believe that women (or men) never achieve an intelligence above the moronic with moral impunity so long as one does not treat women (or men) as morons. Or one might hold that there are some beliefs (such as the one just noted) which would render it rational or easier to mistreat persons, and it is wrong to hold such beliefs, though it is not sufficient to make it wrong to hold a belief that one has, and knows one has, better reason to think false than to think true. But these perspectives are very different from that of the one who holds the principle stated at the beginning of this paragraph. This principle sets high standards for beliefs; if the gist of the previous discussion is correct, then, given this principle, few sorts of beliefs indeed are such that one ought to do anything but suspend one's judgment with regard to them.

EPISTEMOLOGY WITHOUT EPISTEMICALLY CERTAIN FOUNDATIONS

A somewhat more modest principle which does not require foundationalist assumptions or use foundationalist concepts requires that one believe only those propositions which one has better evidence for than against (characteristically, that is expressed as a requirement to *proportion* belief to evidence, but we need not consider this feature of the principle). Since the process of taking one proposition as evidence for another which in turn is evidence for another either ceases at some point with propositions which require no further evidence or else one has no evidence for any proposition, some propositions must be accepted without one's having propositional evidence for them. Put another way, inferences require premises from which one infers as well as conclusions to which one infers; unless some propositions may serve as premises without having first to be inferred from yet other premises, knowledge by inference is impossible; inferred knowledge presupposes noninferred knowledge.[17] This, of course, raises the question as to which propositions one is entitled to accept, or one is justified in believing, without there being propositional evidence for them—without one's having inferred them from other propositions which were already known to be reliable.

Foundationalism and scepticism share the view that knowledge requires epistemic certainty, and reasonable belief requires knowledge. The foundationalist implausibly alleges, and the sceptic plausibly denies, that there are *epistemically interesting* propositions (in the sense defined earlier) which are known or reasonably believed. It seems rather clear that in this dispute, the sceptic is right, and that one who rejects scepticism must reject the tenets that scepticism and foundationalism share. There has been some hesitation to do this on the ground that the only alternative to *foundationalism or scepticism* is sheer conceptual anarchy where anyone is as reasonable in believing anything as anyone else is in believing anything else. If it seems implausible that foundationalism, or else scepticism, is true, it seems just as implausible that if Ralph believes that the moon is an onion, Ralph is reasonable in so believing, or that if Ralph believes that the earth as a whole is larger than his left foot, but his brother believes Ralph's left foot is larger than the universe as a whole, each one's belief is as reasonable as is the other's. But how is one to hold that Ralph's belief about the moon, and his brother's belief about the earth, are unreasonable if one has no foundations of belief to appeal to?

KNOWING AND PROVING

It is sometimes held that a person is reasonable in accepting a proposition only if he or she can prove that proposition. It was noted above that anyone who endeavors to satisfy this condition, however, with regard to some proposition **P** must either offer a circular argument (deriving **P** from **Q**, and **Q** from **R**, and **R** from **S**, and **S** from **P**), which allows the argument to stop somewhere, but at the price of providing no justification for **P**, or else fall into an infinite regress (deriving **P** from **Q**, and **Q** from **R**, and **R** from **S**, and so on forever), which never ends and so never ends with a

17. Reasoning similar to this lies behind a view which one might call "weak foundationalism"—a view, roughly, which says that knowing has to begin somewhere, so there must be noninferred knowledge, but that the propositions so known need not be ones about which one cannot be mistaken.

proposition which has been justified; but then the whole argument, up to any point whatever, remains without justification, since (on the epistemic doctrine in question) what is not proved is not known, and the premise on which the argument rests lacks proof. So if one can know anything, one must know something without having to prove it.[18]

REASONABLE BELIEF WITHOUT EPISTEMIC CERTAINTY

Suppose that Ralph believes he has a head, basing this belief on the sorts of experience which leads any of us to have this belief—experiences perhaps easier to recognize than to describe. His belief lacks epistemic certainty, and does not follow from any set of propositions regarding which he has such certainty. Yet it hardly seems an unreasonable belief on Ralph's part, foundationless (in the foundationalist sense) though it be. Ralph appears to have evidence for it—evidence comprised of his seeing his head reflected in mirrors and windows, having sensations in it, feeling it, feeling the effects of objects on it (feeling *with* it, so to say), and so on. Unless he has good reason to think these experiences deceptive, he has good reason to have his belief.[19] This remains so, even if it is not logically impossible that his belief be mistaken although his experiences support it, and even if it does not follow from any set of beliefs regarding which it is impossible that Ralph be mistaken. If the proposition *There are physical objects* is contradictory, because the concept of a physical object is the concept of something that, were it to exist, would have logically incompatible properties, then Ralph's belief cannot be true; in part at least, it is reflection on the notion of a physical object, not simply appeal to experiences of the sort indicated, that is required to decide this issue.[20]

This reminds one of the possibility that was explored in more

18. And were one to know that one can know nothing without having proved it, one would have to know it without proving it, or else know it by proving it on the basis of something known without its having to be proved. So one can "know" this claim only on the condition that it is false.

19. Cf. Axioms 1–3, Chapter 1.

20. Perhaps it is the case that if *"There are physical objects" is consistent* is true, then it is necessarily true; that it is true cannot be determined without conceptual analysis. In this respect, belief in objects and belief in God are similar. Cf. the discussion of the interrelations of experiential and "systematic" considerations in assessing theistic belief in Chapter 1.

detail earlier. Possibly a claim is confirmed by experience if two things are true—the experience has an object or content appropriate to the claim in question, and the claim is logically consistent (and a coherent part of a coherent network of claims). If one states it thus, one has but the barest of epistemic suggestions. This suggestion was explored in Chapter 1 in a discussion which dealt with both perceptual and numinous experiences. What was developed there was an epistemology of reasonable belief in the absence of epistemically certain foundations.

THE ETHICS OF BELIEF AND PERMISSIBLE BELIEFS

Let a *basic* belief be one which is believed by someone who does not infer it from other beliefs he or she has; in this sense of "basic," a proposition that is basic for one person may, but also may not, be basic for another. Two questions arise: (i) what sorts of propositions is one epistemically justified in accepting as basic? (ii) what sorts of propositions is it permissible to believe? Those who think there is an ethics of belief presumably will think there is an ethics of *basic* belief; it would require explanation, at least, were one to hold that there was an ethics of belief, but only of nonbasic beliefs. One who holds there is an ethics of belief, then, who also holds that it has to do with whether one is epistemically justified in holding a belief[21] will hold that when (i) has been answered, it will be easy to answer (ii).

CONDITIONS OF EPISTEMICALLY JUSTIFIED BELIEF: NECESSARY, SUFFICIENT

Stating the sufficient conditions for being epistemically justified in holding a basic belief, however, seems to be extremely difficult. Foundationalism's attempt seems natural, but mistaken; yet to hold that if one does accept a belief as basic, one is epistemically justified in doing so, no matter what that belief may be, seems just absurd. My believing that pigs can fly is not a belief I am epistemically justified in having if I am careful not to rest my belief to this effect on any other belief I may have. But what alternative is there between foundationalism and epistemic anarchy?

One step toward an answer, perhaps, is to note that at any rate there are obvious sufficient conditions of one's *not* being epistemi-

21. If one is, one's doing so is right; otherwise, it is wrong.

cally justified in holding a basic belief that **P**. Some, at least, will also be epistemically sufficient conditions for holding a basic belief that **not-P**.

Suppose Ralph knows that (a) **P** is a contradiction, or (b) **P** is such that, if it were true, one could not have any reason to think it (or its denial) true, or (c) **Q** is true, and if **Q** is true, then **P** is not; surely if Ralph knows (a) or (b) or (c) then Ralph is not justified in believing that **P** at all (and so not justified in adopting belief that **P** as a basic belief). Thus, it is a necessary condition of Ralph's being epistemically justified in holding belief that **P** as a basic belief that (to the best of Ralph's knowledge, any relevant ignorance being not his fault) **P** is not a contradiction, nor is **P** such that if it were true, one could have no reason to think it (or its denial) true, nor is there any proposition which Ralph knows to be true which is incompatible with **P**. Further, if Ralph knows that **not-P** is a necessary truth, or that **Q** is true and **Q** entails **not-P**, or perhaps that if **P** is true, then **P** cannot be known (or reasonably believed) to be true, then Ralph is justified in believing that **not-P**. So we have some small part of an account of the conditions of justified belief.

As noted, these seem also to be conditions of Ralph's being justified in holding any *nonbasic* belief, and this feature of the statement of necessary conditions of being epistemically justified in holding a belief seems unlikely to be remedied so long as *basic* means simply *is not inferred. Not being inferred from some other proposition* is not an intrinsic feature of a proposition, and for any proposition **P**, presumably one can hold belief that **P** as basic by deciding that there is no other proposition **Q** such that, if one rejected **Q**, then one would also reject **P**.

One sort of restriction on this concerns logical limits on what one can do regarding one's beliefs—for example, if **P** is a conjunct of **Q** and **R**, or entails **Q** and/or **R**, one can hardly decide to make belief that **P** basic in a manner which allows one to reject belief that **Q**, and/or belief that **R**, and yet retain belief that **P**. The second sort of restriction is this. The view that there is an ethics of belief does not require that one be able to alter one's beliefs upon another's demand or one's own choice, and at a moment's notice. It does require that one be able either to "shelter" one's beliefs by avoiding situations in which they may be attacked or even assessed, by oneself or another, or deliberately to expose them to challenge and possibly abandonment, so that one's beliefs are neither (like one's attention) fixed on a proposition or not as one wills, nor (like one's original DNA coding) utterly beyond one's control, but rather (like one's weight) subject to one's influence, over time and through effort, if one wishes. Thus these restrictions are important, but not ones which rule out there being any such thing as the "ethics of belief."

THE ETHICS OF BELIEF AND PERMISSIBLE FALSE BELIEFS

If there is an "ethics of belief" at all, then it seems there are, or may be, circumstances in which a person may hold a belief which he or she is not epistemically justified in holding, but not be wrong for doing so, even if the belief is false. Suppose, for example, that belief that **P** is innate to Ruth in the sense that Ruth is born with a set of dispositions which, once triggered by experiences of a sort every person is likely to have, produce a belief that **P**, and do so in such a way that Ruth finds belief that **P** entirely easy and natural, though she has no reason to think **P** true, and though **P** is in fact false. It seems not logically impossible that these conditions be satisfied by some person with regard to some belief, and clear that if they were, the person would hold a false belief but not be culpable for so doing. Perhaps these exact conditions are never satisfied, but it seems likely that similar ones are—that in any particular culture there be some beliefs which people in that culture find it entirely easy and natural to accept, which enjoy widespread acceptance within the culture, which there is subtle pressure or influence to accept (not necessarily by anyone's intention that this be so), and which are false, or at least which most of those who accept them have not subjected to any sort of epistemic assessment. Yet it may not dawn on anyone to question them, and likely will be beyond the powers of many to ferret them out and investigate them on their own, and it seems unduly harsh to hold that such persons are guilty of an epistemic fault in holding such beliefs; to do so would suppose them possessed of the sort of leisure and inclination, if not the intellectual powers, which Descartes possessed as he wrote his *Meditations On First Philosophy.* Such "culturally produced beliefs," as we may call them, seem not (morally) *improperly* held, though their holder lacks epistemic justification for them.

This suggests a distinction which can be marked as follows:

where the belief in question is *basic,* Ruth's belief that **P** is *permissibly basic* if and only if Ruth is *epistemically justified* in believing that **P**, and Ruth's belief that **P** is *not impermissibly basic* if and only if Ruth's having **P** is innate or culturally produced, whereas Ruth's belief that **P** is *impermissibly basic* if and only if Ruth's belief that **P** is neither *permissibly basic* nor *not impermissibly basic.* Or, one might say, being epistemically justified in having a belief makes it *right* that one have it, but not being so justified does not automatically make it *wrong* for one to have that belief, since one may not be culpable for having the belief in the absence of epistemic justification.

THE SCOPE OF CULTURALLY PRODUCED BELIEFS

Among the beliefs that are culturally produced (and so epistemically unassessed, whether true, or false) there are likely to be beliefs about the nature of human beings, the existence and properties of gods or God, the fate of individuals, what a good life consists in, whether the nonhuman world is friendly or hostile or neutral (or some mixture of these) to human well-being, and the like. In turn, these beliefs will affect actions, and other beliefs, in a variety of ways. As some sociologists of religion put it, such beliefs serve to define the "meaning" of the cosmos and to define the "place" of the individual within it. The implication seems to be that without some such beliefs, whether theistic or not, most persons, at least, would have a hard time functioning—would find it difficult to function in their various social roles of parent or child, leader or follower, farmer or hunter, skilled or unskilled laborer, or whatever. A strict ethic of belief would entail that persons who held such beliefs were wrong in doing so, because (even in those cases, if any, in which these beliefs were true) the persons who held them were not epistemically justified in holding them—not only not epistemically justified along foundationalist lines, but likely not epistemically justified along the lines presented by any plausible account of how it is one provides evidence of appropriate sorts for the propositions one believes, or rationally decides between basic beliefs.[22] In this respect, a strict ethic of belief seems harsh.

One might argue that the harshness was only apparent, and that the real harshness lies in the view that, unprotesting, "allowed

22. Unless it is rational to accept basic beliefs simply on the authority of "everyone" accepting them.

the masses to remain in abject superstition," or the like. One element in the dispute as to whether a strict ethics of belief is itself cruel is its contention that persons who are not very well placed to do sophisticated, or even unsophisticated, epistemology are morally wrong to accept "culturally produced beliefs" which provide a "meaning" to their lives by giving them a "place" in the scheme of things concerns whether the influence, morally considered, of the effects of holding religious belief is evil—an assessment likely to vary depending on what particular beliefs are in question. Such an assessment is made very difficult because it is hard to tell what actions were caused by a person's or community's religious beliefs as opposed to other beliefs they held; perhaps a person who holds religious belief **R** and nonreligious belief **A** will thereby act in one way, and one who holds **R** and nonreligious belief **B** will thereby act in another; what, then, is **R**'s role in producing the former person's actions? The assessment, fully rounded out at least, would also require that we know how the person or community would have acted had they *not* held the religious beliefs in question, and this seems likely often to be imponderable; but then we will not know whether they would have acted better, worse, or (morally speaking) the same, had those beliefs not been present. These issues arise, independent of questions about what beliefs shall count as "religious" and what system of morality shall provide[23] the scales for weighing the various relevant consequences of religious belief. Neither attempting such assessment nor speculating as to its results will profit us here, and no such attempt will be made.

SOME CONSEQUENCES OF A FOUNDATIONALIST ETHICS OF BELIEF

A strict ethics of belief, we saw, will make epistemically unjustified belief wrong. Some, at least, of the problems such an ethic faces perhaps by now are clear. If epistemic justification is construed along foundationalist lines, very few (sorts of) beliefs are justified (and acceptance of foundationalism is not among them); thus most of the (sorts of) beliefs people have, including all cases of believing epistemically interesting propositions, are beliefs they are wrong in having. It would help little to suggest that people are not wrong to

23. Presumably in a way that begs no questions regarding moral perspectives sanctioned by the religious traditions under review.

have at least those beliefs required for survival, or even to require that they only act as if they had those beliefs while really suspending their judgment about them; any such stratagem would be based on beliefs about what beliefs are required for survival, or about what actions are so required, or the like, and any such beliefs are not epistemically superior to those others which have been weighed on foundationalist scales and found wanting. On the other hand, should epistemic justification be construed along nonfoundationalist lines, then a strict ethics of belief will await the appropriate nonfoundationalist account of justification. However that may go—at least on any version that has much plausibility—it seems clear that a great many persons will have beliefs which they have not justified in any such way as that which the account prescribes. Nor will it be reasonable to think that, under the conditions under which these people live, they realistically could be expected to have discovered, and then applied, the appropriate procedures for justifying beliefs. But none of this will entail that those who are able to do so ought not to believe only those propositions which they know to be epistemically accredited.

TWO EPISTEMIC STRATEGIES: FALSIFICATIONIST AND CONFIRMATIONIST

Consider, then, what perhaps is the most important issue that discussion of the ethics of belief raises.

Providing evidence for beliefs, we saw, must begin somewhere—not merely temporally, but logically; unless there are some propositions we can know or reasonably believe without having to base them on our knowledge or belief regarding further propositions, we can know or reasonably believe nothing at all. But where may one begin? One answer is: wherever it is not impermissible to begin. Roughly, we may begin with any proposition we do not know, or reasonably believe, to be false. Another answer is: only where it is permissible to begin. Roughly, we may begin with any proposition we know, or reasonably believe, to be true. Each answer has its point. The strategy the first answer suggests is one of falsification: one tries to find epistemic fault with propositions tentatively held and retains those which are faultless so far. The strategy the second answer suggests is one of verification: one tries to find confirmation of propositions and accepts only those for which it is found.

In fact, of course, when we (temporally) begin our epistemic assessments, we do so with a corpus of belief on which to operate. Assuming foundationalist procedures are discredited by the considerations mentioned above, we have two nonfoundationalist strategies—one falsificationist, one confirmationist. Construed along "ethics of belief" lines, we have, respectively, *One ought to reject any belief which we come to know, or have good reason to think, to be false* and *One ought to reject any belief which we do not find good reason to think true.* Relative to our beginning set of beliefs, one will be conservative and retentionist and the other radical and rejectionist. The strategies are not identical; propositions which are included among those one already believes which one has no reason to think true, but also no reason to reject, will be kept if one follows the former strategy, thrown away if one adopts the latter.

CONFIRMATIONIST STRATEGY

The point of the confirmationist, rejectionist strategy perhaps can be put along these lines. Suppose one considers that there are many propositions that one believes, and reflects that likely a goodly number of them are false; further, of the very many propositions one does not now, but might come to, believe (excluding the contradictories of the propositions one does believe) exactly half are false. One needs some basis for deciding what beliefs to add; it seems only reasonable to accept those which somehow are epistemically accredited. Insofar as one is able, at least as they come to mind, one might as well require the same of the beliefs one already has if they are to be retained. Appeal to authority cannot be a basic or primitive means of accreditation; at the very least, one will need independent reason to accept the claim that the particular authority is authoritative, and that the proposition in question actually is sanctioned by the authority in question, and the authority will have to posess its own means of recognizing truths. There need not be only one way of a proposition's becoming accredited, or one sort of confirmation. *Seeing that* **not-P** *is a contradiction* is one; *having an experience* **E** *which, if veridical, substantiates* **Q**, *and having no reason not to think* **E** *veridical,* perhaps, is another; *being the best explanation of well-founded data* is a third. There may be any number; the confirmationist strategy requires, so far as possible, that there be *some* epistemic accreditation or other for every proposition which one continues, or begins, to accept.

Two relevant points may be granted by the confirmationist

without the position being compromised. One is that reasonable persons may disagree over whether a proposition has been accredited; presumably one's obligation is to "call them as one (reflectively) sees them," epistemically speaking. The other is that any nonepistemically-certain foundations, or basic or noninferred beliefs, there may be may later cease to be foundationalistic or basic beliefs without having been rejected or discarded. Suppose, at time **t**, one's reason for accepting proposition **Q** is that **P** *but not* **Q** is a contradiction (i.e., *If* **P** *then* **Q** is a necessary truth) and **P** is confirmed by an experience **E** such that if **E** is veridical, **P** is true, and there is no reason to think that **E** is not veridical. Suppose also that at **t P** requires, and has, no propositional support; **P** does not follow from some other propositions one believes, and **E** (and perhaps experiences relevantly like **E**) are **P**'s only evidential support. At **t**, then, **P** may be *foundationalistic* in the sense of *supporting other propositions without its having propositional support.* At **t + 1**, suppose, a hypothesis **H** is discovered which has some experiential evidential support, and which is incompatible with **P**, and a theory **T** also is discovered which is powerfully supported and entails **P**. Presumably **P** will be retained, but no longer only, or perhaps mainly, because of its (direct) experiential support. At **t + 1**, **P** no longer will be foundationalistic.

Another relevant point may be granted by the confirmationist, again without compromise. Almost any logically contingent proposition one believes, *foundationalist* or not, may be granted to be *defeasible.* A defeasible proposition is one such that it is logically possible to state conditions such that, were they to obtain, the proposition in question would be false, and such that, were one to discover they obtained, one would be justified in taking the proposition to be false. Logically necessary truths, of course, are not defeasible; at least many logically contingent truths, including those of the form **S** *believes that* **P** *is a necessary truth,* are defeasible, and nothing prevents a consistent confirmationist from granting this.

One might, then, put the confirmationist strategy in terms of a homely slogan: a proposition must have something going for it, epistemically speaking, if it is within our epistemic rights to accept it. The falsificationist strategy's counterslogan would be: a proposition must have something going against it, epistemically speaking, if it is not within our epistemic rights to accept it.

Neither falsificationist nor confirmationist need deny that some propositions are epistemically certain, though they will be correct in denying that any of these is epistemically interesting.[24] A falsificationist can grant that reasonable persons may disagree over whether a proposition has been falsified, that a proposition may be falsified in one way at one time and in a different way at another, and that all or at least most types of logically contingent propositions are defeasible.

FALSIFICATIONIST STRATEGY

A falsificationist will differ from a confirmationist concerning the availability of confirmations. Notoriously, that **P** entails **Q** and that **Q** is true does not entail that **P** is true; indeed, the argument form *if* **P** *then* **Q**; **Q**; *therefore* **P** is not only a fallacy, but a classical one called *affirming the consequent.* Appeal to fallacious forms of argumentation, of course, will confirm nothing. Strict foundationalist procedures, beginning only with epistemically certain propositions, as noted, will confirm very little. Beyond that, the falsificationist notes, the standard confirmation procedure is two-fold: establish singular statements by appeal to confirming experiences (in the way the confirmationist strategy commands) and then infer universal statements from confirmed singular ones. Essentially, the falsificationist's quarrel is with stage two. Suppose **A1** *is* **B**, **A2** *is* **B**, and **A3** *is* **B** are all confirmed, where **A1**, **A2**, and **A3** are particular observable and observed objects, and **B** is an observable property each has been observed to possess. Thus *Some* **A**'*s are* **B**'*s* is confirmed. The falsificationist thus asks: how are we to justify some such proposition as *All* **A**'*s are* **B**?[25] The conclusion plainly is not entailed by the premises; **A1**, **A2**, *and* **A3** *are* **B** or *Some* **A**'*s are* **B** or *Many* **A**'*s are* **B**, etc., does not entail *All* **A**'*s are* **B**. The standard confirmationist strategy is to argue that *All* **A**'*s are* **B** (or at least *The next observed* **A** *will be* **B**) is made more probable by **A1**, **A2**, *and* **A3** *are* **B** than it would otherwise be. Of course one needs a "large enough" sampling of **A**'s, and reason to think the experienced **A**'s comprise a "fair" sampling (or at least no reason to think they do not), and no **A**'s that are experienced *not* to be **B**, and it must be the case that were we to experience an **A** that was not **B** we

24. In the sense of "epistemically interesting" defined above.

25. The cases where one supposes one has observed *all* the relevant items tend to be rare and rather uninformative, and even then the supposition that all relevant cases *have* been observed requires justification.

could note this lack on A's part; and the like. Suppose these, and other relevant, conditions to be met. The problem remains, the falsificationist argues, that *If* A1, A2, *and* A3 *are* B, *and conditions* C1, C2 . . . C^n *have been met, then all* A's *are* B is not a necessary truth, and if we insert "probably" between "then" and "all" the new proposition the resulting sentence will express also is not a necessary truth. Nor is it a proposition for which we have experiential confirmation; to suppose we did would be to begin once again with singular propositions and then try to derive some such proposition as *If* A1, A2, *and* A3 *are* B, *and conditions* C1, C2 . . . C^n *have been met, then probably all* A's *are* B from them, and that would require some further proposition which had no experiential support, unless of course we tried to derive it . . . and so on.[26] Nor is any significant difference made if we were to move to some such claim as *Ninety-two percent of* A's *are* B after having experienced ninety-two A's that were, and eight A's that were not, B. The *universal* versus *statistical inductive generalization* distinction is not crucial here.

Systems of knowledge, however, generally contain universal propositions (or statistical generalizations), not merely singular ones, and these propositions, the falsificationist contends, are not accessible to confirmation. But they can be falsified. Comparison between world and statement cannot confirm them; counterexample can falsify them. Since general or universal propositions constitute the core of conceptual systems, it is falsification, not confirmation, which is most germane to their assessment. Induction, the confirmationist hope for confirming general propositions, the falsificationist treats as no more reliable than the fallacy of affirming the consequent. The confirmationist position is that there are two kinds of reasoning, deductive and inductive; the falsificationist position is that there are two kinds of reasoning, deductive and bad. With the denial of the soundness of inductive justification of universal propositions by reference to particular propositions plus some "principle of induction" not itself known to be true or reasonably believed, confirmation of universal propositions is unavailable, the falsificationalist insists, and only falsification tests remain. *Having survived numerous and stringent falsification attempts,* or the like, replaces *being confirmed.*

26. The falsificationist, then, tends not to be persuaded by answers to, but instead to be persuaded by, Hume's critique of induction, and to be deductivist in approach.

The confirmationist, one might say, is most impressed by the fact that *The apple is red* is true if and only if the apple is red, and that in the case of red apples one can observe the apple and see that it is red and see that this state of affairs corresponds with what the statement says is so. The confirmationist thus accepts the correspondence view of truth, and since what it is for a system of thought—a world view—to be true is just for the propositions that comprise it to be true, the true world view corresponds with the way the world is. True, we cannot make the comparison between the whole world and a given world view that we can between the red apple (or, perhaps, the fact that the apple is red) and *The apple is red,* but what we can do is go at the comparison piecemeal, and insofar as we can assess a world view it is by this sort of comparison. Falsification just gets rid of error; until we have confirmation of a view, we only know that it is not discredited *so far.*

A falsificationist is most impressed by the fact that one cannot compare a view of the world with the world; the former cannot be "held before the mind" all at once if it is complex enough to be plausible, and the latter certainly cannot be so "held." What is true for world views as a whole is also true of various of their propositional components—for example, universal propositions. So tests are required other than comparisons. But a view's passing one test is not any guarantee at all that it will pass another. If one's confidence in a view increases the more tests it passes, this is a matter of our psychology; it by no means follows, nor is it true, that it is less likely to fail the seventh test, already having passed six, than it was to fail the sixth, already having passed five, or even than it was to pass the first, not having passed one as yet. There just is no such thing as confirming a world view, save insofar as confirmation is a matter of lacking disconfirmation after strenuous effort to falsify. Thus a falsificationist may embrace a correspondence theory of, but nonetheless press (roughly) a coherence test for, truth.

SOME VIRTUES OF THE STRATEGIES

Confirmationist strategy obviously has its point. There is a surfeit of already formulated general conceptual schemes, or world views;[27] no doubt others can be formulated. Short of such grand generality,

27. The histories of philosophy, science, and religion, for example, are filled with them.

there are universal propositions and particular propositions in enormous abundance. Why accept any claim, or set of claims, which, so far as one can tell, possesses no epistemic credentials?

Epistemic credentials vary; there is no one sort that a proposition of whatever sort must have or lack. To some rough degree, various disciplines reflect various methods of testing various types of claims; just as one may attempt to emasculate metaphysics by adopting some (in intent) extremely stringent theory of meaning, so one may attempt to emasculate epistemology by adopting some (in intent) extremely stringent theory of testing.

Let a proposition **P** be *logically certified by Ruth* if and only if *Ruth discovers that* **not-P** *is a contradiction,* and **P** be *perceptually certified by Ruth* if and only if there is some state of affairs **A** which is sensorily or introspectively accessible to *Ruth* such that **A** *obtains* entails **P** *is true,* and *Ruth* perceives **A**, Ruth knows **A** *obtains* entails **P** *is true,* and infers **P** *is true* from **A** *obtains.* If one holds (1) *For any proposition* **P**, **P** *is testable (verifiable or falsifiable) only if there is some person such that he or she (in principle) can logically or perceptually certify* **P** and (2) *For any (alleged) proposition* **P**, **P** *has truth value only if* **P** *(in principle) is testable,* one (in intent) emasculates metaphysics (and religion). It seems highly implausible that one can perceptually or logically certify (1). If one cannot and if (2) is true, then (1) has no truth value. Then the emasculation will be only in intent, not in fact.

Or, one might hold (1), and reject (2), thus (in intent) emasculating metaphysics and religion since then one will have no way of testing the propositions of metaphysics or religion (or many scientific claims). But then one will also have no way of telling whether (1) is true or not, so the emasculation, again, will be, not in fact, but only in intent.

One, of course, might expand the notions of logical certification and perceptual certification; any defensible account of the latter, for example, presumably will include reference not only to telescopes, microscopes, cloud chambers, and the multitudinous extensions of our senses that the sciences provide but also—at least equally important—to the various methods used in the natural and social sciences, varying from physics to archaeology and textual criticism. One might, then, so enrich "perceptual certification" as to make it include something like "any method of testing propositions in which sensory or introspective observation plays an evidential role"; correspondingly, one might so enrich "logical certification" as to make it include something like "any method of testing propositions peculiar to mathematics (including geometry) or logic; plus considerations of logical consistency, which apply universally." Even so enriched, it is not clear that *Every method of testing the truth value of a proposition involves perceptual certification or logical certification* is true; there may be defects which call a plague on the conceptual house of systems that have them which fall outside even these generous and vague limits.[28]

Nonetheless, it seems eminently reasonable for those able to do so to ask what sort of epistemic virtue beliefs already held may have, and what epistemic strengths propositions proposed for belief or entertained with interest may possess. This is not to require propositional evidence for every proposition accepted; *observing a state of affairs which confirms* **Q**, for example, may provide powerful, nonpropositional support for **Q**; and *seeing that* **not-P** *is a contradiction* may provide powerful nonpropositional support for **P**. "Nonpropositional" here does not mean "support which cannot be expressed in propositions"—there is and can be no such evidence or support—but rather stresses that experience can provide evidence for propositions which are reasonably believed, or known, without their having been inferred from other propositions. Or, if it is the case, as some have maintained, that perceptual experience itself is propositional—that seeing is always or sometimes a matter of *seeing that,* and so on through the other sensory modalities—then one can say that it is propositions which are perceived to be true which (perhaps among others) are known but not inferred.[29]

Given the rich variety of kinds of epistemic virtue—of evidential (perhaps including nonpropositional) support—that a proposition may enjoy (or lack), it seems that confirmationism is not unreasonable in suggesting that a proposition that lacks any such support is the epistemic analogue of a person whom everyone knows, no one is prejudiced against, and no one will say a word in favor of—it is not to be trusted.

28. Chapter 8 argues that there are.

29. One way of putting this view would be to say that facts, not things, are the objects of (all or some) perceptual states, or (all or some) perceptual states that are epistemic or knowledge-giving, or the like. On it, "see" will have one sense in "I see that 2 + 2 = 5" and another in "I see that the chair is brown," but each sense of "see" will stand for an epistemic state whose "object" is propositional.

This does not mean that falsificationism is mistaken. Confirmationism seems most plausible concerning propositions which are particular, and relatively inessential to conceptual systems. Propositions which are essential to, or whose deletion would require considerable revision of, complex conceptual systems may be much harder to confirm; their epistemic fate may be more tightly tied to that of the system itself. If falsificationist reservations about induction are correct, and/or in any area of inquiry in which appeal to induction is ineffectual even if those reservations are misplaced, testing of universal propositions presumably will come by way of falsification, and "verification" of a proposition indeed will be a matter of its having been given splendid opportunity of being falsified without its having suffered this fate. The same will be true of particular propositions which have general ramifications or "carry systems with them"—for example, *God exists.*

Suppose a conceptual system **A** has these advantages: (i) all or some of its essential propositions enjoy some evidential support—some "perceptual certification" (of the enriched sort) and/or some "logical certification" (of the enriched sort), and (ii) it has been exposed to a variety of well-conceived falsification attempts, none of which have succeeded.

It seems likely that if it is also the case that (iii) **A** contains logically contingent propositions of various types, so that (iv) evidence from a variety of disciplines is relevant to **A**, the situation (i) and (ii) characterize will provide a quite favorable epistemic situation for **A**; it will be reasonable to accept **A** unless some system **A1** is logically incompatible with **A**, and the evidence for **A1** is far better than that for **A**.

It may be difficult to decide whether there is more evidence in favor of one complex conceptual system than there is supporting another, where there is some for each and neither has been falsified. Happily, then, it may not be necessary, given this perspective, to decide whether one of two competing complex conceptual systems provides a *better* explanation of data which seems to support both; perhaps instead the weight of assessment should fall on attempts to falsify both, and insofar as falsification-independent considerations are not involved in disputes about which of two such explanations is "better," not much rests on how such disputes end; perhaps, that is, independent of falsification considerations, the notion of "better explanation" has little content in such cases as those just characterized.

One question, then, is whether there is any "perceptual certification" of monotheism; another is whether there is any "logical certification" of monotheism (using both senses of "certification" in the vague, wide, enriched sense).

CONCLUSION

It was argued earlier[30] that there is experiential certification of theism, provided one can discover or critically elicit uniformity of description of the alleged object of numinous experience, and it also was argued that the differences between perceptual and numinous experience were not such as to negate the possibility of experiential certification by numinous experience. Thus, on the assumption mentioned, the answer to the first question is affirmative.

It was argued earlier[31] that there is data which theism explains or illuminates and correlates. This raised the question as to whether other explanations are better. This question, in turn, is rejected in favor of a method of assessment, to be discussed later,[32] which specifies ways in which conceptual systems can "go wrong."

Confirmationism, perhaps, is most plausible regarding singular existential propositions (perhaps ones which are observational, or toward the observational end of the observational-theoretical continuum). Falsificationism, perhaps, is most plausible regarding universal propositions (perhaps ones which are essential to conceptual systems). The proposition *God exists,* however, is both singular and existential on the one hand, and essential to a conceptual system on the other. This makes it appropriate to raise regarding it *both* the questions raised at the end of the preceding section. No attempt will be made to answer the second question (concerning "logical certification") until the end of Chapter 8.

SUGGESTIONS FOR FURTHER READING

Chisholm, Roderick and Robert Swartz, eds. *Empirical Knowledge.* Englewood Cliffs, NJ: Prentice-Hall, 1973.

30. In Chapter 1.
31. In Chapter 2.
32. In Chapter 8.

Delaney, C.F., ed. *Rationality and Religious Belief.* South Bend, IN: University of Notre Dame Press, 1979.

Gutting, Gary. *Religious Belief and Religious Scepticism.* South Bend, IN: University of Notre Dame Press, 1982.

Hollis, Martin and Steven Lukes. *Rationality and Relativism.* Cambridge, MA: The MIT Press, 1982.

Lakatos, Imre and Alan Musgrave, eds. *Criticism and the Growth of Knowledge.* New York: Cambridge University Press, 1970.

Wilson, Bryan, ed. *Rationality.* Oxford: Basil Blackwell, 1970.

Yandell, Keith E. "Some Prolegomena to the Epistemology of Religion." *International Journal for the Philosophy of Religion,* 12 (1981), 193–215.

PART THREE
THE NONCOGNITIVIST CHALLENGE TO MORALITY

ANALYTICAL TABLE OF CONTENTS TO CHAPTER 5

be swept away, however, if we could discover ways to assess ethical theories rationally. 182

11. One type of ethical theory is *strict ethical egoism,* a proponent of which contends that intrinsic value is solely a matter of what is in his or her own personal interest. 183
12. But ethical theories are practical only if they allow us to determine which actions are right, and since (i) not more than one proponent of strict ethical egoism can be right at any given time, and (ii) any given proponent of strict ethical egoism can in principle make as good a case as any other for being the only person whose interest has intrinsic value, strict ethical egoism is not a practical ethical theory. 184
13. A consistent proponent of strict ethical egoism cannot value friendship or love. 186
14. In order to accept strict ethical egoism, we would have to make very substantial revisions regarding that which is appropriate material for moral reflection. 187
15. In this respect strict ethical egoism conflicts with "the moral phenomena" (i.e., common moral experiences), which are related to ethical theories in a manner that is epistemically similar to the manner in which perceptual experiences are related to scientific theories. 188
16. This suggests that in addition to a consistency criterion for ethical theories there are other criteria that require an ethical theory either to agree with or to justify changes in (i) our sense of when it is appropriate to reflect morally, and (ii) our sense of what properties are "right-making" and "wrong-making"; strict ethical egoism neither meets these criteria nor justifies not doing so. 191
17. Since *persons* as well as *actions* fall within the scope of moral evaluation, consideration of "good-making" and "evil-making" properties should be included in the criteria. 193
18. A practicability criterion for assessing ethical theories is also available, as is a second sort of consistency criterion—making six criteria in all. 193
19. Another ethical theory—*hedonism*—identifies the good with pleasure, and the evil with pain, but this would seem to suggest that enjoyment of another's misfortunes, or malice, is morally good. 194
20. *Being pleasurable* is in fact neither a necessary nor a sufficient condition for *being good.* 195
21. Distinguishing between nonintentional (simple) and intentional (complex) experiences by means of the values of their objects or the capacities exercised in having them leads us out of hedonistic theory. 195
22. Another popular ethical theory—*utilitarianism*—is based on the *utility principle,* which contends that an action is right if it alone of all actions open to an agent is the one that will bring about the greatest happiness for the greatest number in the long run. 197

23. But an action might satisfy this description and involve torture for pleasure. 198
24. The utility principle can be supplemented and supported by the *commensurability principle,* which says that if any two items have value, then their value is measurable in the same terms and is quantitatively comparable. 198
25. A consequence of the commensurability principle is that the morally trivial may outweigh the morally significant without the former ceasing to be trivial. 199
26. The fact that utilitarianism fails to generate or preserve justice suggests another criterion for assessing ethical theories. 200
27. Utilitarianism is plausible if persons are no more than sets of conscious states than if they are substances, or "continuants," and this fact suggests that utilitarianism is not actually metaphysically neutral as it is alleged to be. 203
28. It is not clear how utilitarian calculations are to be made in everyday situations. 204
29. Since *act utilitarianism* and *rule utilitarianism* are extensionally equivalent, whatever serves as a counterexample to one will also serve as a counterexample to the other, and neither seems acceptable as an ethical theory. 205
30. *Formalism* is an ethical theory that holds that a right action is one whose maxim can be universalized consistently, whereas its opposite cannot be. 207
31. But formalism seems to suggest that wrong actions may turn out to be right (or at least permissible); if this is not the case, then the theory is at the very least unacceptably obscure regarding precisely what its results amount to, and so is impracticable as an ethical theory on that account. 209
32. In any case, in subjecting various ethical theories to rational assessment—to relevant, nonarbitrary critique (regardless of whether or not the details of the critique are impeccable)—it seems at least to have been established that moral skepticism is incorrect in its contention that such a critique is impossible. 211

CHAPTER 5

THE PROBLEM OF MORAL RELATIVISM: DO MORAL CLAIMS HAVE TRUTH VALUE?

MORAL RELATIVISM

Christian theism (in common with other varieties of monotheism) contains a morality—at any rate, some ethical theories are, and others are not, compatible with its doctrinal claims. At the very least, once one has developed articulate concepts of God, humanity, and salvation, there will be consequences for morality—unless, of course, there just is no such thing as morality.[1] In fact, it has been thought that, morally speaking, anything is permitted and nothing is forbidden, a view called *moral relativism.* One wonders whether anyone actually believes this, believes for example that such moral principles as "All and only those actions performed by black-haired persons over seven feet tall who are left-handed and prefer eggs and sausage to eggs and bacon are right; all others are wrong" or "One ought always so to act as to maximize the degree to which the world manifests redness" or "The good life is that in which one possesses a collection of rusty paper clips numbering over a million" are as plausible, as reasonably believed, or as nearly true, as any other ones. That there is no moral knowledge (or reasonable belief) entails that one who accepts any one of these is epistemically no better or worse off, by virtue of so doing, than is one who accepts the view that actions which cause great suffering and bring no benefits are wrong or that the good life consists in the realization or development, insofar as possible, of one's nature as a human being. Given

1. Cf., e.g., Exodus 20 or Romans 12, both of which base ethical claims on prior theological claims.

the denial of moral knowledge (or reasonable belief), those who love to torture infants for pleasure, and those who abhor this practice, will differ only as those who prefer their peanut butter chunky and those who prefer their peanut butter smooth. Still, people claim to believe that morality is not a matter of knowledge or reasonable belief at all. One thing that has moved persons toward this view is their acceptance of cultural relativism. Another is the conviction that there is no way of rationally assessing moral claims. These considerations, then, merit examination.

Perhaps it is worth noting that the moral relativist does not entirely escape all commitment to propositions with moral content. The cannibal, presumably, supposes eating human flesh not to be wrong, and so to be permissible or else right—permitted, or else obligatory. Part of what this entails is that the cannibal thinks it is all right to eat human flesh. The nonrelativist noncannibal, presumably, supposes such activity to be wrong. Holding that nothing is either morally right or morally wrong, the moral relativist will not agree with the nonrelativist noncannibal. But the cannibal is also a nonrelativist, holding (as noted) that eating human flesh is morally permissible, if not sometimes morally obligatory. The moral relativist will have no truck with such notions as morally permissible or morally obligatory, but his or her view nonetheless is to the effect that it is all right to eat human flesh. Nothing is morally wrong, the relativist contends; so the relativist will contend that eating human flesh, or torturing infants for pleasure, is not morally wrong. Granted that this is neither recognized nor intended by the relativist to be a moral commitment of any sort; the moral relativist countenances no such thing. But it does not follow that moral relativism, entailing as it does the view that it is all right to eat human flesh, does not involve its proponents in a moral commitment nonetheless—to commitment, that is, to propositions whose truth is incompatible with the truth of propositions of the forms *It is right to do* A and *It is wrong to do* A.[2] And plainly enough, it does involve such commitment, for on the question as to whether it is all right to eat human flesh, the relativist sides with the cannibal.

CULTURAL RELATIVISM

One support for the claim that moral relativism is true is the claim that cultural relativism is true. Cultural relativism is the thesis that

2. Where A is replaced by the description of a particular action or of a type of action.

nothing is viewed everywhere as right, or everywhere as wrong; there is nothing every culture takes to be right and nothing every culture takes to be wrong. It is often noted that, even should this be true, it does not follow that there is nothing that is right and nothing that is wrong. That no one believes that an action is right does not entail that it is not right; that everyone believes an action is right does not entail that it is right; similarly for an action being wrong. Thus, even if cultural relativism is true, moral relativism does not follow.

MORAL PRINCIPLES, RULES, AND JUDGMENTS

It is not easy to tell whether cultural relativism is true. Distinguish between moral judgments, moral rules, and moral principles. A moral rule says that a certain sort of action—*saying what is false with intent to deceive,* for example—is wrong without saying why. A moral principle says that if a type of action has a certain feature—for example, *treating persons as a means only, and not as ends-in-themselves*—then it is wrong, without saying which actions possess this feature. A moral judgment says that some action is right or is wrong and will be defended by appeal to a moral rule; moral rules are defended by appeal to moral principles. The descriptions of types of actions which appear in moral principles tend to be so cast as to be maximally general (within the bounds of morally relevant properties), whereas the descriptions of the types of actions which appear in moral rules tend to be so cast as to be maximally specific (within the same limits).

MORAL DISAGREEMENT: BASIC AND NONBASIC

Two persons can make different moral judgments and yet agree on moral rules. Suppose Sam says that A is right, and Sally says A is wrong; both may agree that actions of kind K1 are right and actions of kind K2 are wrong, but disagree over whether A belongs to K1 or to K2. Or one (or both) of them may simply make a mistake in reasoning from shared moral rules. For that matter, Sam and Sally may disagree about moral rules but agree about A. Suppose A belongs to both kinds K3 and K4. Sam accepts a rule that says *If an action belongs to* K3, *it is wrong* and Sally accepts a rule that says *If an action belongs to* K4 *it is wrong,* but neither holds the other rule, and indeed rejects the other's rule when he or she hears it formulated; then Sam and Sally agree about whether A is wrong—they agree about a moral judgment but disagree about moral rules.

Or, Sam and Sally may disagree about rules, but agree about principles. Suppose both agree that any type of action that has feature **F** is wrong, but disagree as to whether actions of kind **K1** have **F**. If Sam thinks they do, Sam will hold *Actions of kind* **K1** *are wrong*; if Sally thinks they do not, and that they have no other wrong-making feature, Sally will hold *Actions of kind* **K1** *are not wrong.* Or Sam or Sally, or both, may reason invalidly from principle to rule. Of course, Sam and Sally might agree on rules but disagree on principles, both holding that *Actions of type* **K2** *are wrong,* with Sam holding that because he holds *Actions of type* **K2** *have feature* **F1**, *and actions which have* **F1** *are wrong* and Sally holding that because she holds *Actions of type* **K2** *have feature* **F2**, *and actions which have* **F2** *are wrong*; yet each may reject the other's moral principle. Only disagreements regarding moral principles are *basic* moral disagreements, and a cultural relativism that is even apparently suggestive of moral relativism presumably holds that moral principles vary as one moves from culture to culture.

This can appear to be so, when it is not. If, in one culture, the elderly are put to death in the closest thing to euthanasia the culture is aware of (sending them off on an ice floe, or leaving them alone under a tree in the forest), whereas in another they are cared for when they cannot care for themselves, this need not reflect a difference in values. It may reflect only a difference in what the resources of the cultures can bear doing for the elderly, at least as those cultures see things; it may reflect a belief in one culture to the effect that senility in this life causes senility in the afterlife (so the merciful course of action is euthanasia at first sign of senility) and a lack of any such belief in the other culture.

In order to tell, then, whether two cultures do differ by way of basic moral disagreement concerning a type of action, one has to know that there is sufficient agreement as to what a particular course of action involves—what its qualities and consequences are—along with a disagreement about its moral status, which is not merely a disagreement in moral judgment or about moral rules but which is, or traces to, a disagreement in moral principles. Actually discerning this in a given case is not an easy task; failure to discern it is failure to discern basic moral disagreement about a type of action.

There are, then, various sorts of moral disagreement besides basic moral disagreement; discernment of two cultures' views concerning both the nonmoral and the moral properties of an action is required before one can tell whether there is basic moral disagreement between them; even great difference in behavior or institution, by itself, is not enough to show that such disagreement exists.

Some anthropologists and social psychologists have distinguished between things intrinsically valued, or valued for their own sake, within a culture, and things extrinsically valued, or valued for the sake of something else which they cause or contribute to. They have argued that the greatest cross-cultural diversity concerns what is extrinsically valuable; this is not surprising if there is some agreement on what is intrinsically valuable but also a diversity of views about how what is intrinsically valuable can be obtained. Such things as knowledge, beauty, love, and pleasure, they contend, are regarded as intrinsic values in most if not all cultures. Moral principles will be formulated in the light of what is taken to have intrinsic value.

Persons tend not to be fools, and if some thing was valued in every culture, that would lend credence to the view that it was valuable, just as a thing's being valued in no culture whatever would lend credence to its lacking value. But in neither case would these conclusions be *entailed*. What every culture valued might be worthless, and what none valued might be a pearl of great price; few may know, while thousands err, in matters of morality as elsewhere. If every culture thought that it was right and obligatory to eat any practicing anthropologists within its boundaries, this would not make the practice right; if every culture thought it was wrong for persons to be friends, this would not make friendship wrong. These things would merely show to what a miserable condition things had come.

In sum, then, it is not clear that there is universal basic moral disagreement, but it is clear that universal basic moral disagreement would not show that nothing was right, and nothing wrong, any more than universal agreement that something is right (or wrong) shows that it is right (or wrong).

MORAL SCEPTICISM

In many circles, to call a statement a "value judgment" is to condemn it to epistemic perdition—to say that it is not true or false, or is impossible to defend rationally, or is arbitrary, or the like, and certainly to claim that no one can be rationally justified in accepting it. The position variously expressed in these terms is *moral scepticism.* In particular, such views have been held about moral rules and moral principles and attempts to relate morality to human nature. Such statements as *Torture for pleasure is wrong* or *Preventing someone from being punished for what they did not do is right,* which say that a particular type of action is right or wrong, express moral rules. Such statements as *One ought always to treat persons as ends in themselves and never merely as a means to some end one has* and *One ought always to perform that action which will bring about the greatest amount of happiness in the long run for the largest number of those affected,* which provide grounds for saying that a type of action is right (or wrong), express moral principles. Such propositions as *One ought so to act as to realize one's nature* explicitly express a connection between human nature and proper conduct. Moral scepticism will range over propositions of each of these types. The basic rationale behind moral scepticism is the assertion, or assumption, or at least suspicion, that there is no way, or none that is known, to decide rationally between competing moral claims.

As was the case with scepticism generally, so with scepticism about ethics in particular; there are various perspectives which are sceptical after one fashion or another, and to reject or refute one is not therefore to have rejected or refuted another, let alone all. Correspondingly, it will be hard indeed to be sure one has discussed every variety. What one can do is to challenge the assumption, common to every variety, that rational assessment of competing moral claims is impossible.

ONE VARIETY OF MORAL SCEPTICISM: EMOTIVISM

On one account of the matter, an apparent statement to the effect that torture for pleasure is wrong is alleged to be neither true nor false, and to say nothing more than that expressed by something like "Torture for pleasure, no!" It seems clear that an argument of the form *If torture for pleasure is wrong, then those who torture for pleasure are not to be encouraged; torture for pleasure is wrong; so those who torture for pleasure are not to be encouraged* is valid, and that the portions of the argument that occur before the *so* (the premises) provide some reason for accepting what follows the *so* (the conclusion). But if this is correct, then the second premise—which expresses a moral rule—has truth value; it is either true or false, contrary to the view in question.

Another problem with this view is this. Suppose Ralph thinks that his taking money from defenseless people, even if they go hungry for want of funds, is both fun and perfectly permissible, morally speaking, though he grants that perhaps this is not obligatory for those who do not happen to fancy it, whereas Ruth thinks this behavior simply wicked. Then, apparently, Ralph and Ruth disagree. On the view under review, they do not disagree, for were they to disagree, their disagreement would be over whether *Taking money from defenseless people is morally permissible, even though they go hungry for want of funds* is true (Ralph thinking it is and Ruth thinking it is not) and also over whether *Taking money from defenseless people is morally wrong, whether or not they go hungry for want of funds* (which Ruth embraces and Ralph rejects) is true. If neither apparent proposition really is one—if neither what Ralph's favored sentence expresses nor what Ruth's favored sentence expresses is true or false—then Ralph and Ruth, contrary to appearances, do not disagree. This certainly *is* contrary to appearances, and the attempt to say that they "merely disagree in attitude" but do not disagree about the truth or falsehood of any propositions does not help; the attitude Ralph has toward taking money from defenseless persons is positive—but his taking this attitude is not only a matter of having a *pro* feeling toward an activity, but also of his believing that engaging in this activity is permissible. Taking a moral attitude toward **x** ordinarily, if not always, will involve having moral beliefs about **x**. But if this is so, "replacing" beliefs by attitudes will not get rid of beliefs.

THE BASIC QUESTION RAISED BY MORAL SCEPTICISM

Why, though, go against the appearances? If one holds that (i) if moral proposition **P** is true or false, then there is some way of telling which **P** is, or (ii) if one is reasonable in thinking that **P** is either true or false, then one has some way of telling which **P** is, and (iii) there is no (or: one has no) way of telling whether **P** is true or false, then one will conclude (iv) **P** is not (or: one has no reason for thinking that **P** is) either true or false. While one could escape accepting (iv) while accepting (ii) and (iii) by rejecting (i), the crucial thing would seem to be to see whether the challenge (iii) presents can be met. If there is no way of deciding whether a moral proposition is true or false, whatever that proposition may be, then ethics is no science or discipline at all. So the basic question is whether there is some way of deciding whether moral propositions are true or false.

ANOTHER VARIETY OF MORAL SCEPTICISM: INDIVIDUAL SUBJECTIVISM[3]

Various theories about the nature of ethics can be construed as endeavoring to answer this basic question without having to develop anything substantial along the lines of a theory of how moral propositions might be justified. One such theory says that a proposition of the form *Action* A *is right* simply means *I approve of* A; since (roughly) morally to approve of A is to believe that A is right and feel positively toward A, this theory strictly includes more than its proponents intended. Replace it, then, by a view which holds that A *is right* means *I have positive feelings with regard to* A, and ignore the problem that without any propositional context or content, moral *pro* feelings are not distinguishable from any other *pro* feelings. It remains true that *I have a pro feeling toward* A *but* A *is wrong* is not (as the view would require) a contradiction. Again, on this view, if Ralph reports A *is right* and Ruth contends A *is wrong,* they do not disagree, for Ralph only says that he has positive feelings toward A and Ruth that she has negative feelings toward A. This, too, goes deeply against the appearances; yet, on this view, what Ralph says when he asserts that A *is right* is either true or false, for Ralph either has, or else lacks, the feelings which, on this view, Ralph thereby reports.

SOCIETAL SUBJECTIVISM: ANOTHER VARIETY OF MORAL SCEPTICISM

The same sorts of issues arise with respect to other, similar views. Consider the suggestion that A *is right* means My *society contains*

3. One might argue—and with point—that since subjectivism ascribes discernible truth value to moral propositions, it is not moral scepticism, strictly speaking; this is so. But subjectivism ascribes no truth to moral propositions conceived as other than statements about feelings—to propositions about what is right or wrong independent of how we feel. In this respect, subjectivism contrasts with the views shortly to be considered, beginning with ethical egoism. Nothing in the argument here depends on whether subjectivism of any sort is regarded as a variety, or merely a conceptual cousin, of moral scepticism. These remarks apply both to individual and societal subjectivism.

institutions which include or favor doing **A**. *My society contains institutions which include or favor doing* **A** *but* **A** *is not right* is not a contradiction as the view would require. The view would allow two members of the same society to disagree about what was right only at the price of changing the subject; they would be disputing over whether a particular sort of action was favored by the institutions of their society, not about whether it was right. But on this view members of different societies could not disagree about moral matters, for each would be reporting the situation relative to the distinct institutions of their different societies.

An individual can be mistaken about what the institutions of his society favor. Nonetheless, a curious consequence follows from societal scepticism. One could make it right to torture for pleasure by arranging that one's society included an institution that favored it, just as on the view that **A** *is right* means *I have positive feelings regarding* **A**, one could make **A** right merely by coming to have positive feelings regarding it. Further, given societal scepticism, actions such that one's society has no institution which either includes or favors them, or refraining from them, are morally neutral no matter what these actions may be. Given individual scepticism, the same holds regarding actions concerning which one has no positive or negative feelings. None of these contentions is very plausible.

THE RATIONALE FOR MORAL SCEPTICISM

None of the views thus far discussed seems to have much initial plausibility. Why would anyone hold them? One reason was mentioned: one might think there was no way of telling whether a moral proposition was true or false unless some such view was true. One might then find something else that could be done—discovering whether one had positive feelings toward a way of acting, or discovering what the institutions of one's society involve, or the like—and identify deciding whether a moral proposition is true or false with that other, accomplishable thing by means of identifying an action's being right with one's feelings about the action, or the like. Then one will have, not the reality, but the appearance, of having discovered the truth value of moral propositions. If one is fortunate in what one feels positively toward, or in what the institutions of one's society include or favor, one will have the appearance, though not the reality, of having confirmed true moral propositions.

Perhaps another attraction of the sort of view just examined is that it has the appearance of altogether escaping metaphysics, and perhaps also epistemology; at least, no abstruse or abstract epistemology seems to be required. So long as one step—defining moral rightness and wrongness in terms of feelings, or in terms of social institutions, or the like—is accepted, perhaps (with the exception of that one step) this is so; nonetheless, the exception is significant.

The issue, of course, is not "merely verbal"; the fact that the views that have been discussed are formulated as definitions should deceive no one into thinking that they are verbal issues. Like honest witnesses in a courtroom or competent scientists reporting an experiment, proponents of an ethical theory are trying to say what is the case—to "tell it like it is"; and, of course, not all witnesses or scientists or proponents succeed. An action should be called "right" only if it is right; the theories concerning positive feelings and institutions held the attraction of suggesting that an action's being right was somehow identical to very familiar (nonethical) phenomena. Still, these views seem subject to very powerful objections, and if they, or theories like them, are the best one can offer by way of ethical theory, them perhaps there is no truth (or falsehood either) about ethics after all.[4]

TRANSITION TO NONSCEPTICAL, NONSUBJECTIVISTIC THEORIES

It is easy to overlook two facts: (i) the theories just critiqued are ethical theories, and (ii) they do not bear up well under examination. The view, then, that any moral theory is as plausible, or reasonable to accept, as any other will be false if there are ethical theories more plausible than these; the view that there are no criteria for rationally assessing ethical theories seems already refuted by the fact that there are criteria which these theories do not satisfy.

4. One might object that the views criticized thus far are *metaethical* theories, and that it is possible that there are ways of deciding between metaethical theories although there are none for deciding between (substantive) ethical theories. The objection, obviously, depends on there being a distinction between ethics and metaethics which is genuine and yields the result that all the theories thus far discussed are metaethical. It also requires that it really be possible that metaethical theories be rationally assessable and (substantive) ethical theories not be. One who holds these positions will expect that clearly substantive ethical theories be rationally assessed in such a way as to support ethical cognitivism; what follows attempts to do just that.

Perhaps the best way to proceed is to consider other ethical theories, in something like a series of ascending plausibility, and see what other sorts of objection can be raised to them. Then it may be possible to characterize a general procedure for assessing ethical theories.

STRICT ETHICAL EGOISM

Consider, then, strict ethical egoism. The strict ethical egoist holds that exactly one sort of thing has intrinsic merit, or is valuable for its own sake, or as an end, namely his or her own interest; "interest" may be construed in any of many different ways by a strict ethical egoist. The strict ethical egoist also holds that exactly one sort of thing has extrinsic merit, or is valuable for the sake of something other than itself, or as a means, namely what contributes or furthers or enhances his or her own interest.[5] Further, one thing is intrinsically evil, according to the strict ethical egoist, namely the injury or loss of his or her interest, and only one sort of thing is extrinsically evil, namely what detracts from his or her interest. Finally, the strict ethical egoist holds that the only (or only overriding) obligation is to promote that which has intrinsic value.

SUCCESSFUL ETHICAL THEORIES AS INHERENTLY PRACTICAL

One thing that an ethical theory is supposed to do is to provide an answer to the question "What shall I do?" on particular cases of moral action[6] and, in that sense, to be *practical.* This is not the only thing that an ethical theory is concerned with, and perhaps it is not the most important; but it is one function of such a theory. Granted, it may be that a theory—even a very good one, or even the true one—will not perform this function well, or at all, in a particular case; one might lack the information needed to tell what course of action might be best, or one might make a mistake in one's reasoning so that what one concludes is not what follows from the theory,

5. "Ethical egoism" is often used to refer to the view that each person ought to do what will (or what it seems most likely will) further his or her own interest. Hence the adjective "strict" here to distinguish the sort of egoism under discussion. The task of evaluating the view just described is left as an exercise for the reader.

6. Cases in which action is appropriate and in which what one does will be either right or wrong.

or the like. No theory can rule out such possibilities, and in fact, no matter what theory one adopts, one will face such difficulties. But the difficulties should not arise from a theory itself, but only sometimes in the context of applying it to cases.

A CRITIQUE OF STRICT ETHICAL EGOISM

Suppose Sam and Sally are both strict ethical egoists. Each is clear about what has intrinsic value: Sam is clear that only Sam's interest has intrinsic value, and Sally is clear that only Sally's does. Even if the same actions turned out to maximally further the interests of each, clearly Sam and Sally disagree with one another about *why* those actions should be done, and it is highly implausible that the same actions and events that maximize Sam's interest always do the same for Sally's, and conversely. Suppose Sam and Sally learn of each other's positions and want to know the truth of the matter, ethically speaking; they want to know whose interest really is the only intrinsically valuable item in the universe, each being a bit shaken, perhaps, by the initial confidence of the other. What can Sam say to Sally, or Sally to Sam, which will establish Sam's position (but not Sally's) or Sally's (but not Sam's)? Each supposes that his or her interest alone is possessed of intrinsic value; only one can be right (though both can be mistaken). But what will rationally support one supposition without also supporting the other? Sam can point out that Sam is a person, that Sam's interest is unique, that Sam is not Sally, that Sam is rational, that Sam is made in God's image, that Sam is autonomous, that Sam is sentient, and the like; but then Sally in each case can point out that the same thing, or the converse thing in the case of "Sam is not Sally"—namely that "Sally is not Sam"—is the case regarding Sally. Presumably, whatever of these claims one can make, so (with the limitation noted) can the other. It appears that any reason that Sam can give to Sally for supposing that Sam's interest alone is of intrinsic value can be given right back by Sally; indeed, almost every reason Sam can give Sam for thinking that only Sam's interest has intrinsic value is one that Sam can see can be given by others as well. The exception is that Sam's interest is Sam's and not another's; as noted, Sally can note that Sally's interest is Sally's and not another's and ask why that is not as good (or bad) a reason for Sally's interest being the only intrinsically valuable item as Sam's interest being only Sam's is for thinking that only Sam's interest has intrinsic value.

By now, two things seem clear. One is that Sam has no reason to offer to Sam, or to Sally, which is a good reason for thinking that Sam's interest alone has intrinsic worth. The other is a consequence of this, namely that when Sam faces a choice between an action that will further Sally's interest (but not Sam's) and another that will further Sam's (but not Sally's)—say, where doing **A** will further Sally's interest only and refraining from doing **A** will further Sam's interest only—Sam has no better reason for thinking that doing **A** is right than for thinking that refraining from doing **A** is right. Even allowing refraining from action to be a sort of action, this is not a case of two actions being equally meritorious; they are incompatible actions, and (on strict ethical egoistic terms) each has as good a claim (or as bad) to being right as the other, *and only one can be right if strict ethical egoism is true.* But if Sam has no more or better reason to think Sam's interest alone possessed of intrinsic worth than Sally's, then Sam has no more reason to think that actions that promote Sam's interest are right than to think that those that promote Sally's interest are right.

ETHICAL EGOISM NOT PRACTICAL

The strict ethical egoist, then, seems to face two problems: (i) committed by the view itself to the thesis that only his or her interest has inherent moral worth, he or she is not able to offer (to self or other) any good reason that shows that it is false that if the interest of one person has that status, then so does the interest of any; (ii) since the view entails that only actions done to promote the interest of the one and only individual whose interest has inherent or intrinsic moral worth are extrinsically good, the strict ethical egoist, being unable to offer any good reason to think that the one person whose interest has inherent worth is **X** rather than **Y** or **Z** is *a fortiori* unable ever to identify which actions are extrinsically good. Hence, in the sense specified above, strict ethical egoism is not practical and so is defective as an ethical theory.

One might try to save strict ethical egoism by adding to it a doctrine concerning what is good or what is in one's interest, to the effect that it is in one's interest that the interest of others always be well served. This will save nothing, for this states only a second-order interest; it does not tell us what anyone's actual first-order interest is, and requires supplement by a doctrine that does. Suppose the supplement comes by way of the claim that a person's interest is that his or her rational capacities be developed and employed as fully as possible. Then strict ethical egoism will entail that the development of one person's rational nature to the fullest extent possible is inherently good, and the development of anyone else's at best is good as a means to the end of the development of that one person's rational nature. The doctrine that says that this person's interest encompasses the development of the interests of others can only treat the development of the interest of others as means subservient to the end of that one person's rational development, and if there is competition between persons regarding who shall blossom into rational maturity, morality (of a strict egoist sort) requires that pride of place go always to the one person whose interest alone possesses value as an end-in-itself. Perhaps the development of someone else's rational capacities at some given time might even override the development of the rationality of him or her whose development possesses intrinsic value, but only if in the long run his or her development thereby is served.

ETHICAL EGOISM AND FRIENDSHIP

Other features of strict egoism might be noted. If, as seems correct, two persons can be friends if and only if each (rightly) views the other as possessed of inherent moral worth, then no strict ethical egoist can accept friendship as valuable, since it denies that as many as two persons have this property.[7] One might think that something like strict ethical egoism was true but not suppose that *he* was the fortunate person whose interest alone possesses intrinsic moral value; he might ascribe this status to someone else—say, to Ralph. Then he might hold that friendship for himself and others was possible so long as Ralph is excluded, for persons other than Ralph are of equal moral worth (their interest is of value only insofar as it serves Ralph's); but if friendship is as described above, in fact it is not possible, even for persons other than Ralph, since persons other than Ralph lack (and so cannot rightly view each other as having) inherent moral worth if strict ethical egoism is true. Further, a sort of "moral worth" which excludes one from the possibility of friendship not only is not morally very attractive, but an ethical theory

7. The same holds for respect and love.

which finds no place for friendship (or respect or love) as a high value is not very plausible.

ETHICAL EGOISM AND MORAL REFLECTION

A further feature of strict ethical egoism is worth mentioning. Moral reflection seems appropriate at least whenever human well-being is at issue—whenever actions are considered which will affect the well-being of individuals and groups. Strict ethical egoism, of course, denies this. Suppose that Ralph is a strict ethical egoist, and holds that only his own interest has intrinsic value. It is likely that however "interest" is understood, a great many things may not affect Ralph's interest, particularly given that "interest" must be so characterized as to be compatible with strict ethical egoism. Since there will be a great many instances of suffering, injustice, malice, hatred, and the like which will not affect Ralph's interests at all, then strict moral egoism dictates that they are morally neutral, neither good nor evil. If they affect Ralph's interests affirmatively, then they are good, however much suffering (malice, hate, injustice, or the like) they seem to, and actually do, involve. Only if they affect Ralph's interests negatively are they (extrinsically) evil, and then for that reason only, no matter how much suffering (etc.) they include.

With these criticisms of strict ethical egoism in mind, perhaps it is possible to state some general criteria for assessing ethical theories.

CRITERIA FOR ASSESSING ETHICAL THEORIES: A CONSISTENCY CRITERION

Even without reflection on strict ethical egoism, it seems clear that some such criterion as the following is true: (C1) *An ethical theory which contains a self-contradictory moral principle, or two or more incompatible moral principles, is false for that reason.* One has to be careful here. Suppose an ethical theory **T** entails that, for reasons **R1** and **R2** performing action **A** at **t** is right, but for reasons **R3** and **R4** performing action **A** at **t** is not right; further, suppose that (given **T**) **R1** *and* **R2** is as weighty a reason for doing **A** as is **R3** *and* **R4** for refraining from doing **A**, but not more so. Then, given **T**, doing **A** at **t** is neither right nor wrong, but rather is morally neutral. That **T** entails **A** *is right (for reasons* **R1** *and* **R2***)* and **A** *is wrong (for reasons* **R3** *and* **R4***)* does not show that **T** is false. What would show that **T** was false was that, given **T**, possessing a particular feature—

say, *saying what is false with intent to deceive*—by itself should both be a reason for taking an action to be right and a reason for not taking an action to be right (i.e., for taking it to be morally neutral, or else wrong).[8]

MORAL REFLECTION AND MORAL RELEVANCE

Perhaps reflection on the perils of strict ethical egoism can prove instructive relative to further criteria for assessing ethical theories. It was noted that strict ethical egoism seems to conflict with what, independent of this view, one would think it relevant to consider morally. That an action would cause enormous suffering, for example, seems something to be considered when weighing whether the action should be performed, and the suggestion that it is, or even might be, morally irrelevant seems absurd; yet strict ethical egoism has this consequence. It is not easy to specify exactly what makes it appropriate to reflect morally about an action; it is easier to identify cases in which such reflection is appropriate, and cases in which it is not, than it is to state such a criterion. It would be a sensitive conscience indeed which worried over whether one ought to tie one shoe before the other, or button one sleeve before the other, for example; these are not matters of good or evil, or right or wrong, and perhaps it is pathological to think otherwise. That an action will cause suffering, or result in loss of life, or involve saying what is false with intent to deceive, or increase the amount of hatred in the world makes it appropriate to reflect morally about the action and count for the action's being wrong. That an action will bring great satisfaction, or result in saving lives, or involve speaking the truth, or increase the amount of compassion in the world makes it appropriate to reflect morally about the action and count for the action's being right. That a course of action involves an abortion, or includes giving someone a beating, or contains giving aid to a needy person renders moral reflection about it appropriate, in a way in which a course of action involving the changing of position of some grains of sand, or the displacement of a few dust particles in the air, or the breaking of a few dead twigs does not. These observations rest, if one likes, on a pretheoretical sense of

8. In one jargon: an ethical theory is self-contradictory if it views the same property (in the same contexts) both as right-making and wrong-making or both as right-making or wrong-making and morally neutral.

what is morally relevant—of what features of an action make moral reflection about it appropriate. Obviously it is possible that there be disagreement about whether a particular feature has this distinction, and mistakes can be made about this matter; still, given a list of properties of the sort mentioned above, sorting them (as was done) into those which rendered moral reflection appropriate, and those which did not, seems not beyond our abilities and while an ethical theory may radically realign the way in which this distinction is made, some justification is required if it does so. An ethical theory will confirm the "common sense" view, or the view dominant in the culture in which it is offered, insofar as those cases in which its principles are either conformed to or violated by an action coincide with those cases about which, common sensically, it is appropriate to reflect morally. Roughly, these criteria have to do with which cases involve actions affecting human well-being, either for good or for ill. It is possible reflectively to assess the appropriateness of a proffered reason for reflecting morally regarding an action, and to question restrictions on those whose well-being is considered, so that one need not be sheerly a prisoner of untutored "common sense" or one's culture, and such reflection need not be locked within some ethical theory. An ethical theory on which the fact that a given course of action would cause great suffering simply is no reason whatever to reflect about it morally is a highly implausible theory.

THE INTERACTION OF MORAL EXPERIENCE AND ETHICAL THEORIES

Persons, it seems, have a variety of sorts of experiences—sensory, introspective, reflective (if one may use this term to describe such experiences as *seeing that one and one are two* or *seeing that self-contradictions are always false*), religious (of various sorts, perhaps), aesthetic, and—most relevant to present purposes—moral. Thus one can feel a duty or obligation to keep a promise, or to refrain from striking out in anger; one can resent one's being unjustly treated; one can repent one's sins; one can regret that one failed to do good, or be remorseful that one did evil; one can feel deeply guilty for what one has done (or left undone). The phenomenology of such experiences seems not much investigated,[9] and the fact that one

9. Perhaps, for example, remorse *necessarily* is, and regret *may* be, a "moral emotion."

can "feel an obligation" to do **A** even though doing **A** is wrong and that guilt-feelings can be pathological has sometimes led philosophers, psychologists, and others to dismiss them as aberrations. In fact, our capacity to have such experiences, and the attitudes and beliefs into which they are embedded (or which are embedded in them), seems significantly related to our being moral agents. Nor are such experiences always misdirected. One can feel an obligation to act rightly, or feel guilty because one is, or take satisfaction that justice has been done (when it has), and the like. Sometimes, such experiences are appropriate to their targets—sometimes the properties of the objects of such feelings, attitudes, or responses justify our having these feelings, attitudes, or responses.

These experiences are "common" in the dual sense of "frequent" and "shared"; it may be expected that a moral theory will interact with these "moral sentiments" as they are sometimes (perhaps not altogether aptly) called.[10] More accurately, a moral or ethical theory may be expected to interact with the (relatively pretheoretical) moral beliefs, attitudes, and emotions of its adherents—and these beliefs, attitudes, and feelings will interact with the theory. The theory may be expected to accord with, or perhaps confirm, them on some occasions, but to conflict with, and perhaps correct, them on other occasions, but also perhaps to be confirmed, or corrected, by them. Perhaps if one is outraged when the members of one race are unjustly treated, but not bothered when the members of another race are similarly treated, reflection on one's ethical theory may lead one to be outraged on both sorts of occasions. Or perhaps if one is inclined to suppose that only individual persons can do anything that is morally right or wrong, whereas institutions or companies or national policies are morally neutral, the reflection that institutions or companies or policies do produce results at which one feels resentment, or which elicit moral satisfaction and approval, may cause one to expand the scope of one's theory to include consideration of institutions, companies, or national policies. As the moral life involves such things as appeals to rules and principles and such feelings as remorse and guilt and being obligated to act in one way rather than in others, so the assessment of ethical theories involves consideration of the ways in which such theories interact

10. Perhaps "the moral phenomena" or "common moral experience" is a better term.

with—accord with, confirm, change, contradict, correct, are altered by, etc.—the moral phenomena.

Common moral experience, or the moral phenomena, then, plays a role relative to the assessment of moral theories not altogether dissimilar to that which perceptual experience plays relative to scientific theory—minus, perhaps, the important aspect of predictability.[11] The theory will have to come to terms somehow with the phenomena—perceptual phenomena in the case of a scientific theory, moral phenomena in the case of an ethical theory. This does not mean that the theory always must accord with or confirm the phenomena. The scientific theory may entail that the object that appears to be there is not (or lacks properties it seems to have); the ethical theory may entail that the action that is resented is not morally objectionable, or that one should not feel the guilt regarding having done A that one does feel (or that one should feel guilt that one does not). But then, in each case, some account of why the phenomena are misleading is owed, and the account may discredit the phenomena—or the theory. It seems likely that there is no mechanical rule the application of which will tell one where the discredit lies; probably one will have to examine matters case by case. No phenomenon (perceptual or moral) is incorrigible or indefeasible; but no (scientific or ethical) theory is unquestionable, and the declaration of a phenomenon as misleading requires justification.

One of the significant ways in which ethical theories and the moral phenomena or moral experience interact, as we have seen, has to do with considerations of moral relevance.

RIGHT-MAKING AND WRONG-MAKING CHARACTERISTICS

There is another facet to the matter. Not only are there features of actions, or possible effects of actions, which make it appropriate to reflect morally regarding them, but there are also what are sometimes called good-making or right-making characteristics, as well as evil-making or wrong-making ones. An ethical theory which held that the fact that a course of action which would cause great suf-

11. Or perhaps not; for example, perhaps one can predict that if a moral theory is otherwise correct, a person who adopts it and lives by it will (say) resent an unjust action (or experience other of the moral phenomena) in at least roughly predictable or anticipatable ways.

fering, or involve much torture for pleasure, or spread plenty of hatred and malice, or include "punishing" persons severely for things they never did, or required making a practice of saying what one knew to be false with intent to deceive was *for that very reason* a morally good course of action would be highly implausible. The same goes for a theory that entailed that a course of action which involved bringing great satisfaction to many, or freed persons from being at the mercy of torturers, or brought about plenty of compassion and kindness, or prevented innocent persons from being punished for what they never did, or involved making a practice of speaking the truth was *for that very reason* evil or wrong.

CRITERIA FOR ASSESSING ETHICAL THEORIES: RELEVANCE, RIGHT-MAKING, AND WRONG-MAKING CRITERIA

Perhaps, then, some such criterion as the following captures the force of the preceding considerations. Let us say that a moral principle *supports* the features which the (pretheoretical) moral phenomena, or moral experiences, take to be those whose presence in a course of action renders it an appropriate object of moral reflection and whose absence renders it an inappropriate object of moral reflection (call such features *relevance features*) if its constitutive ethical principles are followed, or else violated, in such cases. A moral principle *confirms* those features possession of which, according to moral experience, makes or tends to make a course of action right (call these *right-making features*) if so acting conforms to the principle and *confirms* those features possession of which, according to moral experience, makes or tends to make a course of action wrong (call these *wrong-making features*) if so acting violates the principle. Then: (C2) *An ethical theory should be such that its constitutive moral principle or principles either support the relevance features discovered by common moral experience, clarifying and organizing them, or else justify altering or rejecting them.*[12] Further, (C3) *An ethical theory should be such that its constitutive moral principle or principles confirm common moral experience regarding what are right-making features, clarifying and organizing them,*

12. As Plato's Socratic dialogues make plain, common moral experience, or "the moral phenomena," are not completely consistent; the same is true of perceptual experience, and one role of theory (in ethics and in science) is to adjudicate between conflicting experiences, i.e., between conflicting judgments to the effect that things really are as the experiences on which they are based represent them as being.

or else justify altering or rejecting them. Finally, (C4) An *ethical theory should be such that its constitutive moral principle or principles confirm common moral experience regarding what are wrong-making features, clarifying and organizing them, or else justify altering or rejecting them.* Strict ethical egoism has deep problems meeting any of these criteria.

GOOD-MAKING AND BAD-MAKING CHARACTERISTICS

Of course, other things besides actions are appropriate objects for moral reflection, and one can (and should) expand the notion of *relevance feature* to cover this fact. Some such objects of reflection (in particular, persons) will be not right or wrong, but good or evil, and one can (and should) expand the notion of a *right-making feature* into that of a *right-making or good-making feature* (the property *involving speaking the truth* will be right-making relative to an action, and *being honest* will be good-making relative to a person). Similarly, the notion of a *wrong-making feature* can (and should) be expanded into that of a *wrong-making or evil-making* feature (the property *exhibiting malice* will be wrong-making relative to an action, and *being-malicious* will be evil-making relative to a person). *Relevance features,* then, will be so construed that a relevance feature is a feature of an action *or a person* such that its possession by an action is right-making or else wrong-making, *or that its possession by a person is good-making, or else evil-making.* Not every property a person has is *good-or-evil-making,* or is relevant to the moral assessment of a person; ordinarily, *having red hair, being left-handed, preferring peppermint or chocolate to vanilla, liking to wear brown clothing,* and *wearing a tie* will be morally irrelevant features. Let (C2–C4) hereafter be construed in such a manner that these expansions are built into them. A strict ethical egoist will take it that only she is intrinsically good and others are extrinsically good only insofar as they succeed in furthering her interests, and thus will be as radically revisionist regarding relevance features concerning the morality of persons as regarding the morality of actions, and as radically revisionist regarding good-making and bad-making features as regarding right-making and wrong-making features, in each case with as little reason.

CRITERIA FOR ASSESSING ETHICAL THEORIES: A PRACTICALITY CRITERION

A good ethical theory is practical; it will be possible, not always (for reasons noted earlier) but often, for one who understands the theory to tell which actions are right and which are wrong according to that theory. It will be possible for one who understands the theory to tell what sorts of persons, according to the theory, are morally admirable, and what sorts are morally defective. Thus: (C5) *An ethical theory that is not practical is radically defective.* If the argument presented earlier concerning strict ethical egoism is correct, it is not a practical ethical theory, and so is radically defective.

CRITERIA FOR ASSESSING ETHICAL THEORIES: ANOTHER CONSISTENCY CRITERION

The philosophical interest of strict ethical egoism is minimal; it has no high degree of plausibility as an ethical theory. The concern here has been to ask *what is wrong with it?* with a view to eliciting criteria which satisfy this condition: *an ethical theory's failure to meet them is reason for rejecting it*. Perhaps one further criterion can be milked from our consideration of strict ethical egoism, namely: (C6) *If ethical theory* T *ascribes inherent moral worth, or intrinsic value, or status as a moral end-in-itself, to one person, then* T *is defective if it does not ascribe that status to all persons.*

ANOTHER ETHICAL THEORY: HEDONISM

Hedonism is a theory about what is good; it says that what is intrinsically good is pleasure (and absence of pain). Anything else is good extrinsically, or as a means, only insofar as it brings about pleasure (or absence of pain). It says that what is intrinsically evil is pain (and absence of pleasure); anything else is evil extrinsically, or as a means, only insofar as it brings about pain (or absence of pleasure).

COUNTEREXAMPLES TO HEDONISM: EVIL, AND MORALLY NEUTRAL, PLEASURES

Hedonism then maintains that it is necessary and sufficient for an action's being right that it produce pleasure (or absence of pain) and necessary and sufficient for a state's being good that it be a state of pleasure (or absence of pain). Suppose Ralph takes great pleasure in the misfortune of others. He does not bring them about, since there is plenty of misfortune in the world, and plenty of news about it, so that there is no need for that; he simply rejoices in the misfortunes of others. That Ralph rejoices in others' misfortunes seems to be a defect in Ralph's character; to the degree that he does so, he is evil. But, if this is so, it is so despite the fact that Ralph *takes pleasure* in the misfortunes of others, perhaps living only for those states in which he does so; thus it seems that being pleasurable is not sufficient for a state's being good. The same thing can be seen in another way; drinking a good cup of coffee, or slowly devouring a piece of German chocolate cake, or even scratching an annoying itch, can be pleasurable, but they seem quite irrelevant to morality. Perhaps being the sort of person who enjoys providing good coffee and cake for others is having a variety of virtue; it does not follow that enjoying the pleasures of the palate is a matter of having attained to a state of moral virtue of any kind. One's continually taking a drug which produced states of euphoria, and encouraging others to do the same, seems an unlikely model of virtue; a *Brave New World* society in which the few rule and are euphoric with power and the many are enslaved, though euphoric from *soma*, seems a far better candidate for a society that has maximized pleasure than for a society that has achieved a virtuous state of affairs.

"BEING PLEASURABLE" NEITHER NECESSARY NOR SUFFICIENT FOR "BEING RIGHT" OR "BEING GOOD"

If (as now seems clear) *being pleasurable* is not a sufficient condition for a state of affairs being good, perhaps at least it is a necessary condition of the same. But this too seems dubious. Suppose that Ralph, though lying would bring him financial reward and though he finds speaking the truth psychologically wearying, does tell the truth, taking no particular joy in so doing, but recognizing his duty nonetheless. Is there no moral value in what Ralph has done, because it involves no state of pleasure? Would lying be right, because Ralph would escape the effort of speaking the truth and enjoy the money he got for lying? That it involve pleasure seems not a necessary condition of an action's being right. So being pleasurable seems neither a necessary nor a sufficient condition of an action or a state being right or good. Without denying that causing pain is evil, or that Ralph would be a better person if he could take some satisfaction in doing right, or that it is a virtue in a person that he or she takes delight in bringing innocent pleasure to others, it seems clear that hedonism fares ill in connection with (C2) through (C4).

SIMPLE VS. COMPLEX HEDONISM

Hedonism of the sort thus far considered might be called *simple* hedonism. One can be *in* pain; one can also be pained *at* something.

Using language introduced earlier, *being in pain* is not intentional ("has no object") and *being pained at* is intentional; both include a negative hedonic tone, so both are intrinsic evils for a hedonist. The experience one gains from scratching an itch is not intentional (in the technical sense noted earlier); one might call it *being in pleasure.* On the whole, pleasurable states are intentional; one is pleased at one's acceptance, or by the cake's deep chocolate taste, or the like; often there is a positive hedonic tone to an intentional experience. It is the fact that positive and negative tones can be present in intentional experiences that allows hedonism to offer its standard response to the objection that it is a dehumanizing sort of view—that according to it a satiated pig is morally superior to an unsatiated person. The idea is that one can rank pleasurable experiences by considering their objects. Perhaps on this account the pleasures which are not intentional simply take last place; in any case, the idea is that if Ralph is pleased, successively, by the taste of an apple, the pattern exhibited by a crossword puzzle, and the complexity of Paul's argument in Romans (the examples do not matter to the point being developed) Ralph ascends into progressively "higher" or "more valuable" states. But the most, if not the only, plausible reason for saying this is either that the *objects* of these states are themselves to be rated in terms of their value (*tastes, pattern, argument* comprising an ascending value hierarchy) or that the *capacities* involved in these experiences—the capacities whose exercise makes the experiences possible—are of increasing value (*tasting, recognizing a pattern, appreciating an argument* forming a value hierarchy). Either way, however, one ranks pleasures not on their own, but in terms of their correlation with objects or else capacities (or both). It seems highly implausible that one rank what is *intrinsically* valuable on the basis of hierarchies of what is only *extrinsically* valuable; if so, then hedonism, contrary to its intent, involves viewing something other than pleasure as intrinsically good. The degree of value possessed by a pleasure, on this line of reasoning, is determined by the degree of value possessed by something other than pleasure, and, apparently, the consequence is that objects that are intellectually more complex, or capacities that involve more complex exercise of the intellect, possess higher degrees of intrinsic value, so that in answering the objection that if hedonism were true, "a pig, satisfied, would be better off than Socrates, dissatisfied," hedonism takes up a line of reasoning that leads straight out of hedonism.

Hedonism provides an example of a view about what is valuable which is subject to powerful criticism, as strict ethical egoism provides an example of a view about how what is valuable is to be distributed which is subject to powerful criticism; still, the reflections about hedonism just presented do not seem to provide the rationale for any new criteria for appraising ethical theories, though they provide further illustrations of a theory which has deep problems which the old criteria highlight.

ETHICAL THEORY: UTILITARIANISM

Consider, next, the view that there are a variety of intrinsic goods—pleasure, friendship, knowledge, health, and the like; that the possession of such valuable items is to be called happiness; and that the proper principle of distribution is that which requires the maximization of happiness.[13] As standardly put, that action is right which, of all those open to an agent on a particular occasion, will result in the greatest happiness for the greatest number of those people affected in the long run; this is the *utility principle,* and the ethical perspective it serves as sole moral principle is *utilitarianism.*

Utilitarianism is a very popular ethical theory. For one thing, it seems democratic; every person's happiness (or every person whose happiness is affected) counts when one comes to consider which action will maximize happiness. For another, it claims to eschew all metaphysics and to be compatible with any religious perspective whatever. Again, allegedly, it is an ethical theory with but one moral principle, and so it will not suffer the embarrassment of providing two moral principles which may turn out to conflict with one another in various cases.

Whether utilitarianism is radically revisionist regarding relevance features in part depends on how many and what sorts of

13. Jeremy Bentham and John Stuart Mill were hedonists, so early utilitarianism was hedonistic; G. E. Moore was not a hedonist but was an "ideal" utilitarian, holding a view like the one just described. One could state utilitarianism along the lines of maximizing *possession* of knowledge, friendship, etc., or along the lines of maximizing *satisfaction* in knowledge, friendship, etc. The discussion below will not worry much about this ambiguity; the critique offered can be made of either variety, and will sometimes be cast in terms verbally more appropriate to one than to the other.

values it recognizes; the sort of utilitarianism described above, perhaps, so far as relevance features go, is not radically revisionist. In any case, the utility principle is more complex and deceptive than it might seem.

A COUNTEREXAMPLE TO UTILITARIANISM

Suppose that an island society is comprised of ninety-nine persons whose greatest joy is observing another person being tortured, and one person who does not countenance torture at all. Friendship flourishes among the ninety-nine, though the one finds friendship difficult with those whose taste in enjoyment is so different from his own. It may be that friendship and pleasure are maximized within this society by the ninety-nine turning the one into a subject of study and experiment in such a fashion that their science—at least so far as it concerns human endurance and pain thresholds and the like—flourishes at the same time as pleasure is maximized; maximizing happiness may require that one be tortured that many may flourish, particularly if artistic creativity heightens and mutual commitment deepens among the ninety-nine as they together explore the varieties of torturing the one. That this is painful for the one does not show it to be wrong; sometimes pain is necessary if health, say, or great art, is to be achieved. True, all the pain goes to one, and all the happiness goes to the ninety-nine; but that is defensible along utilitarian lines by noting that, not just pleasure, but happiness is maximized.

THE COMMENSURABILITY PRINCIPLE

One point of the example is that there is no guarantee whatever that even such atrocities as torture for pleasure may not be justified by appeal to the utility principle; no type of action is inherently wrong (or right) and in each case everything depends on how the calculation goes. In order to be clear as to what this involves, it is important to state plainly the assumption that lies behind the utility principle. This principle requires that one always so act as to maximize happiness. The idea is that (i) for any two items **X** and **Y**, if **X** and **Y** have value or worth, their value is measurable in common terms—all value is expressible in common coin, and (ii) the total value of any set of items is calculable by totaling the positive value, totaling the negative value, and subtracting the negative value from the positive; the collective value is a function of distributive value.

The proposition (i) expresses is the *commensurability principle,* and (i) plus the utility principle provide the backing for (ii).

ANOTHER COUNTEREXAMPLE

A consequence is that, as it were, a "big" value can be outweighed by many "little" ones. Suppose Ralph has $2,000 and can get no more, and is a utilitarian. His mother needs a life-saving operation which costs $2,000 and is available only on a "cash-and-carry" basis; Ralph's nest egg is her only hope. Ralph can spend his money only in one of two ways. One is for his mother, but Ralph has never been especially enamored of his mother, and would not miss her much, and should he deny her the operation he can keep others from knowing about it, so his reputation will not suffer. The other way he can spend his money is on ice cream cones. Ralph likes children, and likes being liked by them; he notes that at $1 per triple-decker cone, his money can yield 2,000 cones. At 20 licks a cone, that is 40,000 licks; at 10 positive hedons a lick, that yields 400,000 positive hedons. Reflecting that his mother tends to depression anyway, Ralph sees his clear utilitarian duty and contributes his money to a fund which will buy 2,000 cones for children who otherwise could not purchase them. He informs his mother (at the cost of ten negative hedons) and is surprised that she does not praise the rectitude of his decision.

UTILITARIANISM AND TRIVIALITY

It is easy to claim that this is slanderous toward utilitarianism; but exactly in what manner is this so? What, exactly, in utilitarianism, whose perspective (i) and (ii) clarifies, entails that the pleasure of 40,000 licks of an ice cream cone does not outweigh in value a few extra years of life by an old woman who tends to be depressed? If human life is a value for utilitarianism, it is one among many; indeed, the natural perspective for utilitarianism seems to be that a human life is but a set of experiences, each of which has its own positive or negative value and each of which is counted when one asks whether a person's life as a whole is worthwhile. The more one penetrates this perspective, then, the more it seems that Ralph has been right on target in his reasoning. So far as he can see, his mother will not live a very happy life; the children will love the cones; Ralph likes the children better than his mother. Maximization of happiness requires buying the cones; the unrealistic feature of the story lies in the assumption that Ralph can spend his money only in one of two ways, and if we expand the possibilities this will in no way mean that of the two ways considered, the one Ralph chose is not morally better, given utilitarianism, or that any of the other choices will be better, on utilitarian grounds, or that if some other choice is better (on utilitarian grounds) then this choice will be morally preferable to Ralph doing what for all the world seems his clear duty by his mother. Utilitarianism seems to allow, and seems inevitably at times to require, that what is morally trivial (if not irrelevant), in great quantity, morally outweigh the morally important, without the trivial ceasing to be trivial by the sheer fact of its high cardinality. If this is objectionable, and it certainly seems to be so, the problem lies, not with the story or example, but with utilitarianism.

UTILITARIANISM AND JUSTICE

Another objection to utilitarianism, no less potent for being standard, is that there is no necessary connection, and indeed there often will be conflict, between the action which will maximize happiness and that which will manifest justice. Suppose ten persons invest $100 in a common venture which by common agreement shall last for two years and then be dissolved with its worth split evenly among the investors; it runs its economic course and is worth $10,000 at its end. Set aside the legal considerations and the matter of people keeping their word; still, it seems clear what should be done, namely what is just, assuming no one contributed anything other than the initial funds, either monetarily or otherwise. What is just is that each person should receive one-tenth or $1,000 at the venture's end, just as each contributed one-tenth or $100 at the venture's beginning. Even if one person would be absolutely ecstatic at his receiving $9100 and the other nine getting their original investment back, and even if this would result in a better overall use of the money, justice—and presumably morality—requires an equal distribution of the profits. Analogously, one—not the only—problem with the plan involving ninety-nine sadists torturing one nonsadist was that even if this arrangement maximized happiness it did not distribute happiness equitably; one person got none.

The deceptiveness of the utility principle in this regard is this: it is easy to assume that because everyone's happiness is considered when one is asking what will maximize happiness, this will result in everyone's happiness being respected by the outcome; this simply is not so. Suppose ten persons will be affected by action **A** and by action **B**, and **A** and **B** exhaust the alternatives; suppose further that **A** will yield each person six units of happiness and four units of unhappiness, for a net happiness surplus of twenty, but that **B** will yield nine persons nine units each of happiness and one of unhappiness, and the tenth person one unit of happiness and nine of unhappiness, for a net happiness surplus of sixty-four units of happiness. Justice requires that **A** be done; maximization of happiness requires **B**. So utility and justice are not identical, and may conflict.

If one says that **X**, because it has properties **A**, **B**, and **C**, belongs to kind **K**, and grants that **Y** has **A**, **B**, and **C**, then if one denies that **Y** is of kind **K**, one is inconsistent unless there is some discernible, relevant difference between **X** and **Y**.[14] If one claims that it is right that Sam do action **A1** in circumstances **C1**, holds that Sally is similar in *all* morally relevant ways to Sam, and **C2** is similar in *all* morally relevant ways to **C1**, and knows that Sally is in **C2**, then in all consistency one can only hold that Sally should perform action **A2**, which in all morally relevant respects is like **A1**.

Considering cases which fall *outside* the scope of morality, if one judges differently regarding cases which are similar in all ways relevant to the judgment made, one judges inconsistently; one's judgment is wrong in the sense of being epistemically mistaken, whatever else it may be. But considering cases which fall *within* the scope of morality, if one judges that persons ought to act in morally different ways even though they are similar in every morally relevant respect and are in circumstances which are similar in every morally relevant respect, one's judgment is *unjust*, whatever else it may be.

CRITERIA FOR ASSESSING ETHICAL THEORIES: CONSISTENCY AND JUSTICE

One can state as a further criterion: (C7) *An ethical theory* **T** *in which cases which are similar in every morally relevant respect are judged as being morally different is false and sanctions injustice.* It is false because if two cases are similar in all morally relevant respects, they cannot be morally different or belong to different moral classes, or the like; but to be inconsistent in matters of ethics is also to be unjust, in

14. For example, that while **Y** is **A**, **B**, and **C**, it is also **D**, whereas **X** is not, and if anything is **D**, it does not belong to **K**.

judgment if not in conduct. Unless utilitarianism is to fall prey to (C7), its utility principle, then, must be supplemented by a principle of justice. If this is so, then the utilitarian claim that the utility principle is the only moral principle that is required is false. Since that claim is essential to utilitarianism, utilitarianism is false.

A defender of utilitarianism might argue that whenever an application of the utility principle requires that person A be treated differently than person B, there is an intrinsic morally relevant difference between them—namely that treating them the same will not, and treating them differently will, maximize utility. This need not be due to any morally relevant difference in capacities or opportunities between A and B; it need only be that the sum total of human happiness, or satisfaction, or the like, insofar as it is affected by the way A and B are treated, is higher if they are treated differently. How differently? As differently as is required to maximize the sum total of human happiness or satisfaction, however that is distributed. In fact, however, this is not an intrinsic difference between persons at all and so is not a morally relevant difference between them; it is simply a difference in the results of treating persons in one way as opposed to treating them in another.

One could *say* that happiness will be maximized by everyone always being treated justly, but there is no reason to think this is so; after all, everyone always being treated justly is one extreme, and no one being treated so is the other, and between the extremes are myriad other scenarios. One would have to see which scenario maximized utility, or happiness, or satisfaction. *A priori,* the odds are equally bad for any alternative; whatever the outcome, justice is the prisoner of, and to be pursued by the utilitarian only insofar as it happens to coincide with, maximization of happiness.

By now a certain picture emerges as a fair or accurate way of representing utilitarian ethical theory, such as it is. Each person is obligated to act so as to maximize the sum of human happiness in the long run. To this great goal each one is to be prepared to sacrifice all. It may be that sacrificing all is exactly what is required, for there are no limits on what may turn out to be "moral" in the sense of being approved by the utility principle. That one person be tortured by many, that a whole people be systemically eliminated, that a race be enslaved, that an innocent person be "framed" and sentenced for a crime someone else perpetrated, and so on through a long series of courses of action which seem morally horrendous—

morally "unthinkable"—are not unthinkable for the consistent utilitarian; the question—the *only* "moral" question—is what courses of action will maximize utility or happiness or satisfaction. *Any* course of action that has that feature is right and obligatory, whatever other properties or consequences it may have. Nothing is forbidden unless maximization of happiness forbids it, nothing is so horrendous but that maximization of happiness can make it right.

UTILITARIANISM AND PERSONS

Presumably this perspective is most plausible on, and perhaps it requires, a view of a person on which a person does not *have* but literally *is* a set of conscious states, each state being either *plus*, *minus*, or *neutral* relative to containing satisfaction, or else a view on which a person *has* conscious states but only the states, and not the person, have moral value. These views are competing metaphysical perspectives. Since the latter view leaves open the possibility, at least, that one ascribe value to the person who has the states—even a value incommensurate with that ascribed to the conscious states themselves—the former view seems safer for one who wishes to maintain a utilitarian stance. On the latter view, persons, in effect, are factories for the production and sustenance of conscious states. On the former, a person at a time is a set of simultaneous conscious states and over time is a succession of such sets. If this is not what a person is, at any rate it is then possible to argue that persons, being "owners" of such states, are the proper locus of value, and that utilitarianism misplaces the locus of value—it puts a value on conscious states which belongs only to persons. If persons *are* but bundles of conscious states, this objection cannot be made. If this line of reasoning is correct, the alleged metaphysical neutrality of utilitarianism is highly questionable.

Nothing is so horrendous but what its being required by maximization of happiness makes it right—is this a *critique* of utilitarianism? Suppose everyone else could be made much happier, so that the sum total of happiness rose immensely—even maximally—by one innocent person being condemned to suffer; maximization of happiness or not, this seems clearly wrong. If the assurance is offered that maximization of happiness could or would never require such a thing, the assurance is empty; there is no guarantee whatever that it will not require this and many other things like it. That, in a way, is the whole point of utilitarianism—that such claims as *Tor-*

ture is wrong and *Making the innocent suffer for things they have not done* are only rules of thumb which are justified, if they are justified at all, by appeal to the utility principle, and that the *only* basis for taking an action to be right is that its performance increases the sum total of happiness of those affected. In this respect, utilitarianism runs deeply against common moral experience.

UTILITARIANISM AND UTILITARIAN CALCULATIONS

How it is to be determined whether an action will increase this sum is a problem. Actual examples of calculations are rare, even in the writings of utilitarians. The project of calculating how an action will affect the sum total of human happiness is mind-boggling. Even if one restricts the task to trying to answer "Which of the actions now open to me will bring about the greatest happiness for the greatest number of those affected by it?", and one conveniently (if arbitrarily) assumes that the effects of one's action will soon end (or, more plausibly, holds that one can only take into account the foreseeable consequences of one's action), a hard look at one's situation reveals two things. One is that there is no clear method for answering the question—*many* actions are open to an individual on any occasion of possible action, and even trying to list them mentally would be enormously time consuming; more basically, what moral point would be served by doing this? The usual reply is that utilitarianism does not require this, since we already know which *sorts* of actions usually maximize satisfaction and enshrine this in moral rules. But this more dodges the point than meets it, for the rules are supposed to be arrived at by calculating the results of particular actions, or of adopting or rejecting practices or institutions or kinds of action, on maximizing happiness.

The other is that, without having made, or being clear about how to go about making, any such calculations, we know that torture for pleasure is wrong; the utilitarian, knowing this too, supposes that what makes it true is that torture for pleasure will not maximize satisfaction. Whether torture for pleasure will, or will not, maximize satisfaction depends on the circumstances; sometimes it will, and sometimes it will not. But its wrongness will not vary as does its maximization (or otherwise) of satisfaction.

ACT VERSUS RULE UTILITARIANISM

Act utilitarianism holds that while we often will not have time to apply it directly to actions and must rely on moral rules as rules of thumb, when it is possible one's obligation is to apply the utility principle directly to individual actions. *Rule* utilitarianism holds that our obligation is to apply the utility principle directly to practices, or *kinds* of action, and only thereby, and hence indirectly, to individual actions. The idea is that one will get different results as to what actions are right, depending on whether one is an act or a rule utilitarian.

Suppose five persons own factories which discharge an equal amount of pollution directly in the river that supplies water for their town. Each is the wage earner for a family of six, each operates a factory whose profit margin is just adequate to keep the wolf from the door, and each cannot afford to filter his or her factory's pollution because the filtering device this would require is prohibitively costly. The river could handle the pollution from any one, but not from more than one, of the factories—certainly not from all five. Each person can argue that the pollution of his or her factory does no harm—the river can handle that amount of pollution—and the pollution filter would cost enough so that its purchase would produce bankruptcy. None of the factory owners knows how to do anything but operate his factory, and each has been forgiven an enormous debt provided he continue to operate his own factory. So each is morally justified in acting as he does—namely, continuing to pollute the river—if act utilitarianism is true. But if practice, or rule, utilitarianism is true, then apparently one can argue in a different vein. One can note that the practice of polluting the river will have most unfortunate effects on the river, and on those who use it as a water source; since the city needs water, and has no other source, the common good requires that the factories cease to pollute the river, even if this wreaks great hardship on the five owners. The collective consequences of the acts of polluting fail to maximize satisfaction though the distributive consequences succeed in maximizing it.

THE EXTENSIONAL EQUIVALENCE OF ACT AND RULE UTILITARIANISM

So they do. But this does not establish a genuine difference between act and rule utilitarianism. The rule utilitarian, as does the act utilitarian, embraces the utility principle as the only moral principle. A moral rule exercises authority only in subservience to the utility principle; moral rules are rules of thumb, not moral principles in disguise. There will be exceptions to moral rules, even for the rule utilitarian—namely, those actions which maximize utility though they violate the rules. For the rule as for the act utilitarian, the utility principle alone is exceptionless; to opt for a rule over the utility principle when they conflicted would be to abandon utilitarianism. A rule which condemns an action which (if treated as an exception to a rule, and as setting no precedent and establishing no practice) has utility conflicts with the utility principle. So a utilitarian, under such circumstances, will set aside the rule and perform the utility-possessing action. Presumably, then, when the two conflict, a utilitarian is required to follow the utility principle rather than a rule which derives what authority it has from that principle; otherwise, moral rules are being treated as moral principles. Thus the rule or practice utilitarian (as least, in intent) will follow moral rules unless the utility principle dictates otherwise; unless, that is, acting against a rule will maximize utility. An act utilitarian (at least, in intent) will always act so as to maximize utility. The act utilitarian, then, (in intent) applies the utility principle directly to actions, always performing the one that maximizes utility. The rule utilitarian has a more complicated moral life; (in intent) she applies the utility principle to rules, and follows those rules the following of which maximizes satisfaction (i.e., performs actions which contribute to the maximization of satisfaction) save where so doing would violate the utility principle (in which case she violates the rules and performs the action which maximizes utility). So both are obligated always to perform the action that will maximize utility; act and rule utilitarianism are *extensionally equivalent*—whatever is right for one is right for the other, and whatever is wrong for one is wrong for the other. Hence any counterexample to the one is a counterexample to the other.

Utilitarianism, then, seems unacceptable as a moral theory. To the degree that this is so—and even to the degree that this judgment is rationally debatable—it follows that it is false that there is no way of rationally assessing an ethical theory. The task of explicitly relating the critique of utilitarianism presented here to the criteria for assessing ethical theories listed above will be left as an exercise for the reader.

ANOTHER ETHICAL THEORY: FORMALISM

Formalism is one important alternative to utilitarianism. One way of developing formalism is as follows. Let the *maxim* of an action be a description of that act which includes all of the action's morally relevant features, plus the (at least hypothetical) intention of the describer to perform that action, including the end or ends for which it would be done. If **A** is a description of an action by Sam, which includes every morally relevant feature **A** would have were Sam to perform it (so far as Sam can discern them), and **E** is the end for which Sam would do **A**, then something like *Let me do* **A** *in order to achieve* **E** will express the maxim of that action, so far as Sam is concerned.

TWO EXPANDED SENSES OF "CONSISTENCY"

Now suppose Sam is wondering whether he should perform **A**—whether it would be right, or wrong, or morally neutral, for him to do **A**. Formalism's reply to Sam requires that he universalize his maxim, thereby turning *Let me do* **A** *in order to achieve* **E** into *Let everyone do* **A** *in order to achieve* **E**. Then the question is whether the result is consistent. "Consistent" here does not only mean "logically consistent"; the question is not whether it is logically possible that everyone do **A** with the intent of achieving **E**.

One relevant further sense of "consistent" is this: could everyone do **A** without the point of Sam's doing **A**—the end for which Sam would do **A**—being defeated? If the answer is negative, then the maxim cannot be universalized "consistently," or the universalization of the maxim is "inconsistent." Suppose Sam's plan is to remove the books from Sally's library into his own, without Sally's knowledge—an activity Sally would heartily oppose if she came to know of it. Then Sam cannot cordially embrace the universalization of his maxim, which (according to formalism) would run something along the lines of *Let everyone take the books of whomever he wishes in order to enhance his own library*;[15] were everyone to do this, Sam's own library would leave Sam's possession, contrary to his intent. Stealing is wrong, because were everyone to steal, the thief's point

15. Were *the*, or *an acceptable*, universalization of Sam's maxim to run *Let everyone put his books in Sam's library*, or the like, this perhaps itself would be an objection to formalism. Here, I assume the right sort of universalization to be along the lines in the text.

in stealing would not be realized. *Let me steal books from others' libraries that my library be large* cannot be universalized—not everyone can adopt this maxim—without defeating its end; so the maxim cannot be consistently universalized.

A similar, but perhaps not identical, sense of "consistency" is involved in another sort of case. Consider the maxim: *Let me say what is false with intent to deceive, whenever I find this convenient, in order to escape speaking truths I prefer not to utter.* Can this maxim be universalized? Suppose everyone were to do that, what would happen? It seems clear that the liar can succeed only against the backdrop of an institution, or at least assumption, of truth-telling. But putting the universalized maxim into practice would be tantamount to institutionalizing lying when one found that preferable to truth-telling, or to making that into a practice; at any rate, were everyone to say what was false with intent to deceive, whenever they found this convenient, in order to escape speaking truths they preferred not to utter, then (assuming this were discovered, which seems not implausible) the presumption of truth-telling on which the effective liar trades would vanish. People would not expect the truth, and so could not be successfully lied to. Or so formalism supposes.

THE FORMALIST CONTENTION

Formalism, then, offers something like the following characterization of inconsistency: a maxim of the form *Let* **x** *do* **A** *in order to achieve* **E** cannot be consistently universalized if (i) were everyone to do **A**, **E** would not be achieved (even though no practice presupposed by *doing* **A** would be destroyed), or (ii) were everyone to do **A**, an institution or practice or presumption which is required for doing **A** successfully[16] would be destroyed (and so one could not do **A** successfully).

One more notion is needed in order to round out the basic elements of formalism. The *denial* of a maxim of the form *Let me do* **A** is simply *Let me not do* **A**. Then it is formalism's contention that: (i) if the maxim of an action **A** is universalizable,[17] and its opposite is also universalizable, then doing **A** is morally neutral—permissible but not obligatory; (ii) if the maxim of an action **A** is universalizable

16. That is, an institution (etc.) without which one could not *try* to do A and succeed.

17. That is, can be universalized *consistently*.

and its opposite is not, then doing **A** is morally right; (iii) if the maxim of an action **A** is not universalizable and its opposite is, then doing **A** is morally wrong. Should both a maxim and its opposite fail to be universalizable, then presumably one has made a mistake in the original formulation of the maxim.

Formalism can be much more fully developed than will be done here; it will suffice for present purposes if we can show that its assessment is not arbitrary.

A COUNTEREXAMPLE TO FORMALISM

Suppose that Pat lives alone with Pat's father. The father is rich, and Pat (his only heir) suffers from a disease which causes great pain and will substantially impair the quality and length of Pat's life. The father, having a strong personality, has Pat under his power. Pat works for him for wages that make the legal minimum wage seem a princely sum. Nor will the father pay for the operation that would cure Pat, who will outlive him anyway. But the father is good for another five years at least, and the operation will do no good unless performed within a month, in which case Pat will be cured.

Even if what has been said of the father shows his best side, presumably it is wrong for Pat to lace the father's gin with arsenic. But suppose Pat, perhaps in a moment of anger after having been humiliated once again by the father's vicious verbal abuse, does contemplate his murder. Pat formulates this maxim:

(M) Let me take my father's life so that I may pay for an operation that will extend the length and retain the quality of my own.

Suppose Pat is perfectly willing that (M) be universalized, and apply to mothers as well as fathers; suppose also that Pat is willing to be eliminated if the father's circumstances and characteristics are ever Pat's own. The universalization of (M) will be:

(M1) Let everyone take a parent's life so as to pay for an operation that will extend the length and retain the quality of his or her own life.

Now (M1) will only apply, other than vacuously, to persons in need of such an operation as it specifies. One can add to (M), and so to (M1), a specification of the father (parent in (M1)) as miserly, unconcerned with anyone else's welfare, cruel, inconsiderate, rich but stingy, and so on; one can add that money for the operation is obtainable only by taking the father's life. This will restrict the scope of those to whom (M1) applies still further. But without complicating (M) or (M1) further, it seems that

(a) It is not clear that one cannot consistently embrace (M1) in the sense of "consistency" relevant to formalism, and
(b) It is not clear that adding further descriptions of the father's evil character or Pat's good character or other morally relevant features of the circumstance described will alter the fact that (a) records.

If this is correct, then on formalist grounds at least Pat's taking the father's life is no worse than permissible. It is not wrong. It is either obligatory or else permissible. If, as seems plausible, (M)'s contradictory is also universalizable, then according to formalism, following (M) is permissible. Yet, however much one may sympathize with Pat, following (M) seems to be another case of murder.

THE POSSIBILITY OF DIVERGENT RESULTS FROM APPLICABLE MAXIMS

Now one could no doubt find maxims that would fit the case and yield the result that it is wrong for Pat to kill the father. For example, describe the action as taking the life of another. Perhaps the maxim,

(M2) Let me take the life of another so that I may prolong the quantity and retain the quality of my own,

which universalizes into

(M3) Let everyone take the life of another so as to prolong the quantity and retain the quality of one's own life,

yields the desired result. For if (M3) were followed, my life would (or might permissibly) be taken by someone else, which would do little to sustain its quantity or quality.

But we could also describe the action via

(M4) Let me so act as to provide an operation that I need,

which universalizes into

(M5) Let everyone so act as to provide an operation that he or she needs.

(M5) applies, other than vacuously, only to persons in need of operations. At least on the face of the matter, (M4) and (M5) seem not inconsistent in the relevant sense. But consider:

(M6) Let me not so act as to provide an operation that I need,

which universalizes into:

(M7) Let no one so act as to provide an operation that he or she needs.

Again, it is not clear that (M6) and (M7) are inconsistent with one another either. If they are not, then it seems that the action (M6) specifies also is permissible.

Getting the maxim straight, then, is no easy task. Different maxims yield different results so far as consistency goes, so it is important to choose the correct maxim. Yet the clearest and fullest maxim in Pat's case seems to be the first one given, or one much like it, and on it what looks for all the world like murder turns out to be permissible. Perhaps it is true that whatever will not pass the formalist's test is wrong, but it is not true that everything that does pass it is right or that everything that is wrong is captured by the test. This result, of course, even if correct, is far short of what the formalist claims. At the least, then, formalism seems to violate (C4) by making a wrong action permissible, and a similar argument could easily be constructed for the claim that formalism violates (C3) by making right actions only permissible ones. *If* there are intractable problems regarding identifying the correct maxim to use, problems arise regarding (C5), which concerns practicality. But this criticism, and others, will not be pressed here.

CONCLUSION

The reason for not pressing on toward a full-dress critique of formalism, and still other ethical theories, is simple. The basic task of this chapter has been to argue that it is possible to assess ethical theories rationally. But an argument to this effect can hardly proceed in the abstract (though it may be abstract); rather, one needs actual examples of ethical theories which are stated with enough clarity and detail so that their purport is plain. Then one needs to ask whether they are adequate in one specific way or another, and how one tells, and with what results. An attempt has been made to offer relevant and telling objections to a sampling of diverse ethical theories. What is crucial to the overall argument is not that the objections be unanswerable, requiring rejection or at least revision of their targets, though they may be so. What is crucial is that they illustrate the process of rationally assessing competing ethical theories. If they illustrate this process, then the idea of such a process is not vacuous, and if it is not, then the basic rationale for moral scepticism fails.[18]

SUGGESTIONS FOR FURTHER READING

Carter, Curtis, ed. *Skepticism and Moral Principles: Modern Ethics in Review.* Chicago: New University Press, 1973.

A variety of essays criticizing moral skepticism.

Donagan, Alan. *The Theory of Morality.* Chicago: University of Chicago Press, 1977.

Donagan defends the contention that Judeo-Christian/Stoic morality is rationally assessable.

Downie, R. S., and Telfer, Elizabeth. *Respect for Persons.* New York: Schocken, 1970.

Downie and Telfer discuss the concept of a person along nonutilitarian lines.

Fried, Charles. *Right and Wrong.* Cambridge: Harvard University Press, 1978.

A strong defense of the cognitive status of ethics.

Gert, Bernard. *The Moral Rules: A New Rational Foundation for Morality.* New York: Harper and Row, 1970.

Gert challenges moral skepticism and relativism.

van Inwagen, Peter. *An Essay on Freewill.* Oxford: Clarendon Press, 1983.

Krausz, Michael, and Heiland, Jack W., eds. *Relativism: Cognitive and Moral.* South Bend, IN: University of Notre Dame Press, 1982.

Midgley, Mary. *Beast and Man.* Brighton: The Harvester Press, 1979.

______. *Heart and Mind.* New York: St. Martin's Press, 1981.

Singer, Marcus G. *Generalization in Ethics.* New York: Knopf, 1961.

Smart, J. J. C., and Williams, Bernard. *Utilitarianism: For and Against.* Cambridge: Cambridge University Press, 1973.

A debate concerning the relative merits of utilitarianism.

18. It is utterly compatible with this rationale failing that none of the objections considered be the last word in assessing even those theories discussed above, and certainly they are not.

PART FOUR
THE CHALLENGE TO THEISM FROM EVIL

ANALYTICAL TABLE OF CONTENTS TO CHAPTER 6

8. This leaves, however, the question of whether the existence of evil constitutes evidence against the existence of God. 224
9. A probability argument from "sample classes" will *assume* that we have recognized evils that God has no morally sufficient reason to permit, but this assumption is false, and our not knowing what that reason might be is not evidence that there is no such reason. 225
10. Ethical theories contending that worlds containing evils are not worth creating do not fare well either, and there are worlds that not even an omnipotent deity can create. 229
11. It seems that evil will constitute evidence that God does not exist only if we know that there are evils that he has no morally sufficient reason for permitting, and it seems that we can know this only if we know that God does not exist. 237
12. Whatever it is reasonable to suggest that theists ought to be able to provide relative to a theodicy it is reasonable to think that they can provide, so long as theism comports well with plausible ethical theories. 238

CHAPTER 6

IS THE EXISTENCE OF EVIL EVIDENCE AGAINST THE EXISTENCE OF GOD?

That there is evil in the world is evident; the relation of this fact to monotheism is complicated. Judeo-Christian monotheism is a religion of salvation and forgiveness, of judgment and redemption. Such a religion would have no purchase on a world without evil; some of its central concepts would have no application. In such a world, no salvation would be required; there would be nothing to forgive or judge, and nothing from which one needed to be redeemed. *Monotheism is true* entails *There is evil.*[1]

Nonetheless, the fact that evil exists constitutes an essential element in what has perhaps been the most forceful objection to monotheism. Many have found the existence of evil a barrier to their believing that an omnicompetent deity exists; they have thought, or alleged, that the proposition *There is evil* is true, and that it constitutes grounds for supposing that the proposition *God exists* is false. The allegation has been that either *God and evil coexist* is a contradictory proposition or else the existence of evil at least provides evidence against the existence of God. This chapter will investigate that allegation, which comprises the problem of evil.

THE CONSISTENCY STRATEGY

It seems clear that there is no contradiction between the propositions *God exists* and *There is evil.* If three propositions A, B, and C

1. *Monotheism* is here taken to mean something like "a standard set of theistic doctrines" rather than simply the claim that God exists.

constitute a noncontradictory triad, then there will be no contradiction between any two propositions in the triad. The three propositions *God exists, Any evil that God permits is one that he has a morally sufficient reason for permitting,* and *There is evil,* constitute a noncontradictory triad. Hence, between any two propositions in that triad, there is no contradiction. *God exists* and *There is evil* are two propositions in that triad. So between *God exists* and *There is evil* there is no contradiction.

There is a relevant restriction on this strategy. No single member of the triad may itself be a contradiction; each member must either be a necessary truth or a contingent proposition, whether true or false. *The triad need not contain only truths,* for what the strategy deals with is the question, not of the *truth* of a pair of propositions, but their *logical compatibility.* Thus if one wishes to object to the present application of this strategy, the appropriate move will be to contend that at least one member of the triad is a contradiction. If *There is evil* is contradictory, it cannot be that the existence of evil provides evidence against God's existence (though of course if *There is evil* were a contradiction, then since *Monotheism is true* entails *There is evil,* monotheism itself would be contradictory). That *There is evil* is contradictory, however, is hardly plausible; rather, it seems plainly but contingently true that evil exists. On the other hand, if *God exists* is contradictory, then monotheism is false for that reason, regardless of the existence of evil; but then there will have to be a proof that *God exists* is a contradictory proposition.

A CHALLENGE TO THE CONSISTENCY STRATEGY

Perhaps, then, if one wishes to question the strategy at hand, the most promising tactic will be to contend that the proposition *Any evil that God permits is one that he has a morally sufficient reason for permitting* is contradictory. One way of putting the questioner's contention is to claim that it is logically impossible that an omnicompetent deity have a morally sufficient reason for permitting an evil. It is not obvious that this *is* a logical impossibility, however, and so the claim that it is requires justification. Our question is whether this requirement can be met.

One might claim that a being could have a morally sufficient reason for allowing an evil only if that being were defective in some manner—in knowledge, perhaps, or in power—and that since God can, by definition, have no such defects, he can have no morally sufficient reason for allowing an evil. In order to highlight an aspect of this strategy that is crucial to its success—namely, that the proposition *God has a morally sufficient reason for permitting an evil* be not merely false, but *necessarily* false or contradictory—we might present the argument in the following terms: (i) *necessarily, a being has morally sufficient reason for permitting evil only if that being is defective in knowledge or power*; (ii) *necessarily, God (if he exists) is not defective in knowledge or power*; so, it follows that (iii) *necessarily, God (if he exists) has no morally sufficient reason for permitting evil (i.e., it is logically impossible that God possess such a reason)*.

A REPLY TO THE CHALLENGE

This line of reasoning requires that only lack of knowledge or power provides a morally sufficient reason for allowing evil; this contention is dubious. Perhaps it also begs the question against monotheism; one contention frequently made by monotheists, and a claim that is arguably part of monotheistic ethics, is that enduring suffering is an essential element in the development of moral character. One achieves moral maturity only through suffering, and, of course, the achievement is alleged to be worth the cost. The view, then, is that (i) it is logically impossible that a human being achieve mature moral character without undergoing some suffering, (ii) suffering is an evil and achieving mature moral character a good, and (iii) this good, morally speaking, is worth the price of this evil. On this view, then, there is no possible world which includes mature (i.e., maturely good) moral agents but contains no suffering. If it is so much as logically possible that this view is correct, then it is logically possible that God have morally sufficient reason for allowing evil, for if an evil is a logically necessary condition of a good whose occurrence is worth the cost of the evil, God has a morally sufficient reason for allowing that evil, which reason requires no defect in his knowledge and power. Developed, then, along the lines we have been considering, our questioner's strategy requires that it be not merely false, but a contradiction that an essential element in a human being's obtaining mature moral character be that he or she endure suffering.

On behalf of the questioner's tactic, one might note that the monotheistic view regarding mature moral character and suffering, at least as discussed above, is expressible by *It is logically impossible that a human being attain mature moral character without his or her enduring suffering.* An intuitively very plausible thesis has it that if a proposition is logically necessary (is either necessarily true or else a contradiction), it is logically impossible that it be other than necessary, and if a proposition is logically contingent, whether true or false, it is logically impossible that it be other than contingent. Thus, if it is true at all, the monotheistic view regarding mature moral character and suffering is a necessary truth, and if it is false, then it is a contradiction. But this, of course, provides no reason for supposing that this view *is* false, and hence contradictory.

While we have discussed the question of whether it is logically impossible that God have a morally sufficient reason for allowing evil by using a particular example concerning character and suffering, it should not be thought that the questioner is right if monotheism is mistaken in this regard. One might suggest only that undergoing or overcoming some evil or other, not necessarily suffering, is essential to achieving mature character. More modestly still, one might suggest that there are some character traits—fortitude or courage, say—whose possessor must overcome some evils—pain or fear, for example—and whose moral value justifies their moral cost. Any of these views, as well as others, if they are not contradictory, are such as to render it logically possible that God have a morally sufficient reason for allowing evil, thus thwarting the questioner's tactic. This result will accrue if there is some evil such that: (i) there is a good such that it is logically impossible that it occur without that evil occurring, and either (ii) it is logically necessary that that good obtaining is morally worth the price of that evil obtaining, or (iii) it is contingently true that the good obtaining is morally worth the price of that evil obtaining. If some evil is such that (i) and either (ii) or (iii) is true of it, then it is logically possible (since true) that God will have a morally sufficient reason for allowing it.[2] Nor, as we shall see, is it only such evils for which sufficient reasons may be available.

ANOTHER OBJECTION TO THE CONSISTENCY STRATEGY: EVILS THAT CANNOT BE JUSTIFIED(?)

The questioner is not at the end of his tether. Welcoming the concern with particular cases, the questioner may contend that

2. Perhaps the evil must also satisfy this condition: (iv) the good to which it is a logically necessary condition is not such that its existence precludes the existence of some good which has greater value.

while there are types of evils that satisfy the description *evils it is not contradictory that God have morally sufficient reason for allowing*, there also are types that do not. Suffering, perhaps, satisfies this description, whereas, perhaps, *dying an agonizing death* does not. Or, not incompatibly with this suggestion, the questioner may contend that some instances of a type of evil—say, some instances of suffering—satisfy this description (perhaps those which play an essential role in yielding moral growth) and some do not (perhaps those which play no such role). This last suggestion, concerning instances of a type of evil, is not very plausible; it seems that if it is logically possible that some cases of a type of evil be such that God has a morally sufficient reason for allowing them, then this possibility holds for any evil of that type. Perhaps some cases of suffering provide opportunity for moral growth, which opportunity is squandered; it will not follow that it is logically impossible that God have morally sufficient reason for allowing them. If two evils **A** and **B** differ so substantially that God can have sufficient reason for allowing **A** but not for allowing **B**, it seems plausible that this itself is sufficient reason for taking them to be different in type or kind. This pushes us back toward the suggestion that there are types or kinds of evil it is logically impossible that an omnicompetent deity have morally sufficient reason for allowing. What sort of evil might this be?

ALLOWING A PERSON TO DIE AN AGONIZING DEATH

The plausibility of this suggestion relies on its being viewed as a last, and most inelegant, link in a chain; the story, whatever its other components, ends dismally, nor are there any following events which might redeem it. This *lastness*, so to speak, is crucial to the plausibility of the suggestion. Do we, then, know—as the suggestion requires—that death of the body is the end of the person whose body dies? If we *do* know that, then on that ground alone most varieties of monotheism can be rejected, as they include as essential elements doctrines requiring life after death and so are false unless these doctrines are true.

In fact, we do not know that death of the body is the end of the person whose body dies. Perhaps it is true that if monotheism is false, that is the truth of the matter, and if monotheism is true, it is not, and that if one does not know whether monotheism is true or not, one does not know whether the death of the body is the end of the person whose body dies. If monotheism-independent proofs of life after death are scarce, so are disproofs. Further, for the questioner's case to be made, that we do not survive death would have to be, not merely true, but necessarily so; a person's survival of death would have to be a violation of the law of noncontradiction. Otherwise put, doctrines of bodily resurrection, immortality of the soul, reincarnation, and any other conceptions of life after death would have to be logically inconsistent, not merely false. It seems implausible that all such doctrines are contradictory; at any rate, the critic would have to show that they are.

A BRIEF REVIEW OF THE ARGUMENT ABOUT THE CONSISTENCY STRATEGY

That the critic's perspective does require this strong claim can be seen if we remember the ground we have traversed. That *God exists* and *There is evil* are not logically inconsistent was defended in this fashion: if a triad of propositions **A**, **B**, **C** does not comprise a contradictory set, then no other set constructed out of two members of this triad—say, **A** and **C**—will comprise a contradiction. The propositions *God exists, Any evil God permits is one he has a morally sufficient reason for permitting*, and *There is evil* comprise a consistent triad. Hence no set constructed from any two of its members—say, *God exists* and *There is evil*—comprises a contradictory set. So *God exists* and *There is evil* are not logically incompatible.

The restriction of this strategy is that no single member of the set be itself a contradiction.[3] The reason, then, for this restriction is that if a set of propositions contains a contradiction, then any conclusion one wishes may be derived from that set, including the conclusion that any two of its members *are* logically incompatible.

To rebut this argument successfully, the questioner must render plausible the claim that at least one member of the set *God exists, Any evil God permits is one he has morally sufficient reason for permitting*,

3. This is ruled out explicitly by our statement of the strategy if we read "comprises a contradictory set" so that a set that contains a contradiction comprises a contradictory set, or implicitly if we note that any set that contains a contradiction will fail to yield the result at which the strategy aims. For suppose that the set contains **P**, **Q**, and **R**, and that **P** is a contradiction. Then **P** has the form: **A** *and* **not-A**. From **P**, then, **A** follows. From **A**, it follows that either **A** *or* **not-Q**. From **P**, **not-A** also follows. From **A** *or* **not-Q** and **not-A**, **not-Q** follows. So our set contains **Q** and entails **not-Q**.

and *There is evil* is a necessarily false, or contradictory, proposition. That there is evil seems true, and if it is false there is no problem of evil. If the allegation is that *God exists* is contradictory, any grounds there may be for that allegation constitute the basic case against monotheism. So we have concentrated on the middle member of the triad, noting that the questioner requires that it be a contradiction that any evil that God permits is one he has a morally sufficient reason for permitting. Consideration of this requirement led us to consider whether there might be some type **T** of evil such that *God has morally sufficient reason for allowing an evil of type* **T** is necessarily false.

ANOTHER RESPONSE TO THE CONSISTENCY STRATEGY

Perhaps one can find the desired sort of evil among the following: allowing unrequited innocent suffering; rewarding unrepented murder, rape, and blasphemy with everlasting bliss; punishing the innocent; not punishing the guilty. An all-good deity could not perpetrate such things. Nor could he permit them and remain all-good. So not every sort of evil is one God could have a morally sufficient reason for permitting.

A REPLY TO THE RESPONSE

While discovering such a type is necessary to the questioner's case, it is not sufficient for it; there must be evils of some such type. That there be a type of evil such that if God allows it, his doing so has no morally sufficient ground does nothing by itself to blot the divine character; God must have actually permitted such evils.

Even this is not enough to serve the questioner's cause. Suppose it is true both that: (i) it is a necessary truth that if God permits an evil of type **T**, he has no morally sufficient reason for permitting it, and (ii) God has permitted an evil of type **T**. What the questioner's case requires is that (iii) it is *necessarily true* that some evil God has permitted is one he has no morally sufficient reason for permitting—or, if one prefers, it is *necessarily false* that every evil God permits is one he has a morally sufficient reason for permitting. But (i) and (ii) do not entail (iii). They entail only that (iv) it is *true* that some evil God has permitted is one he has no morally sufficient reason for permitting—or, if one prefers, it is *false* that every evil God permits is one he has a morally sufficient reason for permitting. So the most the questioner can derive from (i) and (ii) is the *falsity* of the middle proposition in our triad. This, however, is nothing to the point; the questioner's strategy requires that the proposition in question be contradictory.[4]

Suppose, then, one replaces *God has permitted an evil of type* **T** by *It is a necessary truth that God has permitted an evil of type* **T**. This new proposition, plus *It is a necessary truth that if God permits an evil of type* **T**, *he has no morally sufficient reason for permitting it*, entails *It is a necessary truth that some evil God has permitted is one he has no morally sufficient reason for permitting*—or, to put the same conclusion another way, *It is necessarily false that any evil God permits is one he has a morally sufficient reason for permitting.* Then the questioner—provided some adequate basis could be found for accepting this new proposition—surely would have made the desired case?

In fact, even this is not true. For (a) *It is a necessary truth that God has permitted an evil of type* **T** entails (b) *An evil of type* **T** *exists* and (c) *God has permitted this.* If, for ease of reference, we call the evil in question "Nemesis," then (a) entails both *Nemesis exists* and *God has permitted Nemesis.* Suppose that *Nemesis exists* is a logically contingent proposition; then it is not logically impossible that *Nemesis exists* be false. But if **p** entails **q**, and it is not logically impossible that **q** be false, then it is not logically impossible that **p** be false. So if *Nemesis exists* is contingent, (a) is false, and the questioner's strategy fails for that reason. So that strategy requires that *Nemesis exists* be a necessary truth. Unfortunately for the questioner's strategy, if *Nemesis exists* is a necessary truth, then that Nemesis exists is not a state of affairs God could do anything about, and so not a state of affairs that God permitted. Hence, it is not a state of affairs that God permitted but lacked sufficient reason for permitting. Thus the questioner's strategy fails for that reason.

Perhaps the reasoning behind this last move is not evident. Why is it true that if *Nemesis exists* is a necessary truth, then the existence of Nemesis is not an evil state of affairs that God has permitted? One way of answering this question is to focus on the

4. If we suppose that the set **A**, **B**, **C** is a consistent set that contains only true members, and **A**, **D**, **C** is a consistent set that contains one false member, and that no member of either set is self-contradictory, then an appeal to the consistency of **A** *and* **C** that rests on the consistency of the latter set is as legitimate as an appeal to the consistency of **A** *and* **C** that rests on the consistency of the former set.

notion of a necessary truth. Such a truth is true under any possible conditions God could bring about or allow to occur; it is true whatever God does or fails to do. Another way of answering it is to focus on the notion of an omnipotent God. Roughly, anyway, to say that God is omnipotent is to say that, for any proposition **A**, if **A** is not a contradiction, and if *God makes* **A** *true* is not a contradiction,[5] then God can make **A** true. *There is a Euclidean triangle which has four interior angles* is a contradiction; it is false in all possible conditions. So there is no world or condition God could create that would make it true. This is not a limit on God's power; it is just a fact about contradictory propositions. If *Nemesis exists* is a necessary truth, then *Nemesis does not exist* is a contradiction. For God to be omnipotent does not entail that he can make contradictions true. Any evils that have logically necessary existence, or are logically necessary beings, are not beings God has permitted, or failed to permit, to exist; their nonexistence simply is logically impossible—they will not fail to exist in any world, or under any conditions, that even an omnipotent God creates. Thus, whether *Nemesis exists* is a necessary truth or not, the questioner's strategy fails. Perhaps the thing to do, then, is to admit what seems clearly true, namely that there is no logical incompatibility between *God exists* and *There is evil.* This does not entail that *There is evil* is not evidence against *God exists*; that **p** is logically compatible with **q** does not entail that **p** is not evidence against **q**.

ON ONE PROPOSITIONAL BEING EVIDENCE AGAINST ANOTHER WITH WHICH IT IS LOGICALLY CONSISTENT

That a small child, told by its mother a moment ago not to take any chocolate chip cookies, is found upon the mother's return to have chocolate and crumbs over its hands and face after a manner corresponding to the lowered number of cookies in the jar, does not entail that the child has been disobedient. Perhaps the child's elder

5. *Uranus was not created by God* is not a contradiction. It is true only if both (a) *Uranus exists* and (b) *God did not create Uranus* are true. But God cannot make *Uranus was not created by God* true; in order to do so, God would have both to have, and not to have, created Uranus. For God to be omnipotent requires that he be able both to create Uranus, and able to refrain from doing so, but not that he be able to both create and not create it.

sibling has framed it. Perhaps the cookies spontaneously disappeared and the crumbs and chocolate on the child sprang from nothing. But the evidence suggests otherwise. One proposition can be evidence against another without it (by itself) entailing the negation of the other. Perhaps, then, the thing to do is to drop the questioner's strategy and replace it by the critic's contention that there being evil provides evidence against the existence of God, even though *God exists* and *There is evil* are not logically incompatible. How can this contention be developed?

AN ARGUMENT THAT *THERE IS EVIL* CONSTITUTES EVIDENCE AGAINST *GOD EXISTS*

One way of developing the critic's contention is to argue inductively as follows: (i) there are a great many evils; (ii) if there are a great many evils, then (probably) some of them are evils that God is not justified in permitting; so (iii) (probably) some of them are evils God is not justified in permitting. The argument plainly requires premise (ii), but how is this premise to be justified? The implicit suggestion is that, in a crucial respect, evils are like apples, coins, or bottles: given the conditions that obtain in our world, and given enough apples, some apples will be bruised; given those conditions and enough coins, some coins will be scratched; given those conditions and enough bottles, some bottles will be broken. We know these mundane things because (a) we know how to identify bruised apples as well as unbruised ones, scratched coins as well as unscratched ones, and broken bottles as well as whole ones, and (b) have seen bruised apples, scratched coins, and broken bottles. The implicit suggestion is that we are able to accomplish the same sort of things regarding evils—or else that the same sort of thing is true of evils (namely, that some of them are evils such that, if God exists, then God is justified in permitting them, and some are not) as is true of apples (namely, that some are unbruised, and some are not), and the like, because, in each case, there are so many of them.

A REPLY TO THE ARGUMENT

In fact, however, while we often can discern that some state of affairs is evil, there is no discernible or observable feature of an evil which is either *God's being justified in allowing it* or *God's not being justified in allowing it*; in the case of evils, we do not have something like (a). *A fortiori*; we do not have something like (b) in the case of evils. So we have no grounds of that sort for thinking (ii) is true.

Put another way, the argument under discussion suggests that we will have no reason to think that premise (ii) is true unless we can discover among the evils that have been experienced some evils that have, and others that lack, the property *being such that God has morally sufficient reason for permitting it,* and that we have good reason to think our "sample class" of evils is representative so that we can fairly extrapolate from it to generalizations about the class of evils as a whole. In fact, if we discover even one evil that has the property in question, that discovery all by itself will confirm premise (ii).

The problem remains how we are to tell that an evil has (or, for that matter, lacks) the property in question. Of course, if we know that monotheism is true, then we will know that every evil has that property, and if we know that monotheism is false, we will know that no evil has it. But appeal to evil was supposed to be helpful in solving that issue, not to assume that the issue has already been settled. Short of knowing already that God does exist (or that he does not), the task of discovering that some particular evil has (or lacks) the property in question will be an impossible one—and if it is, the critic has no basis for accepting premise (ii).

THE REDUNDANCY OF THIS ARGUMENT

It is worth emphasizing that, if the strategy implicitly involved in the argument we have been considering were to work, the argument itself would be unnecessary. Suppose one discovered that some particular evil **E** lacked the property *God's being justified in permitting* **E**; then one of course has discovered that God has no morally sufficient reason for permitting an actual evil; and since it follows from the proposition *God exists* that he has a morally sufficient reason for permitting every evil there is, it follows from our having discovered such an evil that God does not exist.

ANOTHER CRITICAL ARGUMENT

Perhaps the critic can build on this fact. It is patent that some evil has this feature: *if God has a morally sufficient reason for permitting it, no human being knows what it is*; indeed, it seems likely that almost every evil has this feature. Or, more modestly, concerning some particular person **N** and some particular evil **E**, it will be true that (iv) *If God has a morally sufficient reason for permitting* **E**, **N** *does not* *know what it is.* Then the critic can argue that (v) *If* **N** *does not know what morally sufficient reason (if any) God has for permitting* **E**, **N** *is not reasonable in thinking that* **E** *is such that God has a morally sufficient reason for permitting it*; so (vi) **N** *is not reasonable in thinking that* **E** *is such that God has a morally sufficient reason for permitting it.*

This argument is considerably less promising than it might seem. If **N** has any reason to think theism true, then **N** has reason to think that what theism entails is true, and theism entails that God has a morally sufficient reason for permitting whatever evils he permits. But the proposition (vii) **N** *has reason to think that theism is true* does not entail that (viii) *there is some evil* **E** *such that* **N** *knows what God's reason for permitting* **E** *is*; so (vii) can be true, even though (iv) is true—even though there are evils such that, if God has a morally sufficient reason for allowing them, **N** does not know what that reason is. Further, if (vii) is true, **N** has reason to think that (ix) *God has a morally sufficient reason for permitting every evil he permits* is also true. The critic, then, must assume that (vii) is false; but the argument does nothing to establish this, and certainly is not supposed to have to make any such assumption.

The argument has additional difficulties as well. What it requires is some such claim as (v') **N** *has reason not to think that some evil* **E** *is such that God has a morally sufficient reason for permitting it*: it must not merely be the case that **N** ought to suspend judgment regarding whether or not God has a morally sufficient reason for allowing **E**; it must be the case that **N**'s not having a reason to think **E** has the requisite property will entail that **N** does have a reason for thinking that it indeed does not have this property. This further step is legitimate only if some such claim as the following is true: (x) if God does have a morally sufficient reason for allowing **E**, then **N** will know what that reason is. But there seems to be no reason to think that (x) is true, no reason to suppose **N** is or must be privy to any reason of this sort, and so this version of the critic's contention also seems to fail.

In sum, it is frequently assumed that one can argue: there are evils such that the proposition (1) *There are evils such that if God has a morally sufficient reason for allowing them we do not know that reason* is both true and embarrassing to theism. It seems true. It is embarrassing to theism only if some such claims as: (2) *If (1) is true, then God has no morally sufficient reason for allowing these evils,* or (3) *If (1) is true, then it is reasonable to believe that God has no morally sufficient reason for allowing these evils.* (1) seems clearly true, but (2) does not seem clearly true, and in order to justify (2) one would have to establish that (1) provided grounds for (2)'s consequent. That we know of no such reason as (1) refers to hardly seems grounds for saying there is none. Nor is it clear that (3) is true and in order to establish (3) one would have to establish that (1) provided grounds for (3)'s consequent. (1) is compatible with a person simply suspending judgment relative to whether such a reason exists; it is also compatible with one's thinking there is such a reason, and doing so with complete epistemic propriety, provided one has some reason to think theism true. So (1)'s truth is not encouraging regarding (3)'s. It may be clear that (1) is not evidence *for* theism, but that hardly seems helpful to the critic's case.

APPARENTLY POINTLESS EVILS

It is not merely the case that there are evils such that, if God has a morally sufficient reason for allowing them, no one knows what that reason is. It is the case that some evils appear, and are, horrendous—ghastly in their nature and consequences. Only one whose experience has been remarkably sheltered could be excused for denying this. Not only does one not see that any good comes from them; it is also hard to see what good could come from them, or what could be such that it was a reason for an omnicompetent being, or any being aware of them and also able to prevent them, to allow them to occur. If theism is not compatible with this, then so much the worse for theism; many intelligent and morally sensitive persons have drawn the conclusion that theism is false for just this reason. But many intelligent and morally sensitive persons have thought this perspective mistaken.

How, exactly, does the argument go? After all, the dispute is about whether a certain permise or set of premises entails, or in some other manner makes it unreasonable not to draw, a certain conclusion. The premise goes something like this: (1) *There are evils which are vicious, horrendous, ghastly, both in their nature and their consequences, and we can see no redeeming features to them or reasons that might motivate an omnicompetent deity to allow them*. The conclusion goes something like this: (2) *Either (2a) There are no such reasons (so God does not exist) or (2b) It is unreasonable to think there are any such reasons (so it is unreasonable to think that God exists).*

The inference from (1) to (2a) or (2b) is similar to the argument just discussed; the basic difference is that this argument states the data more dramatically. (1) does not *entail* (2a); (1) does not *entail* (2b). What, then, exactly is the epistemic connection between (1) and (2a), or (1) and (2b). Presumably, the idea is that there is some one-or-more-membered set of propositions S such that S contains only truths and such that S *and (1)* entails (2a), or else (2b). Attempts to find a premise with *epistemic* content to play the role of S were investigated above; perhaps a different result can be obtained if propositions with *ethical* content are considered.

The move from (1) to (2) is enhanced if one adds some formulation of hedonism, for which only pain (or reduction of pleasure) is intrinsically evil, only what produces pain (or pleasure-reduction) is extrinsically evil, only pleasure (or reduction of pain) is intrinsically good, and only what produces pleasure (or pain-reduction) is extrinsically good. The only moral point suffering could have from this perspective is as a contrast—a change of pace—that in certain contexts might give pleasure all the more zest. Given a hedonistic ethic, then, there is great promise of beginning with (1) and ending with (2). But then either the critic must establish the truth of hedonism or else show that, whether hedonism is true or false, at any rate monotheism entails it. Otherwise, appeal to hedonism will not help. This particular argument will not succeed. Monotheism does not entail hedonism, and hedonism is false. But perhaps other ethical theories will fare better as potential bridges from (1) to (2).

WORLDS AND EVILS

In fact, one might try to begin, not with ethical theories, but with very basic, rather abstract, propositions as candidates for S (i.e., for being true and, together with (1), entailing (2)). Consider, then, the claim that (1a) *Any world containing no evil is morally better than any world containing some.* Then, as (1)—i.e., *There is evil, etc.*—is true, if we add (1a) and (1a) is true, it will follow that (1a1) *Our world is morally worse than any world which does not contain evil.* But (1a1) is not (2); it is neither (2a) nor (2b), and it entails neither. It will have to be supplemented, then, if it is to serve as a bridge between (1) and (2).

Supplementing (1a1) will be futile, because it is false. Consider two worlds, one (World **A**) comprised of a single pebble everlastingly rolling around a single circular hollow iron band, and another

(World **B**) comprised of a million moral agents whose long history of righteousness and justice, with deeds of great goodness, is blemished only by one child once stealing a penny from its mother's purse, this wrong action being followed by repentance and forgiveness. Given (1a1), **A** is morally better than **B**, since **B** contains an evil and **A** does not, though **A** contains no moral good either; but **B** seems morally far superior to **A**.

Perhaps the thing to do, then, is to replace (1a1) by (1b) *If worlds* **A** *and* **B** *both contain moral good, and* **B** *contains some moral evil but* **A** *does not, then* **A** *is morally better than* **B**. But suppose world **B** is as before whereas **A** is a world in which moral choices are few and rather insignificant, though what few there are, are made rightly. Then it will be very plausible indeed that **B** is morally superior to **A**, contrary to (1b). This moves us to (1c) *If worlds* **A** *and* **B** *contain equal moral good, and* **B** *contains moral evil but* **A** *does not, then* **A** *is better than* **B**. Perhaps (1c) is true; added to (1), does this get one to (2)? Not by itself; (1) says that really terrible things occur, and (1c) says that of two worlds which are morally equal, save that one of them contains some evil, the one without evil is better. (1) and (1c) do not entail (2).

WORLDS GOD CANNOT CREATE

One might argue that if a world **A** is better than another world **B**, then plainly an omnicompetent being will not create **B**. This is false for two sorts of reasons. Suppose **A** is a world in which all moral decisions are made rightly, and **B** is a world in which some moral actions are made rightly and others are made wrongly. Let a *moral action* be one performance of which is either right, or else wrong, and is free, where *action* **C** *of person* **S** *at time* **t** *is free* if and only if *at* **t**, **S** *in fact can perform* **C** *and* **S** *in fact can fail to perform* **C**. If God ordains that **S** do **C** at **t**, or creates the world in such a fashion that **S** shall do **C** at **t**, then **S** is not free with respect to doing **C** at **t**; the same goes, of course, if God ordains that, or creates the world so that, **S** shall refrain from doing **C** at **t**.

It turns out, then, that (in one sense) God cannot create world **A** or world **B**. Worlds **A** and **B** contain moral actions, and hence free actions. If to create a world is to ordain everything that occurs in it, God cannot create **A** or **B**. Of course, God can bring about an environment in which **S** can live, and bring **S** into being, granting **S** the ability to choose freely with regard to **C**. It is sometimes presented as a limitation on divine omnipotence, or divine sovereignty (the providential exercise of omnipotence), that there should be free agents, or persons capable of free action. But if *there being (free) agents* is one possibility, and *there being no (free) agents* is another, presumably making the former possibility actual is at least as much an exercise of creative power as is making the latter possibility actual; and presumably *being providential over a world containing (free) agents* is at least as much an exercise of sovereignty as is *being providential over a world containing no (free) agents*. If God creates Ralph as a moral, and so free, agent, then God cannot also determine, in each case of Ralph's acting, what Ralph shall do. But then if God creates Ralph unfree, then God cannot also leave it up to Ralph, in each case of Ralph's acting, what Ralph shall do. One might as well argue, then (as some absurdly have), that to create at all limits sovereignty, since if God brings **X** into being this forfeits the golden opportunity of *not* doing so, and if God fails to bring **X** into being this forfeits the golden opportunity to create **X**, so that either way sovereignty is lost; only an everlastingly inactive deity is fully sovereign in the sense of keeping all his options open. One defect of this line is that a God who thus far has created no **X** has forfeited the chance to have already done so, and hence, on the view of sovereignty in question, has lost his sovereignty already. Another defect is that so fragile a sovereignty is not worth having.

There are some states of affairs an omnipotent deity cannot bring about. He cannot bring it about that *Ralph does, but also does not, exist at time* **t**. Nor can he bring it about that *Uranus is an uncreated planet*. The former would require that God create Ralph at **t**, or create him prior to **t** and sustain him in existence at least until **t**, but also that he do neither of these things. The latter would require that he create the planet Uranus, and also that he not. The proposition *Ralph exists, but also does not exist, at* **t** is a contradiction; it is logically impossible that any state of affairs correspond to it, so it is misleading to speak of God's "not being able" to create a state of affairs corresponding to that proposition. *Uranus is an uncreated planet* is not a contradiction; it is logically possible that a state of affairs correspond to it. But it is not possible that God, or any agent, bring about that state of affairs.

The relevant points can be put as follows. Let **R** refer to the proposition concerning Ralph's existence, and **U** refer to the proposition concerning Uranus. **R** is a contradiction; no state of affairs could correspond to **R**; there is no possible action described by *making* **R** *true* because **R** is a contradiction. **U** is not a contradiction; a state of affairs could correspond to **U**; there is no possible action described by *making* **U** *true* because it is inconsistent with **U**'s *being* true that anyone so act as to *make* it true. There is nothing mysterious or peculiar about **U**. It is possible that there be an island that no one ever discovers; it is not possible that someone discover an island that no one ever discovers. It is possible that there be a scientific theory no one ever posits; it is not possible that one posit a scientific theory which no one ever posits. It is possible that there be a number one higher than any number any human being ever specifically thinks of; it is not possible that someone specifically think of a number one higher than any human being ever specifically thinks of. The island can be discovered, or the theory posited, or the number specifically brought to mind; once this happened, the *no one ever discovers, posits, or specifically thinks of* part of the description is rendered false. Analogously, an omnicompetent deity can create Uranus; once he does, it exists, but of course not as an *uncreated* planet.

There is no possible action described by *making* **R** *true* or *making* **U** *true;* omnipotence does not include or fail to include such actions, since there are no such actions to be or not to be included within the range of omnipotence.

Returning to the critic's contention, then, a world in which all agents always chose rightly might indeed be better than a world in which those same agents (or others as like them as possible) sometimes chose wrongly; but God (in one sense) cannot create that world. God creates the conditions under which agents exercise their autonomy, and creates autonomous agents who then exercise that autonomy either rightly or wrongly. It seems not inappropriate to say that under such circumstances, in a modest way, agents are cocreators of the universe that results—cocreators in the sense that the moral conditions that obtain in the universe are functions, in part, of their morally relevant choices and actions as the physical conditions that obtain in the universe are functions, in part, of their choices and actions regarding cities and highways. If to create a world *simpliciter* is to create a world so that every property it ever has is determined by the creator at the moment of its creation, God cannot create *simpliciter* a world containing moral agents. So he cannot create *simpliciter* a world in which all autonomous agents always choose rightly.

Perhaps he also cannot create *simpliciter* the "best of all possible world." He cannot do so if it contains moral agents. He also cannot do so if it is true, as Aquinas thought, that *no* world is such that creating it exhausts what an omnicompetent being can do regarding moral worth; then, as there is no "best possible world," there can be no such thing as creating it. Even to create a world with an infinite number of moral agents is compatible with that world's not including Ralph, another moral agent, whose existence in that world may not be incompatible with the existence of the infinite number of agents already there; and if Ralph is added, perhaps there is always a Ralph who is related to the universe which includes Ralph in the same way as Ralph was to the universe that did not include him.

In any case, it would seem that the critic eventually runs directly into a most inconvenient fact: that world **A** is better than world **B** does not entail that God ought to create **A** rather than **B**, even if those are the only relevant choices, since it may be that *God creates* **B** *simpliciter* is a contradiction and so describes no possible action at all. Furthermore, it may be that for any worlds **A** and **B** such that **A** is morally better than **B**, there is also a world **C** that is better than **A**, and a world **D** that is better than **C**, and that all of these truths are *necessary* truths, so that the proposition *Either God creates a world* **W1** *such that a world* **W2** *would be better had he created it (assuming he could create it), or else God does not create at all* is also true and necessarily so. Apparently, this will be so if (in some sense) there is an infinitely ascending series of descriptions such that each describes a world still more elegant morally than its predecessor. Then God's obligation, so to speak, is to create some world such that it is better that it exist than that it not exist.

Perhaps it is true that there are certain worlds that God cannot create *simpliciter*, and perhaps it is true that among those he can create *simpliciter* it is always true that, for any world he were to create, he could create a better one, so that *Ralph can conceive of a better world than ours* is not evidence for *God did not create our world* or *God should not create a world such as ours*; perhaps it is also true that although our world could be better in ever so many ways, that fact does not in itself constitute any evidence at all that God did not create it. Even if these contentions are in fact true, however, they do not exhaust the critic's resources.

ON CREATING ONLY MORALLY SUPERIOR PERSONS

The critic might proceed from the plausible assumption that some moral choices are morally more significant than others—that in ordinary circumstances, the theft of a quarter is plainly less evil than a murder, say, and the sacrifice of one of one's kidneys to save another's life is plainly more admirable than giving a quarter to charity. If a *moral saint* is a moral agent who makes very many significant moral choices and always makes them freely and rightly, then one might presume that a world containing a large number of moral saints will be morally much the richer for this fact, and it might be argued that a God possessed of omnicompetence would create only moral saints. Or, just to be safe, one might lower the requirement to include simply *morally superior persons* (those being persons who fall short of being moral saints only by virtue of having performed a few morally insignificant wrong actions, among many right actions, early in life). Then one could argue that God perhaps will also create morally superior persons, but that if he is all-good, all-knowing, and all-powerful, he will not create any creature who will become less than a morally superior being—he will not create any Hitlers, Borgias, and Genghis Khans. And since our world contains an undeniable abundance of pesons who fall far short of being morally superior beings, let alone moral saints, one might argue that God did not create our world, contrary to the contention of theism, and so theism must be false.

As it stands, this argument is not very powerful. There are many persons who are not morally superior beings (perhaps *no* persons achieve even this status), and yet it seems overly harsh to suggest that it would be morally better that they not exist, or that their existence is a blot on the universe. It seems likely that everyone who loves someone else loves someone who falls short of being a morally superior being, but would disagree (and plausibly so) with the view that it would be morally preferable had the object of his or her love never so much as existed.

One might tighten the reasoning behind the objection along the following lines. It is logically possible for only moral saints, or only moral saints and morally superior beings, to exist. A world in which everyone is a moral saint, or at least is morally superior, is a better world than ours (perhaps it is about as much as we can expect along the lines of a "best possible world"). Since it is a logically possible world, it is one God could have created. If God exists, and is omnicompetent, it should be the world that actually exists. But it is not true that the actual world contains only moral saints, or moral saints and morally superior beings; so there is no God.

This line of reasoning is defective in various ways. For one thing, while it is logically possible for only moral saints to exist, whether a moral agent becomes a moral saint or not depends on choices freely made by the agent: God cannot create *simpliciter* even one moral saint, or morally superior being (or one grievous sinner, for that matter). Perhaps the idea is that God should create only those agents who, if created, would so choose as to become moral saints, or at least morally superior beings. But it is *not a conceptual question* whether there are *any* persons who, if created, would always or usually choose freely and rightly. Perhaps there is none—at least that would seem to be a fair conclusion to reach if we are to judge by what moral agents do exist (or, more accurately, if those persons who actually do exist are in fact moral agents created by God, and are a fair sample of persons who might be created). At any rate, if we can reason inductively about this matter, the inductively justified conclusion would seem to be that if other persons had been created in place of those who actually were created, we can suppose that they would likely be of much the same moral quality. Perhaps there are exactly seven persons in all of history who, if created, would always choose freely and rightly, and perhaps they lived so long ago that there is no surviving record of their existence. Perhaps there are seventy such, all of whom will be created in the year 2000. Perhaps there are billions of them who have been created on other planets. One such speculation is as worthless as another; the relevant point is that sheer reflection will not tell us whether there are any such persons or not (nor will it tell us, in the event that there are such persons, whether they may already have been created or have yet to be created).

Another problem is that, as noted above, it is not the case that if **X** is better than **Y**, then God ought to create **X** rather than **Y**. It may be that for any thing God has created, he could have created something better; this would suggest that God would have to choose between either not creating anything at all or else creating something such that he can be criticized for being able to do better than he did. If there are worlds God could create such that it would be better for him to create them than not to create them, and no world that would be the best he could create, then it will be true both that (i) for any world God creates, he can do better, and (ii) it is better that God create than that he not create. Then God will be subject to the "criticism" noted above, even though, so to speak, he has "done the right thing." In fact, however, "criticism" that can be made under such circumstances is no criticism at all.

Furthermore, the fact that it is extremely good for God to create persons (if any) who will become moral saints does not entail that it is not very good for him to create persons (if any) who will become rather ordinary persons, morally speaking. No matter how many persons there are who, once created, will become moral saints, there seems no reason to think that God somehow does wrong, or other than right, in *also* creating persons who, once created, will merely become morally adequate.

Once one recognizes that the question of whether there are any persons who, if created, would become moral saints, or morally superior persons, is *not* a conceptual question, not a matter that can be decided by reflection alone (it is empirical only in the broad sense of *not being conceptual*), the cogency of the objection under review is greatly diminished, if not eliminated altogether; the defects of the objection, taken together, are too great for that objection to constitute a successful way of putting the critic's contention.

EVILS WITHOUT ANY KNOWN PURPOSE

Even if the critics' objections are groundless, however, it would still seem to be the case that theists have to admit that they do not know what the morally sufficient reason is that God *ex hypothesi* has for allowing many or most or perhaps almost all evils. There need be nothing about the reason (which might be a set of different reasons) that renders it *in principle* unknowable, or incommunicable, or the like; the theist simply does not know what it is.

The only reason we might have for holding that God has any such reason is whatever reason we have to think theism true; the only reason we might have for holding that God has no such reason is whatever reason we have for thinking that theism is false; if we have no reasons for thinking theism to be true and none for thinking it to be false, then we also have no reason to justify us in holding that God either has or lacks such a reason. Putting it differently, it is a necessary truth that *if (and only if) God exists, he has a morally sufficient reason for permitting whatever evil he permits*; whatever reason we have for holding that the proposition *God exists* is true, we have for thinking the proposition *God has a morally sufficient reason for permitting whatever evil he permits* is true; and whatever reason we have for holding that the former proposition is false, we have for thinking the latter proposition is false; and if we have no reasons, pro or con, regarding the former proposition, we have no reasons, pro or con, regarding the latter.

That there is mutual implication between propositions **P** and **Q** does not entail that **P** and **Q** are equally accessible epistemically. It might be that the only way to know whether **Q** is true or not is to determine whether **P** is true or not, and that we can determine whether **P** is true without first having had to determine the truth value of **Q**, whereas we cannot determine the truth value of **Q** unless we already know the truth value of **P** and also know that the proposition **P** *if and only if* **Q** is true (or at any rate that **P** *implies* **Q** is true). It may be that although (G1) *God exists* is true if and only if (G2) *God has a morally sufficient reason for permitting every evil that he permits* is true, so that (G1) and (G2) imply one another, we nevertheless cannot tell whether (G2) is true in any other way than by discovering whether (G1) is true and knowing that *(G1) if and only if (G2)* is true (or at least that *(G1) implies (G2)* is true).[6]

If this is so—if the truth value of (G2) is epistemically accessible only through our determination of the truth value of (G1)—then appeal to the alleged falsity (G2) as evidence against theism is otiose. Since (G1) is obviously essential to theism (by virtue of the fact that it expresses its basic tenet), it must be assessed directly whether favorably or unfavorably, and not through (G2).

THEISM AND THEODICY[7]

If the preceding line of reasoning is correct, it is also important regarding the problem of evil. The importance can be highlighted

6. If we know that (G1) is true, we can know that (G2) is true by knowing that (G1) implies (G2), or by knowing that (G1) and (G2) are related by mutual implication, whereas if we know that (G1) is false, we will have to know that (G1) and (G2) imply one another or that (G2) implies (G1) in order validly to conclude that (G2) is false.

7. A *theodicy* is an attempt by a theist to *explain* the fact that there is evil.

as follows. If the propositions *God exists* and *God has a morally sufficient reason for permitting every evil that he permits* are both true, then the existence of evil is not evidence that God does not exist. So *There is evil* is (and thus can be known to be) evidence that *God exists* is false only if the proposition *There are evils that God has no morally sufficient reason for permitting* is (and is known or reasonably believed to be) true. But it is hard to see how one could know or reasonably believe this latter proposition without already knowing that God does not exist (and so having to know this on the basis of some grounds *other than* the problem of evil).

However important this consideration may be, it remains true that the theist will not be able to specify the *ex hypothesi* reason for allowing an evil. By itself this fact does not seem damaging, inasmuch as it seems unreasonable to require that a theist be able to do this, involving as it does the possession of a piece of information beyond the scope of normal human comprehension. But it does not seem unreasonable to expect that those theists capable of dealing competently with ethical theory should specify something of the sort of things that, if true, would constitute morally sufficient reasons for some of the evils that obviously exist. Even this expectation needs carefully qualified statement, however; it is not reasonable to expect a speculative account of the cosmos that, if true, would constitute a reason for a particular evil to have been allowed.

THEISM AND ETHICAL THEORY

What this qualification amounts to can be stated along these lines. Suppose an infant drowns. Perhaps a theist reasonably might be expected to say something about whether death is an evil, and if so what sort of morally sufficient reason, in general, there might be for allowing it. If a theist *never* could say any such thing about any evil—not from lack of intelligence or training, but because no sufficiently rich content can be attached to the notion of a morally sufficient reason in the sense in which it has occurred in the discussion thus far, then perhaps there is not much force in the suggestion that God has any such reason (though it could nonetheless be used in applications of *the consistency strategy*). But the theist, however well trained, is not reasonably expected to tell stories about, say, the infant's afterlife in which its death by drowning plays an essential, or at least a significant, role in the infant's post-drowning life in heaven, or the like.

What this apparently reasonable demand amounts to, then, is this: the theist is neither responsible for giving speculative accounts of how a given evil might fit (in a morally elegant manner) into the biography of the one it befell, nor allowed to keep the content of "morally sufficient reason for allowing evil" at the level of "reason that does not make those who possess it culpable for allowing the evil they permit" (except to the extent that the consistency strategy is in view); something between these two extremes might reasonably be thought possible if theism is to deal plausibly with the fact of evil. Perhaps nothing more is at issue here than this: if theism is true and interesting, it should have something illuminating to say with regard to evil. Perhaps it is *this* issue, rather than the claim that the proposition *There is evil* provides some presumptive evidence against theism, that lies at the core of the critic's contention. At least, perhaps this is so if theism's "having something illuminating to say with regard to evil" is understood to involve its having something illuminating to say about good as well as evil, and how evil might itself be made to serve a good purpose without thereby ceasing to be evil.

The implication of these considerations would seem to be that unless theism can provide an ethical theory or theories (or at least the beginnings or nucleus of an ethical theory or family of ethical theories) in which, so to speak, evil can be seen as having some point—as not being what an earlier generation of philosophers would have called a *surd* (i.e., an inexplicable entity not plausibly viewed as primitive, a thing conceptually indigestible, at least by the theories at hand)—then this is itself something to the epistemic discredit of theism. Independent of any consideration of the problem of evil, it seems true that a theism that has no consequences regarding ethics, and from which nothing of relevance to ethical theory can be derived, is "conceptually thin" in so significant a way as to require explanation. Perhaps here critic and theist can agree: if the content of theism does not allow us to generate an ethical theory that is rationally defensible and for which the existence of evil is not a surd, then we can conclude that theism cannot illumine or yield understanding concerning the existence of evil, despite the fact that it should do so—and in that case the fact that there is evil would constitute evidence against the existence of God after all.

What seems appropriate, then, is a discussion of (at least one variety) of theistic ethics, and a consideration of this might provide relevant content to the notion of a "morally sufficient reason" as it appears in the proposition *Necessarily, if (and only if) God exists, then God has a morally sufficient reason for permitting whatever evil he permits.*

There are various ways of developing a theistic ethic, of combining the philosophical tradition in ethics (itself not unaffected by the claims and concepts of monotheism) and the conceptual resources of a monotheistic theology. Any such attempt is subject to critique on both philosophical and theological grounds; obviously this is true of the following briefly introduced general themes relevant to a discussion of theistic ethics.

THEISTIC ETHICS AND THE PROBLEM OF EVIL

The concern here is with theistic ethics and the problem of evil. One theme relevant to this concern relates to the connection between good and evil. It would seem that at least some goods are logically impossible without corresponding evils; if fear is an evil and courage a good, for instance, then since it is logically impossible to have courage without having conquered fear, there is at least one good that is logically impossible without a corresponding evil: the proposition *Ralph is courageous, but has never conquered fear* is a contradiction. When a good **G** and an evil **E** are related in the manner that fear and courage are, the evil is a logically necessary condition of the good—that is to say, evil **E** is a logically necessary condition of good **G** if and only if the proposition **G** *exists, and* **E** *does not* is a contradiction. Pain and fortitude are related in that way; so are suffering and compassion (if the mere appearance of suffering might be sufficient for the existence of compassion, then the appearance of suffering where there is no actual suffering is itself presumably an evil). Theists often argue that these and similar moral goods are highly valuable, and that a moral universe will contain them—but then that universe will also contain evils.

At least two objections can be made to this line of reasoning. One is that the goods in question are good only insofar as they involve the amelioration of evils; like the backscratcher, they derive their value only from what they relieve, and so their value is purely extrinsic. The other objection is that although it is true that genuine courage cannot exist without fear, its emotional and behavioral counterpart can; at any rate, emotional states that are psychologically similar (if not identical) to "felt courage" as well as overt behavior that appears to be similar (if not identical) to "courage in action" could exist in a world in which there is no fear. Perhaps this sort of world, with its high-quality simulation of genuine courage, as it were, would be better than one containing genuine courage, since with genuine courage comes the evil of fear; and perhaps similar remarks can be made, and conclusions drawn, concerning fortitude and compassion and whatever other goods there are that have evils as logically necessary conditions. On certain assumptions, these objections are powerful, perhaps decisive; the assumptions, however, are dubious.

THEISM, EVIL, AND THE LOCUS OF MORAL VALUE

If we assume that the locus of value is conscious states, then the state of being courageous, or of being fortitudinous, or of being compassionate, may have some moral value; but if we ask why people should want to feel fear so that they could feel courageous, or pain so that they could feel fortitudinous, or whether anyone should want someone else to suffer so that he or she could feel compassionate, the answer seems to be that no one could have these desires and be sensible in so doing. It seems that it would be better by far that there be no need for courage because there was no fear, and no need for fortitude because there was no pain, and no need for compassion because there was no suffering. A hedonistic ethical theory, no doubt, would yield this result, but that is because hedonism finds the locus of value in conscious states. It is not the only ethical theory to do so; nor is it the only ethical theory to draw these sorts of conclusions.

If instead one assumes that the locus of value resides first and foremost not in isolated conscious states, but in enduring persons or moral agents, however, then the question becomes not whether a conscious state that depends upon an evil for its existence is worth the price, but whether an environment that allows for the development of moral agents must contain evils, and, if so, whether the existence of moral agents is worth the price.

EVILS AS LOGICALLY NECESSARY CONDITIONS OF GOODS

Various conditions under which an omnicompetent deity would have morally sufficient reason for permitting an evil can be specified. Previously it was suggested that an evil **E** is logically necessary to a good **G** if and only if the proposition **G** *exists, but* **E** *does not* is a contradiction. It will not be frequent that what is required for Ralph's becoming courageous is some particular fear that he must conquer rather than another; what will be requisite is that he conquer some fear or other. Thus, two cases are to be distinguished: one is that in which a particular evil E is related to a particular good G in such a manner that (i) the proposition G *exists but* E *does not* is a contradiction, and (ii) no other evil E1, of the same sort as E, is such that if E1 replaced E, or had obtained rather than E, then G still would exist (i.e., E is *categorically* logically necessary for G); the other case is that in which a particular evil E is related to a particular good G in such a manner that (iii) the proposition G *exists, but no evil of the sort* E *belongs to exists* is a contradiction, and (iv) another evil E1 of the sort E belongs to could replace E, or have obtained rather than E, and G would still exist (i.e., E is *disjunctively* logically necessary for G).

If we suppose that the positive value of G and the negative value of E counterbalance each other, and also that E is distributively (or categorically) logically necessary for G, then presumably it is morally permissible that G obtain—that is to say, if God permits G, he needs no morally sufficient reason for doing so (or else has sufficient reason for doing so). If we suppose that E is distributively (or categorically) logically necessary for G, but that the positive value of G is outweighed by the negative value of E, then presumably it is wrong to permit E to obtain. If we suppose that E is distributively (or categorically) logically necessary for G, and that the positive value of G outweighs the negative value of E, then presumably it is right that G obtain—that is to say, a being who can bring G about is praiseworthy for bringing G about, and a being who can prevent G but does not is praiseworthy for not preventing G. At any rate, it appears that these results will obtain if one assumes that in each case it is only the relation of E to G that has moral significance—that E is not logically requisite to some other good G1, and is not a sufficient condition for some other evil E1, and the like (including such considerations will complicate the statement of the issues, but not materially change anything).

Furthermore, if one supposes that E is distributively (or categorically) logically necessary for G, and that S can either bring about G or prevent G from coming about (and that only the balance between G and E is relevant to what it is right to do), then (i) if E outweighs G, it is wrong for S to bring about or permit G; (ii) if G outweighs E, it is right for S to bring about or allow G; and

(iii) if **G** and **E** counterbalance each other, it is not wrong for **S** to bring about or allow **G**. If it does not count against S's goodness if S does something that is either right or not wrong, then it does not count against God's goodness to allow an evil that is distributively (or categorically) logically necessary for a good that at least counterbalances that evil. If every evil is so related to its own good in such a manner that the good at least counterbalances it, and if some goods outweigh their corresponding evils (the ones that are logically requisite for them), then, assuming that an omnibenevolent being will cause a surfeit of good over evil, it follows that the existence of evil does not count against God's goodness, and hence that it will not provide evidence that would call his existence into question. It seems logically possible that every evil might be counterbalanced or outweighed by its corresponding good, and also that both evil and God might exist, and if one has no reason to think it false that every evil is so related to its own good, then one has no reason to think that the existence of evil constitutes evidence against the existence of God.

FREEDOM AND EVIL

Let us suppose that Ruth freely acts wrongly. It is obvious that God's permitting her to act in this manner is not a matter of his permitting an evil that serves as a logically necessary condition of her being an agent; it is not a logically necessary condition of Ruth's (or anyone's) being a moral agent that she choose wrongly, but only that she choose freely. So if God has any morally sufficient reason for allowing the evil **E** of Ruth's choosing wrongly, it will not be that it serves as a distributively (or categorically) logically necessary condition of her being a moral agent. Of course, each wrong action might nonetheless be a logically necessary condition of some good or other that at least counterbalances it. It is a logically necessary condition of Ruth's being a moral agent that she be able to act wrongly (*acting* being understood to include *making a choice*) as well as that she be able to refrain from acting wrongly. Whether she acts wrongly or not is up to her.

If Ruth acts wrongly at time **t**, the proposition that tells us she did so is logically contingent (and the same holds if she acts rightly). Any person who is a moral agent—that is, any person who acts rightly or wrongly on enough morally significant occasions to be a creator (or co-creator) of his or her moral character—will act freely and rightly, or else freely and wrongly, on a number of occasions;

if one calls the description of how an agent acts on such occasions that agent's *moral biography*, then the fact that a person has the particular moral biography he or she does is logically contingent. If, then, God has a morally sufficient reason for permitting Ruth to exist despite the fact that her moral biography includes wrong actions (and hence contains evil), then it will be the case that *Ruth's existing (and having the moral biography that she does, which includes evil) is morally better than her not existing*; this may be so, even though *Ruth's moral biography contains evil* is logically contingent, and no evil in that biography serves as a logically necessary condition for any good.

One might object that the assumption that a moral agent must be free or autonomous in the sense characterized above has been challenged. It has been thought logically possible that Ruth be such that she is free even though she is always caused by God to choose rightly, where, of course, *God causes Ruth to choose rightly at time* **t** entails *Ruth chooses rightly at* **t**; or that for any agent—Rita, for instance—who is autonomous and sometimes chooses wrongly, it is possible, and better, that Rita not be autonomous and that God cause Rita always to choose rightly. It is *possible* in that Rita, under those conditions, would be a moral agent and *better* in that a person who always chose rightly (even if unfreely) is morally superior to a person who chooses always freely (even if sometimes wrongly). In turn, however, both of these contentions have been strongly challenged; the disagreement as to whether they are true or not is one of the fundamental disagreements among competing ethical theories. In fact, the basic disagreements concerning the problem of evil are themselves fundamentally disagreements of this sort.

CONCLUSION

The existence of evil is evidence that God does not exist if and only if, beginning with (*P*) *There is evil* as a premise, one can provide a derivation that has (C) *God does not exist* as conclusion, where each line (*L*) between premise and conclusion is known or reasonably believed to be true, and where the sum (*SL*) of the lines between (*P*) and (C) is such that (*P*) and (*SL*) entail (C). It is enormously difficult to provide some such derivation; at any rate, none has been discovered here. So the present conclusion is that the fact the evil exists does not provide any reason for thinking that God does not exist.

SUGGESTIONS FOR FURTHER READING

Hick, John. *Evil and the God of Love.* New York: Harper and Row, 1966.

Provides a philosophical discussion of two types of solution to the problem of evil as they have developed historically in Christian thought.

Mavrodes, George. *Belief in God.* New York: Random House, 1970.

Discusses the problem of evil as an epistemic problem in Chapter Four.

Pike, Nelson, ed. *God and Evil.* Englewood Cliffs, NJ: Prentice-Hall, 1964.

Contains the now standard statements of the critic's argument by Mackie and McClosky (and Hume) as well as replies by Pike and Smart.

Plantinga, Alvin. *God and Other Minds.* Ithaca, NY: Cornell University Press, 1967.

______. *The Nature of Necessity.* Oxford: Clarendon Press, 1974.

______. *God, Freedom and Evil.* New York: Harper and Row, 1974.

______. "The Probabilistic Argument from Evil." *Philosophical Studies,* 35 (1979).

Yandell, Keith. "A Premature Farewell to Theism." *Religious Studies,* 5 (1969).

______. "Ethics, Evils and Theism." *Sophia,* 8 (1969).

______. "Theism and Evil." *Sophia,* 11 (1972).

______. "Logic and the Problem of Evil." In Yandell, *God, Man and Religion.* New York: McGraw-Hill, 1973.

______. "The Greater Good Defense." *Sophia,* 13 (1974).

______. "The Problem of Evil." *Philosophical Topics* (Fall, 1982).

______. "A Proposed Solution to the Problem of Evil." *TSF Bulletin,* 6 (1982).

PART FIVE
THEISTIC RELIGION AND MORALITY

ANALYTICAL TABLE OF CONTENTS TO CHAPTER 7

7. If *freedom* is defined as simply "doing what one wants" and *happiness* is defined as simply "getting what one wants," then these terms will produce highly implausible doctrines. 256
8. The contention that morality is simply a survival technique with whatever rights and obligations there are being generated by contracts and consistency constitutes a view that confuses prudence with morality and ignores the facts that not all obligations can be contractually generated and that justice cannot be the only value; consistency generates justice if it generates anything moral, but in fact it generates nothing moral at all. 257
9. The view that **x** *is right* means *God wills* **x** entails that *God does what is right* means no more than that *God does what he wills* and also necessitates abandoning the notion that God has reasons for declaring things to be right; alternatively, one can regard *God wills* **x** as entailing **x** *is right* because God is omniscient and omnibenevolent, but this does not tell us what is right or why. 259
10. One approach to the construction of a theistic ethic begins by arguing that persons are created in the image of God and then relates this fact to the concepts of *moral agent* and *moral character*; according to this view, the inherent value of all persons is a function of their having been made in God's image—of their being like the Creator in morally relevant ways—and this value remains independent of the individual ways in which persons might act or the character they might develop. 259
11. Particular obligations are entailed by an overarching obligation to develop one's potential as a being that has been created in the divine image (i.e., a being that has rational, moral, and social characteristics and that is capable of *agapē*). 260
12. It might seem reasonable to contend that the *imago Dei* comprises capacities or properties that have inherent value, but this is actually not so, since such value can be ascribed only to persons, not properties. 262
13. The sort of theistic ethics described above bases "act morality" on "agent morality." 264
14. The sense in which even persons have inherent value also has its crucial qualifications. 265
15. An ethic based on agent morality will be nonutilitarian. 265

CHAPTER 7

HOW (IF AT ALL) ARE RELIGION AND MORALITY RELATED?

WHAT HAS VALUE AND WHAT IS VALUED

That one is willing to ascribe truth value to moral claims places one among those whose view in ethics is "cognitivist"; it does not decide what variety of cognitive theory one will hold.[1] The first portion of this chapter will consider various attempts to construct a nontheistic ethical theory which makes no explicit appeal to metaphysics or to anything that is not easily and empirically accessible.

What moral cognitivists often, and understandably, seek is a way of showing that a moral judgment, rule, or principle—a moral claim of some sort—is true which is maximally simple and straightforward, one which appeals to obviously sound data and proceeds from it by lucid and patent inference. One such attempt is to argue: persons value **x**, what persons value is valuable, so **x** is valuable. So long as an appropriate value for **x** is chosen—health, friendship, pleasure, say, rather than illness, enmity, and pain—one can begin

1. Conceivably, one could hold that a moral judgment, rule, or principle was either true or false, but one could never tell which. This would deny the claim that if a statement has truth value, there is (in our possession) a way of finding out what that truth value is, though it would be consistent with the view that if a statement has truth value, then there is (in principle) a way of finding out what that truth value is (though we may not find out what that way is, or if we do find out what it is, we may not be able to apply it effectively). This view would be very similar to sheer scepticism in its effect on ethics; no substantive moral knowledge would be possible. Insofar as the argument to this point has shown that some ethical theories or principles are false, or are more reasonably taken to be false than taken to be true, that argument has force against this weakest possible variety of moral cognitivism as well.

with a proposition which plainly is true. But is it true that what persons (all persons, or most persons, or the majority of persons, or the like) value is valuable? Yes, if "valuable" means "capable of being valued"; but then the conclusion will read "What people do value is something people are capable of valuing." Obviously true, this conclusion is neither something that requires defense (it is a necessarily true proposition that if **S** does **A**, then **S** can do **A**) nor is it a moral principle or the basis for a moral theory. No, if "valuable" means "possessed of moral value"; it is not a contradiction, and it is not always false, that what is widely or universally valued (is *anything* valued by *absolutely* everyone?) lack moral value altogether.

The traditional, and not unreasonable, response is to suggest that one take as valuable (in the "possessing value" sense) what meets this condition: that it is preferred by those who have experienced it and its lack, or it and its competitors, and who reflectively prefer it over its absence or over its competitors. But then this preference will be one held for reasons or else not. If it is not—if this select group of reflective experiences have no reason for preferring as they do—then why should one think that the fact that they prefer as they do is a matter of their having discovered something which possesses moral value? But if they have reasons for their preferences, then either these reasons are reasons for thinking what is preferred has moral value or not. If not, then their preferring what they prefer is no reason to think that what they prefer has value. If so, then it is the reasons that provide the evidence that what is preferred has value, not the sheer fact of its being preferred.

It is easy to say that it is the *being approved by those who reflectively prefer* **x** *to* **x**'s *absence and/or* **x**'s *competitors, having experienced both* that comprises or constitutes *having moral value*, and when it is pointed out that is is not logically impossible that something have the former property and not the latter, and that the preference be based on grounds irrelevant to (or incompatible with) the item preferred possessing such value, to switch, for the moment at any rate, to the view that such preference is only the best reason we can have for thinking that something possesses value. Even that is false. Even reflective preferences can be morally wrong: a preference for evil—including one for what one knows to be evil—is not logically impossible, either for an individual or a group, reflective or not, and what sort of evidential status a person's or group's preferences have depends on their reasons for having them, their grasp of the relevant data, and so on. One can tell whether what all, or most, or the majority of, persons value is in fact valuable only by telling what is valuable, and then seeing if that is what all, or most, or the majority, value. The theory, then, that **x**'s being morally valuable is just a matter of **x**'s being valued is mistaken.[2]

PRESCRIPTIVISM

A different, and more sophisticated, attempt to have a theory that will generate morality from the obvious is prescriptivism. This view notes that the meaning of a moral term such as "right" or "wrong" contains both a descriptive element and an evaluative element. On this view, if a person says, "Action **A** is right," he means "**A** meets ideal **I**, and I favor things that meet **I**." A person who favors a different ideal **I'** would mean something analogous by "**A** is right"—something she would express by saying what her competitor said, but replacing "**I**" by "**I'**." On this view, moral claims have truth value. But the core of the view is the claim that there are competing ideals, and one cannot rationally decide between them.

Suppose Ralph approves of actions that meet ideal **I**. A person may believe that an action meets an ideal when it does not. Suppose this is so regarding Ralph, **A** and **I**. Ralph falsely believes that **A** meets **I**, and so holds that **A** is right. Since Ralph believes **A** meets **I**, and has a pro-attitude toward things he believes do that, and so has such an attitude toward **A**, is it the case that **A** is right? Or is **A** wrong, because **A** fails to meet **I**, and Ralph would withdraw all pro-sentiment from **A** were Ralph to discover that? Perhaps one should distinguish between *Prescriptivism One*, which holds that (P1) **A** *is right* (said by Ralph) means *Ralph believes* **A** *meets ideal* **I** *and Ralph approves of anything Ralph believes meets* **I**, and *Prescriptivism Two*, which holds that (P2) **A** *is right* (said by Ralph) means *Ralph approves anything that meets ideal* **I** *and Ralph knows* **A** *meets* **I**, or the like. For (P1), **A** will be right given the circumstances described above; on (P2) it will not be right. Given (P1), that an action is right does not even require that it meet the ideal, the meeting of

2. If one suggests that knowledge of what is valuable need not be based on reasons, but rather may be basic, this will raise the question of why the expert's claims to immediate moral knowledge should be accepted, especially when they conflict with the judgments of others. A claim to immediate knowledge is not rendered unassessable by virtue of its (real or alleged) immediacy.

which the evaluator supposes constitutes grounds for being approved of. Given (P2), that an action is right does require this, so that a person can believe an action right (or wrong) when it is not. For both views, each ideal is such that, for any ideal incompatible with it, including its opposite, one who rejects the ideal will be equally justified with one who accepts it, since choice between ideals is rationally arbitrary.

THE RIGHT ACTION AND THE OBLIGATORY ACTION

It seems to be the case that, if anything *is* right or wrong, it is so in virtue of the properties it actually has, not because of properties anyone thinks it has. On the other hand, a person's obligations will be dependent on what seems to one to be the case, given information which one properly supposes reliable.

Suppose that an ordinary surgeon performs an operation on George which involves his making a particular small incision which ordinarily is easy to make and causes no complications, but in one case in a billion will kill the patient so that in one case the operation must be performed with that incision omitted. George's case is one of the exceedingly rare ones. If one needs this particular operation, one needs it badly, for one will soon die without it; those who need, and receive, it recover completely. Only a handful of specialists are even aware that one in a billion require the operation without the small incision, and only they could recognize that sort of case. Under such circumstances, viewing the consequences, the right thing to do is to operate on George, omitting the small incision. Given the ordinary surgeon's information, his obligation is to operate as usual. What is right (and would be recognized as such, given all the relevant information) is one thing; what the surgeon is obligated to do is another.

A CRITIQUE OF PRESCRIPTIVISM

Given (P1), this distinction cannot be made[3]; what is believed right *is* right, and so one is obligated to do it. Given (P2), this distinction can be made; what meets the ideal one has arbitrarily adopted, or come to accept but cannot rationally appraise, is right, and one's beliefs do not enter into the matter.

Given prescriptivism, if Ralph says *Meeting the ideal of maximizing*

3. And this is a reason for rejecting (P1).

human self-realization, and being approved for so doing is what makes an action right, and Ruth claims this status for *Meeting the ideal of maximizing human suffering, and being approved for so doing,* whereas Rita holds out for *Meeting the ideal of causing a return to wearing cuff links and collar studs, and being approved for so doing*, Ralph, Ruth, and Rita will not be disagreeing, and should one want rationally to assess their very different ideals, prescriptivism tells one this is impossible. Nor can a prescriptivist consistently say that Ruth and Rita are just not sensible people or are fanatics, if by this is to be understood more than that the prescriptivist happens to hold a rationally arbitrary ideal which they happen not to meet. Why anyone should think that the sheer fact that an action meets an ideal that someone happens to hold, but cannot assess as rationally superior to any other ideal that anyone else holds, makes an action *right*, or somehow morally more distinguished than it would otherwise be, is unclear.

"CREATIVE FREEDOM" AS THE ONLY VALUE

Some people contend that the exercise of *creative freedom* is the only, or at least the only overriding,[4] value—creative freedom being an exercise of personal autonomy that ignores established patterns, or that yields something original, or that is unfettered by past practices, or some such. This view seems inadequate as well. For one thing, a use of creative freedom can be creatively evil: the creative brainwashing, or torture, or enslavement of others is altogether possible, nor would it be any less evil because of being creative. For another, if *absolute* originality (or anything much like it) is in question, three consequences follow: (i) it will be hard to tell whether anything has that feature; (ii) a great many utterly trivial actions can have it—one might be the first person ever to place a rusty nail at the foot of the Washington Monument, for instance, but the absolute originality of the event would in no way obviate its insignificance; (iii) love, friendship, kindness, compassion, providing for a family, giving to those in need, and offering sound counsel to someone who wants it and asks for it are all likely to lack absolute originality, and be in no way the worse for it.

4. Where **x** is an overriding value if and only if for any set S of values not including **x**, if S conflicts with **x**, it is right that **x** triumph; conflicts between cases of the exercise of creative freedom will then be viewed as tragic moral choices.

Without disparaging the expressions of genius in the sciences and humanities, we might note that absolute originality (with respect to any given type or token of action) is essentially irrelevant with respect to moral value. Indeed, seeking and trying to restrict oneself to what is original would put a very great (if not very worthy) restraint on one's autonomy. Slavery to originality is still slavery.

FREEDOM AND REASON

Some philosophers (particularly existentialists) have argued that freedom and reason clash in the sense that genuine freedom can obtain only if one has no better reason to choose one alternative than to choose any other. If one is given a range of alternatives such that there is or even *might* be a reason for adopting any of them, they would argue, one's choice among them will probably not be free, because some alternatives will likely be more reasonable than others, and one could be sure of choosing freely only if one were to choose in the utter absence of any reason for making one choice over another. Some theologians have argued that if God has any reasons for making his choices (including ones about what actions he will, or we should, perform), then his freedom is restricted and his sovereignty lost.

The opposite extreme to this is the view (sponsored by Leibniz) that a perfectly rational being is always such that, if he or she does action A rather than not, there must be a better reason for doing A than not, with the consequence that if actions A and B are such that (i) doing one of them is vastly better than doing nothing or doing neither, (ii) one cannot do both, and (iii) there is no better reason to do either one rather than the other, then a perfectly rational being will not do A (there being no reason to choose A over B) and will not do B (there being no reason to choose B over A), but will do either nothing or something else (even though it is true that doing A or B is better than doing nothing or something else).

But what sort of value attaches to a freedom if the manner in which it is exercised is perfectly arbitrary? If there is no better reason whatever for choosing any action rather than another, then to refrain from choosing any action (i.e., to reject all possible actions) and to choose any given action rather than another will be equally trivial options, and an agent who does either is neither to be praised nor blamed for so doing. The suggestion that only *basic* choices are arbitrary, and that once they are made other choices are nonarbitrary relative to one's basic choice, is nothing to the point: a choice which is "not arbitrary" only in the sense that it fits in with an arbitrary choice already made is equally well, if not better, described as "second-order arbitrary."

If one person chooses the ideal of bringing healing to the sick and another the ideal of slicing as many olives as possible, no doubt some choices will further one ideal and other choices will further the other; if both ideals are such that there is no reason to choose them as opposed to not doing so and no reason to prefer either to the other or to any third ideal, then any choice between the ideals is itself arbitrary. Freedom, or autonomy, has point and its exercise gives dignity only if it is possible to choose wrongly, and hence also possible to make a right choice—only, that is, where there are reasons for choosing one way rather than another. So the existentialist account of freedom is mistaken. So, apparently, is Leibniz's, for should there be equally good moral reasons for choosing **A** or for choosing **B** where these cannot both be chosen, and it is morally neutral whether **A** is chosen or **B**, but morally preferable that **A**, or else **B**, be chosen rather than that some other action be performed or that nothing be done, then it is rational to decide arbitrarily between **A** and **B**.

FREEDOM AS DOING WHAT ONE WANTS

A definition of *freedom* somewhat along the lines of that just discussed might be supplemented by an account of *happiness* in the following manner: we will be perfectly free if we can do whatever we choose, and we will be perfectly happy if we get whatever we want. The implausibility of the doctrine embedded in these definitions can be seen by noting what sort of conditions will yield such freedom and happiness. If Ralph wants only one thing—to scratch his nose—and if he is able to choose and to do only one thing—to scratch his nose—then he will be perfectly free and perfectly happy, given the doctrine these definitions express. Nor do these definitions of freedom and happiness preclude all of Ralph's choices being wrong or his happiness abounding in the doing of evil. For such reasons as these, a well-articulated theistic ethic will require that a morally significant freedom be one that is exercised on morally significant occasions, and that happiness be comprised of something more significant than getting whatever one wants.

MORALITY AS A SURVIVAL TECHNIQUE

One more attempt to construct an ethic within easily accessible bounds—with no explicit appeal to metaphysics, for example, and no initial commitment to moral claims—begins by noting that human beings have certain basic and universal biological and psychological needs, and that every society, just in order for its members (and so for it) to survive, has rules aimed at making possible the satisfaction of these needs. Each person is vulnerable to, and requires cooperation from, every other. There are limited resources for which we all compete, and persons render help to, and even sacrifice for, others within limits which fall short of what optimists desire but surpass what pessimists predict.

Given this general context, then, the view is that one's *interest* is a matter of having one's biological and psychological needs met; morality has to do with interests. Each person actually (or, more plausibly, tacitly) enters a contract in which each agrees that the interests of others, as well as his own, be met. That the needs of one person be met, and those of another not be, is unfair or unjust. This is the extent of morality. When one considers matters other than the satisfying of interests across the board, one passes beyond the realm of morality; anything further which would ordinarily be included within the scope of morality falls instead under the rubric of a "vision of life," or the like.

But how, exactly, is one to get *morality* out of these considerations? If one wants his needs to be satisfied, one may maximize his chances of this occurring if one cooperates with others; this stance is prudent on one's part. On the other hand, suppose one decides he would prefer to pretend to cooperate, risking detection and whatever cost this might bring, for the sake of having others meet his needs (so long as they are deceived) without his having to meet theirs. Perhaps this is imprudent on one's part, but (given this view) why is it *wrong*?

NOT ALL OF ETHICS CAN BE CONTRACTUAL

If the answer is that deceit is wrong, two things should be noted. One is that it cannot be wrong due to the making of a contract, whether explicit or implicit; for if (independent of contracts or mutual promises) Ralph and Ruth, as persons in communication with one another, do not owe one another the truth, no contract can create this obligation, for prior to the contract there will be nothing wrong with a lying contract which promises truth-telling. If lying is not wrong before a contract that makes it so, it is not wrong afterward.

NOR CAN INJUSTICE BE THE ONLY EVIL

If lying is wrong, it is precontractually wrong. Further, if there is injustice, there are wrongs besides injustice. Suppose it is not wrong that Ralph prevents Ruth's basic needs from being met; then why should it be wrong that Ralph allow Sam's needs to be met when he prevents Ruth's from being met? Perhaps because then Ruth's feelings would be hurt as she expired? Then hurting Ruth's feelings is wrong—but that hardly seems plausible if not allowing Ruth's basic needs to be met is not wrong. It cannot be wrong that something is done for or to one person but not another, unless there is something such that it is wrong to do it to a single person, whatever is or is not done for or to another. Injustice, construed as inconsistency in matters of morality, is wrong; but it cannot be the only or basic or primitive or underivative wrong: it presupposes the wrongness of something else.

CRITIQUE OF THE VIEWS THAT MORALITY IS SIMPLY A SURVIVAL TECHNIQUE

If either of these points, let alone both, is correct, the strategy outlined above will fail, for there either will be things that are just wrong—like not allowing that a person's basic needs be met. They are wrong, not from considerations of prudence or contract or inconsistency, but because inherent value resides in being a person at all, or else there will be nothing at all that is wrong. In the former case, the wrongness of depriving a person of having his basic needs met lies in the worth of being a person; from this will stem obligations to help others, and to refrain from doing harm. Even if one is inconsistent in holding (i) I intend to further my own interests (meet my basic needs), (ii) I do not intend to further anyone else's interests (meet anyone else's basic needs), and (iii) my interests are not more valuable than anyone else's, or in holding (iii) plus (iv) I do not intend to further my own interests, and (v) I intend to further the interests of others, that fact is not sufficient to show that anything *morally wrong* is involved. Prudence/imprudence plus consistency/inconsistency do not yield anything that is right or wrong.

THE VIEW THAT "X IS RIGHT" MEANS "GOD WILLS X"

One standard theistic account of morality suggests that "X is right" only if "God wills that x obtain," or the like. This can be understood in various ways. One might suggest that X *is right* just means *God wills that* x *be done*; this has the inelegant consequence that *God always does what is right* means only that *God always does what he wills*, which is hardly what a theist is likely to have meant. It also raises the standard question as to whether God has any reason for making the moral choices he makes. If not, then they are rationally arbitrary, and it is only divine might that makes right. If so, then those reasons, not divine fiat, provide the grounds for saying that something is right. More promising, perhaps, is the view that (i) *God is omniscient* entails (ii) *God knows what is right*, and (iii) *God is omnipotent and omnibenevolent* entails (iv) *If God knows what is right, he will do it*, and (ii) and (iv) entail (v) *God knows, and so does, the right*, though it does not entail that God does what is right simply because he knows it is right; that God knows what is right, and is all-good, entails that. But this does not tell us what is right, or what is good; nor does it tell us why. A different approach—though not one that need yield different moral principles or rules from the last—begins at a different place.

THEISTIC ETHICS AND THE "IMAGO DEI"

Theism characteristically holds that persons, male and female, are created in the image of God. What follows will consider one way of developing this theme so as to relate theism to morality. What follows if persons are created in God's image?

Suppose Ralph is an evil person—dishonest, unkind, and malicious in his better moments. It would still be wrong to take Ralph's life, not merely because this would endanger nice persons like ourselves or because the deed would sully the character of its perpetrator: Ralph's life itself has value. Ralph's life has value, not because it is comprised of a finite (or even an infinite) number of conscious states, but because Ralph is a moral agent. Better, perhaps, Ralph himself, and so his life, has value because he is a moral agent.

MORAL AGENCY AND MORAL CHARACTER

The notion of moral agency is complex. An agent is an autonomous source of choices and actions. To say that Ralph as a moral agent is autonomous with respect to choice or action A at time t is to say that, at t, Ralph in fact can do A and Ralph in fact can refrain from doing A—not merely that *Ralph could do* A *if he chose to do so* (which is compatible with his being unable to so choose) or that *doing* A *is within the scope of someone of his I.Q. and physical capacities* (which is true of his raising his right arm, even if his arms are chained to his side). An agent who is autonomous with respect to a morally significant choice or action A (one which is right, or else wrong) is responsible for doing (or refraining from doing) A; removal of autonomy entails removal of responsibility. In turn, an agent's moral character is a function of the virtues (and/or vices) the agent develops through action over time. A virtue or a vice is a tendency or disposition to act rightly (or wrongly) on a certain sort of morally relevant occasion—to speak the truth (or lie) when asked a question, to refrain from stealing (or to steal) when examining goods for sale, to be kind (or unkind) in contact with others, and so on. Such tendencies are functions of individual choices and actions; many lies will make a liar and many thefts, a thief. It takes time, and some effort, to become either evil—or good. An agent, then, endures and exercises autonomy over time, retaining personal identity as character develops, for good or ill. But since it is wrong to remove evil Ralph from the scene—even if Ralph will never become good or even rise to moral mediocrity, and this sad fact should become known—the value involved in being a person cannot simply be a function of how a person behaves. The value of a person is partly due to what a person *is*, and so only partly dependent on what a person *does*. A vivid way of putting this is to say that the divine image is not lost, even in hell—that *being condemned by God* and *its being better that one exist than not* are not incompatible properties. (This will involve taking some Dominical statements about similar topics as hyperbolic.)

HUMAN NATURE AND OBLIGATIONS: THE CONTENT OF THE IMAGO DEI

Moral character, then, progresses (or regresses) in a particular person as she or he acts or chooses rightly or wrongly; which raises the question again as to what the criteria for that might be. One way of putting the Christian response to this query is in terms of two claims: (i) to be a person is to have been created in the image of God, (ii) a person's fundamental obligation is to mature in the potential built into the *imago Dei.* The former offers a doctrine of human nature, a portion of an ontology; the latter expresses a fundamental moral principle, a part of an ethical theory.

One influential and highly plausible understanding of the *imago Dei* is that being a person involves being *rational* in that rich sense of rationality that involves such capacities as *recognizing necessary truths, making inferences, using language, remembering, adapting means to ends, intelligently anticipating the future, making and using artifacts, discovering empirical laws, developing theories*, and *writing music, or playing it, or at least appreciating it* (and analogously for the other "art forms"), and so on through the wide variety of capacities which enable human persons to develop a culture. Capable of developing and assessing systems of description and explanation, and evaluating alternative courses of action (including, but not limited to, morally significant ones); requiring the company and acceptance as well as cooperation of others to and from whom respect is due; in these respects, and others, persons are rational-moral-social agents, and this constitutes part of persons having been created in the image of God. In these respects, the Judeo-Christian tradition resembles other perspectives: a strong tendency in classical Greek thought, in Stoicism, and a strong strain in recent secular humanism, for example.

It seems correct, however, to add a further feature characteristic of at least Christian ethics, namely the centrality of the capacity for *agape*, which perhaps can be characterized as acting in what one reflectively takes to be the best interest of others without concern for personal benefit, though insofar as possible within boundaries set by acting in what one reflectively takes to be one's own interest. "Interest" here is to be construed in some such way as this: **X** is in one's interest if and only if **X** will contribute to one's maturity as made in God's image. While this perspective does not uncritically embrace whatever a given culture produces or values (what sensible perspective would?), it is by no means anticultural or antiintellectual. It does rank *agape*, or love, in something like the sense characterized above, as among its highest virtues.

INTRINSIC GOODNESS

At least in one version, then, theistic morality holds a view which one might express by saying that for it, persons made in God's image have inherent worth, or intrinsic goodness, or the like. This is not to say that they owe their goodness to themselves; rather, they owe it to their creator. Nor is it to say that they cannot become evil, or will not. It is to say something about the status of *being a moral agent* which is distinct from anything that might be said about how that agency is used or to what effect. But what?

The notion of intrinsic goodness is essentially the notion of something that is good *no matter what*. As such, it is hard indeed to find instances to which the concept applies.

Consider a list of things plausibly viewed as intrinsically good: knowledge, love, friendship, and pleasure. No doubt the list is not complete. It will be enough for present purposes if its members are about as plausible a set of candidates for intrinsic goodness as any.

Knowledge—knowing that something is the case—*is* a good. But is it good no matter what? There are, let us suppose, exactly 100,004 distinct stones in Bascom Hall in Madison. Is having this information not trivial but somehow intrinsically good? I doubt it.

Suppose Robin is escaping from a burning building by crossing a board extending between it and the next. It is true that the board will break when Robin is exactly six feet from the other side. It is also true that Robin, shocked into action by the sound of splitting wood, will leap to safety. But is it probably good that Robin now know in advance that the board will break? Perhaps certain propositions are such that if they are true of a person, then it is better that the person know they are true, no matter what. Perhaps one's being a moral agent is among them. Perhaps a Jew, Christian, or Moslem will hold that it is better to know that God exists and that God loves you, even it you spurn that love. Perhaps an atheist will hold that it is better to know that God does not exist, even if this depresses you. In any case, if knowledge is an intrinsic good, perhaps it is only knowledge of certain very important truths about oneself and one's status in the universe that is intrinsically good. It seems false that just any old knowledge, so to speak, is good to have, no matter what, and so false that knowledge, intrinsically and so in every instance, is good.

Similar remarks apparently apply to our other cases. Love as *eros*, sexual love, can be beautiful and it is a good; it can also be incredibly destructive. Love as *phileo* is friendship. Friendship is good, but a friendship can be so consuming of time and energy that a marriage is ruined or a child left alone so often it feels (and is) deserted. Love as *agape* is self-giving love, acting without consideration of self-gain for the well-being of others. It is the stuff real saints are made of. In the summary of the law and the prophets, we find the words "you shall love your neighbor as yourself." Apparently one can act so chronically for the good of others that one acts to one's own detriment, and it is wrong to do so, however free most of us are from being in danger of this. Perhaps it is not unfair to consider overzealous charity as *agape* run amuck. If so, the woman described in one of Agatha Christie's novels as charitable is a case in point; it was said of her, "You could tell the objects of her charitable activities by their hunted look."

Pleasure is a good. But not just any old pleasant sensation, under any condition, no matter what. So none of our candidates seems good "without qualification" or "no matter what."

Still, ordinarily it is a good thing that one extend one's knowledge, enjoy a pleasurable state, start or enrich a friendship, or act in another's interest without concern for gain—so much that it is not the claim that such a thing is good but the claim that it is not that needs justification. There are things, then, which are good in the sense that they belong to a class or kind that has this feature: if something is a member of that kind, this very fact is presumptive evidence that it is good; one needs a reason not so much for thinking that something of this sort is good as for thinking it is not.

The idea is that if

(i) Action A will extend knowledge, be pleasurable, begin or deepen a friendship, or be in the interest of another without concern for gain,

then we do not need a special further reason for concluding that

(ii) A is good;

but we do need a special further reason for claiming that

(iii) A is neutral or bad.

The reason for (iii) must overcome or override the reason (i) provides for (ii). This is not finding intrinsic goodness; but neither is it finding no goodness at all. If a name for this sort of goodness is needed, "presumptive goodness" will do. Perhaps similar remarks can be made about intrinsic badness, and that a notion of "presumptive badness" can be developed; it will not be developed here. Still, so far we have discerned nothing that is intrinsically good.

PROPERTIES AND PERSONS

Maybe, however, we have been looking in the wrong place. Our candidates roughly have been *properties* of persons. Consider instead persons themselves. Have they intrinsic value? Kant defined a person as one who was accountable for his or her deeds. As it stands, very young children and severely retarded human beings would not be persons by this definition. This can, and no doubt should, be remedied something along these lines: S is a person if and only if S is accountable for S's deeds (S's choices and actions), or S is a member of a species whose members normally are accountable for their deeds.

If we ask why goodness, friendship, pleasure, or love are even presumptively good, the answer concerns the positive role that such features play (or can play) in the developing of human beings as persons or moral agents. Conversely, ignorance, friendlessness, constant pain and deprivation of pleasure, and hate and deprivation of love are bad because of what they do to people. (No doubt this sounds so elementary as to be hardly worth mentioning. If so, that is all to the good. It is not often in ethics that one finds anything so flagrantly true as to be almost foolish to affirm.) If this is true, whether obvious or not, then it is true because of what people are or can be. More formally, a theory of what is good and what is bad, if it distinguishes between these in terms of the effects they have on people, requires the support of a theory of human nature.

ACT MORALITY AND AGENT MORALITY

This suggests a way in which we can rest act morality on agent morality. The idea can be put in some such fashion as this:

(1) Action A is right if and only if A falls under practice P, and P is right;

(2) Practice P is right if and only if P's being followed will promote the development of morally good persons.

What one is to make of (2) depends on the preferred account of a morally good person. One could so qualify (2) that any action which will promote the development of morally good persons is right, even were the practice it would lead to were everyone so to act not promote this.

One can argue that the value of a person is always and only a value for others. It is good that Pat be honest, loving, fair, merciful, friendly, and the like because Chris is thereby benefited. It is good that Chris has these features, for Pat benefits thereby. But this leaves the question as to why Pat or Chris is *worth* benefiting.

One might, in this context, speak of the mistake of pure altruism—that *only other* persons have moral worth—as the reverse mistake to that of egoism—that *only oneself* has moral worth. But of course this leaves us with the question as to what talk of moral worth amounts to and why it should, in some basic or ultimate sense, be ascribed to persons. Perhaps, if any persons have moral worth, all do; but why suppose that any have?

THEISM AND MORALITY

At this point, religion and morality meet, at least in the sense that theism's answer to the query, as we have seen, is that persons are made in the image of God, who possesses preeminent worth. If the general pattern of reasoning exhibited here is correct, the proper thrust of theistic ethics is nonutilitarian; instead, it is "deontological." Fundamentally, what this involves is a rejection of the commensurability thesis and an insistence that the value of persons is not one among many values to be placed into the calculation of what will maximize happiness. Rather, *being a person* has inherent or intrinsic value, and anything else that is valuable gets its value from its being extrinsic to this intrinsic good. A humanist will suppose that this is so, but in a sense which precludes a person's owing this dignity to God; a theist will insist on this debt. One can argue that this position puts the theist under duress to say what reasons there might be to suppose that debt is owed; this is to ask what reason there might be to be a theist. Equally, one can argue that the humanist is under duress to show that the high value humanism places on human nature can be plausibly maintained in a nontheistic world, in which the origin and the prospect of a person are different from a person's origin and (presumably more positive) prospect in a theistic world.

The sense of intrinsic value ascribed even to persons by Christian theism is constrained by certain considerations. It is derived, given by grace; talk of inherent value is compatible with this feature, and emphasizes that human beings, morally speaking, are *ends* rather than mere *means* to other, higher ends. Talk of inherent value concerns the moral status of persons in virtue of the properties they possess, and the moral status of persons is not reduced by the admission—made by any plausible view—that the properties possession of which make persons moral agents are not self-granted. It also seems plausible that a person might exist in circumstances so drastically and permanently bad that no rational agent, however moral, could wish to be sustained in them, or countenance the sustenance of another in them. If so, *being a person* is not a good, *no matter what*, and so not an intrinsic value. That God loves persons presumably entails that God allows no person to come into that most inelegant state. Perhaps it is logically possible that one's wrong choices and actions so poison one's nature and character that the value involved in being a person is overcome thereby, and an omnibenevolent (and otherwise omnicompetent) deity will restrain a person's exercise of freedom so his or her evil stops at least just short of that point. A doctrine of hell cast along these lines will amplify a remark of George MacDonald to the effect that hell is the best that God can do for those who will allow him to do nothing better on their behalf.

The core of the notion of inherent value in the perspective under consideration perhaps can be expressed along these lines: there is nothing which is not a person moral consideration for which outweighs or equibalances the moral consideration due a person. This way of putting things may be cast too much in the shadow of utilitarianism; perhaps the point should be made by saying that nothing which is not a person is a moral agent. Morality concerns only persons, and things other than persons come into it only as they affect persons. (If sentient animals constitute some exception to this, it is by virtue of their resemblance to persons.) So persons are not entities whose prospects are appropriately cast into an alleged commensurability equation; they possess rights which are not subject to calculation of consequences. But this topic is too large to pursue further here.

THEISM AND THE RATIONALITY OF MORALITY

We saw in discussing the moral argument that it is sometimes claimed that if God does not exist, it sometimes is irrational to do what is right—e.g., to die for an unquestionably great cause which will fail if one refuses. Christian theism clearly includes a doctrine of life after death—specifically, a doctrine of the "resurrection of the body and the life everlasting"—so that dying for a cause, while still clearly courageous, will not be as costly from a theistic standpoint as for a perspective which includes no hope of another life. Further, in a theistic world, presumably virtue is rewarded and vice is punished, and it is in fact possible that a moral agent become a morally good person. In these, and no doubt other, ways, morality is "at home" in a theistic universe.

THE POINT OF THEISTIC MORALITY

No doubt the point of morality, theistically conceived, includes survival; it is not exhausted thereby. The fuller point of morality is the development of persons into moral maturity—into beings who imitate God by way of being truthful, just, merciful, forgiving, compassionate, and the like; by exercising *agape*. Perhaps there is no need for a theist to view death as the cessation of growth or as a matter of entering a static life (if that is not a contradiction in terms).

One could put what has been discussed in terms of "imitation" instead of along the lines of "obedience," and this is often and appropriately done. But the point of the obedience is not subservience for subservience's sake, but for attainment of the potential intrinsic to being made in God's image.

MORALITY AND THEOLOGY

It seems clear that a consistent atheist, even if she believes in evil, will not believe in sin. Sin is a theological notion—a matter of God's law being violated, and his person offended. Theism baptizes morality. It does so most shockingly, perhaps, in its suggestion that whenever anyone is wronged, God is wronged. David, having sent Uriah to death and enticed Bathsheba to adultery, tells God that he has sinned only against him, and the sentiment is not corrected. This expresses at least a widely accepted Christian notion, and seems a bit neglectful toward Uriah and Bathsheba. But so to construe things misses the point. God so identifies himself with the cause of Uriah and Bathsheba that to wrong them is to wrong him. It is the converse of the saying that whatever good one does to another, one does also to God; "inasmuch as you have done this unto the least of these my brethren, you have done it unto me."

CONCLUSION

Theistic ethics bases ethics on ontology. The fate of those theories, considered earlier, which tried to escape doing so hardly makes this a criticism; perhaps no actual ethical theory (as opposed to varieties of moral skepticism or relativism) escapes being implicitly or explicitly based on some ontology or metaphysic, however modest, in any case. At least in one variety, Christian theism—nonutilitarian (rejecting the commensurability thesis), resting act morality on agent, and based on the claims that persons are made in God's image and that the basic obligation is to imitate God—ascribes a unique moral status to persons. It sets the notions of right and wrong, good and evil, vice and virtue, and agency and character in a theological context. In part, if the argument of Chapter 5 is correct, this articulation of ethical theory (and other varieties) should be accessible to rational assessment. It is not the purpose of this chapter to provide this assessment, but only to suggest that there are interesting and promising ways of relating theism and morality.

SUGGESTIONS FOR FURTHER READING

Carnell, Edward John. *Christian Commitment.* New York: Macmillan, 1957.

Helm, Paul, ed. *Divine Commands and Morality.* New York: Oxford University Press, 1981.

Henry, Carl F. H. *Aspects of Christian Social Ethics.* Grand Rapids, MI: Eerdmans, 1964.

———. *Christian Personal Ethics.* Grand Rapids, MI: Eerdmans, 1957.

Matthews, W. R., ed. *Butler's Sermons.* London: Morrison and Gibb, 1949.

Mitchell, Basil. *Morality, Religious and Secular: The Dilemma of the Traditional Conscience.* Oxford: Clarendon Press, 1980.

A critical discussion of a number of contemporary varieties of secular morality.

Quinn, Philip L. *Divine Commands and Moral Requirements.* Oxford: Clarendon Press, 1978.

A sympathetic discussion of various versions of divine-command theories of ethics.

Ramsey, Paul. *Basic Christian Ethics.* New York: Scribner's, 1950.

Robinson, N. H. G. *The Groundwork of Christian Ethics.* Grand Rapids, MI: Eerdmans, 1972.

Stob, Henry. *Ethical Reflections: Essays on Moral Themes.* Grand Rapids, MI: Eerdmans, 1978.

Thomas, George Finger. *Christian Ethics and Moral Philosophy.* New York: Scribner's, 1955.

Yandell, Keith E. "Religion and Morality." In *Basic Issues in the Philosophy of Religion.* Boston: Allyn and Bacon, 1971.

———. "The Problem of Evil," *Philosophical Topics*, Vol. 12, No. 3, 7-38.

PART SIX
A PROGRAM FOR RELIGIOUS RATIONALITY

ANALYTICAL TABLE OF CONTENTS TO CHAPTER 8

CHAPTER 8
CAN RELIGIOUS CONCEPTUAL SYSTEMS BE RATIONALLY ASSESSED?

In any of its concrete varieties theism is (or includes) a conceptual system essentially: its rites, institutions, codes, and practices presuppose, embody, and cannot exist without its theology—and the same holds for any religious tradition. This may be obvious, but the point is worth stressing because it is so often denied.

The conceptual system essential to theism contains logically contingent claims (i.e., claims that are not themselves self-contradictory and do not have self-contradictory denials), and the presence of such claims is as essential to the conceptual system of theism as it is to the conceptual systems of all religious traditions: no religious tradition is composed solely of logically necessary truths. This means that theism cannot be confirmed on purely conceptual grounds alone—even though in principle it can be refuted on conceptual grounds alone: any view that can be shown to be logically inconsistent or incoherent is refuted on such grounds—and any view is in principle open to this sort of critique. But not being inconsistent or incoherent is not the same as being true or rationally justified; possessing the former properties is but a logically necessary condition of possessing either of the latter properties.

The conceptual system essential to theism contains logically contingent propositions which are not merely about the existence and immediate psychological or conscious states of persons. A claim is *incorrigible* relative to a person if and only if it is logically contingent and the claim's truth follows from the person's believing it.

Logically contingent proposition **P** is incorrigible relative to Ralph if and only if *Ralph believes that* **P** entails **P** *is true*. Thus, even if statements about one's own existence and immediate psychological states are incorrigible, theism contains claims which are not incorrigible relative to theists (or anyone else)—it essentially contains *corrigible* claims or logically contingent claims which are not incorrigible in that their truth does not follow from someone (or, for that matter, from everyone) believing them. Even idealistic religious traditions contain claims about the existence of minds and conscious states other than those of any particular person, as well as claims about human nature and/or reincarnation and karma and enlightenment or the like, which are not incorrigible, but corrigible. Thus even such traditions are not exceptions to the generalization that theism in common with all other religious traditions contains logically contingent, corrigible, propositions. Every religion, then, essentially includes a conceptual system of the sort described. So no religion is "merely subjective" or involves only "private" claims in any sense incompatible with its making claims which are corrigible, logically contingent, and either true or false (and so being "objective" and "public") in these respects.

CONFIRMATION AS MORE THAN LACK OF FALSIFICATION

The question *What would confirm Christianity?* has this feature: unless one offers reasons which are easily exposed as inadequate, it is staggeringly difficult to answer. To say "revelation from God" simply replaces the question by another: What would confirm that it *was* a revelation? Whatever reason we might have to think the content of the revelation false would be a reason to think it not a revelation at all. Roughly, the sort of thing that would confirm Christianity is the sort of thing that would confirm any general conceptual system were it true and known to be true. But what is that?

Perhaps, if the ethics of belief is of the sort discussed earlier, for one to be justified in accepting a conceptual system need not require very much of the believer; for one to justify a conceptual system, or show it to be, or to be plausibly taken to be, true has higher requirements. What requirements might there be? One answer is this: that the system has been exposed to significant opportunity for epistemic failure without its having epistemically failed. A moral saint is an agent who, having had eminent opportunity for wickedness, escapes the snares of evil; a system is justified which, having had eminent opportunity for falsehood, escapes the snares of error. The analogy, however, exposes a defect. No one becomes a moral saint merely by escaping sins of commission; there are sins of omission to be averted, which is to say, there are right actions to be performed. A moral saint both possesses virtues and lacks vices, and to be virtuous is not merely to be empty of vice. Correspondingly, a conceptual system which only escapes error is not thereby justified. A system one has justified (as opposed to merely not being blameworthy in accepting) must possess some epistemic virtue, must explain some data which requires explanation, solve some problem, provide some sort of intellectual illumination or the like, as well as not be falsified by virtue of failing any of a sequence of appropriate tests. The chapters on religious experience, arguments for God's existence, and religion and morality contended that theism has this sort of virtue; the chapter on the problem of evil argued that it lacked an important vice. What other vices might it possess or lack?

COHERENCE

The propositions *Atlanta is in Georgia, Bill Russell is the greatest basketball center ever to play the game,* and *No University of Wisconsin philosopher is over seven feet tall* are all true. Nonetheless, it is hard to see that together they form a coherent system, that they explain some phenomenon or solve some problem or present some view of the world or a part thereof. Coherence is a matter of mutual relevance of a set of propositions to the explanation of some phenomenon, the solution of some problem, the presentation of some perspective, or the like.

Since lack of coherence argues lack of system, an incoherent system is an unsystematic system, and "coherent system" a near redundancy. A supposed system which lacks mutual coherence among its propositional constituents provides a poor explanation, solution, or perspective, or none at all, and so, short of revision, is a weak candidate for truth.

"TRUE CONCEPTUAL SYSTEM"

A body is healthy if its members are healthy; otherwise, it is at least not fully so. A conceptual system is true if its constituent propositions are true; otherwise, it at least is not fully so.

CONTRADICTORINESS

A contradictory proposition is not meaningless, but false, just as its denial is not meaningless, but true; furthermore, a contradiction is a *necessary* falsehood, and its denial a *necessary* truth. A system essentially containing a contradiction for that reason is false. If two propositions are such that neither alone is a contradiction but their conjunct is, it is a necessary truth that one or the other is false, even if neither of them is a *necessary* falsehood. Thus if neither **P** nor **Q** is a contradiction, but **P** *and* **Q** is a contradiction, a system of which **P** *and* **Q** is an essential part is false.

ESSENTIAL PROPOSITIONS

Propositions are more or less essential to a system to the degree that the explanation, solution, or view the system presents is changed by their removal. The proposition *God exists,* for example, is essential to Christianity, but confusion has reigned in recent theology to the extent that even this has been denied. Reflection is required to tell whether or not—or (continuing the verbal license involved in speaking of *degrees* of being essential) to what degree—a proposition is essential to a system in which it appears. Removal of a proposition from a system may have no significant effect whatever, or it may be tantamount to dismissing the system, or many things in between these extremes. Only careful thought, rather than any hard and fast rule, will tell one what the consequences will be in a given case.

It might plausibly be argued that the failure to meet the criteria of coherence or consistency accounts for most if not all of the defects of conceptual systems, but such an argument will not be particularly useful unless we understand exactly what the implications of a failure to be coherent or consistent amount to. Although an exhaustive exploration of such matters is of course out of the question, it will be worthwhile to survey briefly some rules for assessing conceptual systems.

TWO RULES FOR ASSESSING CONCEPTUAL SYSTEMS

We have thus far concluded that if an explanation or solution or perspective lacks coherence, it is epistemically defective, and that if a conceptual system lacks coherence, it contains propositions that do not relate to one another so as to solve a problem (or explain a phenomenon, etc.); perhaps it will not have a sufficient number of propositions, or perhaps it will contain some irrelevant propositions, or perhaps both. If a conceptual system lacks consistency or contains a contradiction, then of course it will contain propositions that *cannot* relate to one another so as to provide an adequate explanation or solution. It seems appropriate, then, to suggest that an incoherent explanation, solution, or perspective will not be able to provide an adequate account of the truth about the matter in question precisely because it is incoherent—although it might be able to do so if its incoherence is remedied by the addition and/or subtraction of appropriate propositions. We propose, then, the following rules:

(R1) *An incoherent conceptual system, because of its incoherence, cannot provide an adequate account of the truth of the matter in question;*

and

(R2) *A system that essentially contains a contradiction is false for that reason, and cannot be true until the contradiction is removed.*

These rules would seem to be appropriate for assessing conceptual systems, but by themselves they scarcely seem adequate to the task: clearly, a conceptual system can be radically defective even though it does not violate (R1) or (R2). At the very least, (R1) and (R2) would require supplementation to develop the implications of incoherence and inconsistency further, and even that might not be sufficient; despite this, however, the two rules are still relevant to the assessment of conceptual systems.

TWO RULES CONCERNING "TRANSLATION"

One variety of behaviorism suggests that thought is neither more nor less than actual and potential behavior (including verbal behavior). One version of this thesis requires that any proposition to the effect that a person has a particular thought can be restated, or "translated," without remainder into propositions that state that the person in question is behaving, and tends to behave, in particular ways. It might, in discussing this view, seem unfair to begin with an example like *Ralph is assessing the comparative epistemic merits of Bertrand Russell's neutral monism versus Aristotle's substantival ontology*, but perhaps the more modest *Ralph believes his tie is on fire* will not seem too esoteric for the sort of behaviorism in question to handle without too much difficulty. How might the "translation" go?

The task at hand is to translate the proposition into statements concerning observable behavior, and yet there really is no behavior that we could describe as typical for such an occasion as finding one's tie ablaze. Nevertheless, this is also true for a great many quite ordinary beliefs that persons have, and so that does not constitute a serious objection to the example as such: if this version of behaviorism can handle only beliefs that (as the nonbehaviorist would put it) are associated with typical behavior patterns, its scope will be rather limited.

One might suppose *Ralph believes his tie is on fire* "translates" into something like *Ralph shouts "My tie is on fire" and pours water on his tie*. But of course Ralph may be so surprised or alarmed as to be rendered incapable of speech; it is not evidence that Ralph has no belief relevant to his tie being on fire that he does not say some particular thing, or anything at all. To require that the proposition *My tie is on fire* "cross Ralph's mind" may or may not be justified, but in any case is to require something that is itself a thought—a *mental* rather than *behavioral* feature—and so to require it is to require something of which another behavioristic "translation" is required. Perhaps Ralph will pour water on his tie, if he can find some, or look for water if none is readily at hand, provided he believes that water puts out fires of this sort, and has enough presence of mind so to act. But if he believes that the fire will go out harmlessly, or that water will make the fire blaze more strongly, or has any of an indefinitely large number of similar beliefs, he will not do so. What he will do would at least in part seem intractably to be a function to what *other* beliefs he has, so that any attempt to say what Ralph will do if he does believe that his tie is on fire in such a way that his other beliefs are not referred to seems plainly to offer a quite mistaken sort of analysis. The behaviorist reply is obvious: those beliefs too must be analyzed behavioristically.

Obviously, some beliefs are such that when we try to translate proposition (1) *Ralph has belief* **A1** into proposition (2) *Ralph behaves in way* **B1**, we cannot justify proposition (2) without resorting to proposition (3) *Ralph behaves in way* **B1**, *provided he has belief* **A2**; we find that while proposition (1) may entail proposition (3), clearly it does not entail proposition (2). Nor is it plausible that this defect (as it appears to the behaviorist) can be remedied. If indeed the defect cannot be remedied, then behaviorism (at least of the sort in question) will turn out to be false. The reason for its falsehood might be put in this manner: a condition of its truth is that a particular sort of translation or analysis is possible where **P** ascribes some mental state to Ralph, and **Q** ascribes some actual and potential behavior to Ralph, it must be the case both that **P** *is true if and only if* **Q** *is true* and *the truth or falsity of* **P** *is to be determined by reference to the truth or falsity of* **Q** *and not conversely*. It also requires that the meaning or sense of **P** derive in some significant way from the meaning or sense of **Q,** and not the other way around (and also that **P** and **Q** are not such that their meanings or senses are distinct)—but no such behavioristic analysis of all beliefs seems possible.

Were it possible to translate talk of God into talk of, say, "peak psychological experience," then theism would be refuted, or else replaced by something else. It is a necessary condition of the truth of theism that no such translation be possible, and it seems clear that none is. These reflections suggest some such rule as the following:

(R3) *If it is essential to the truth of conceptual system* **T** *that a kind* **K1** *of propositions be translatable or reducible without remainder into propositions of kind* **K2,** *and they cannot be so translated, then* **T** *is false.*

Appeal to this sort of rule has been used to criticize a great many philosophical perspectives.

Conversely, however, if a theory requires that a particular sort of translation be not possible when in fact it is—that clouds not be composed of water droplets, say, or that lightning not be an electrical discharge—then a converse rule will be applicable:

(R4) *If it is essential to the truth of a conceptual system* **T** *that propositions of kind* **K1** *cannot be translated or reduced without remainder to propositions of kind* **K2,** *but they can be so translated or reduced, then* **T** *is false.*

For example, if it were possible to show that God is "contingently identical," say, to the set of all "peak experiences," then theism would be false, or would thereby have been replaced by something else. This, too, has insufficient plausibility to be considered here. Nonetheless, (R3) and (R4) are also relevant to the assessment of conceptual systems.

EPISTEMICALLY SELF-DEFEATING CLAIMS

It is the case with some propositions that if they are true, no one can know that they are true, such as *Nothing exists* and *There are no conscious beings.* Presumably there is no problem or mystery about such cases. No one can know that they are true, for if they were true there would be no one to know them.

Contrast these cases with certain others. Cultural determinism holds that (i) *Every belief one has is determined by one's culture* and (ii) *If one's belief that* **P** *is determined by one's culture, then one does not know that* **P** *is true;* together, (i) and (ii) entail (iii) *No one knows anything.* But the truth of (i) and (ii) does not preclude there being persons who have beliefs. One might say that cultural determinism precludes knowers by precluding knowledge, whereas *Nothing exists* or *There are no sentient beings* precludes knowledge by precluding knowers. So if cultural determinism is true, no one can know it to be true, no matter how many persons there may be, and no matter how great their intellectual capacities may be. In that respect, being a cultural determinist is self-defeating. If one is a cultural determinist, one cannot know that one's position is true; cultural determinism has this epistemic defect.

Whatever point such claims as those considered in this section may have, it does not reside in distinguishing knowledge from reasonable belief. For "know," then, in the preceding paragraphs of this section, one may as well read "know, or reasonably believe." Further, one might describe a claim whose truth would entail there are no persons (and so no knowledge) as *vacuously* entailing that there is no knowledge; such a view precludes knowledge only because it precludes potential knowers—its truth would preclude there being persons. And one might describe a position, like that of cultural determinism, whose truth would allow there to be persons, but would disallow persons from possessing any knowledge and from having reasonable beliefs, a *nonvacuously* entailing that there is no knowledge or reasonable belief. A claim that *nonvacuously* entails that there is no knowledge or reasonable belief is not a claim one can reasonably accept; in that sense, it is *epistemically self-defeating.* Cultural determinism, then, is epistemically self-defeating. It is not the only view that has this discouraging feature.[1]

Suppose that one claims both that (i) there is a difference between belief that is, and belief that is not, reasonable, and (ii)

1. A view which entails no persons exist cannot reasonably be accepted either, but the reason this is so seems to be captured along such lines as those suggested by (R11) below. Only *human* persons are in view in the criteria developed here.

that every belief that anyone has is analyzable without remainder into actual and potential behavior on the believer's part. Given (ii), it should be the case that the distinction between belief that is and belief that is not reasonable can be made in terms of one sort of behavior and another sort. This is not very plausible; in any case, suppose it is false—suppose that (iii) the distinction between belief that is reasonable and belief that is not cannot be made in terms of any distinction between one sort of actual and potential behavior and another. If (iii) is true, then either (i) is false or (ii) is; and if (i) and (iii) are true, then (ii) is false. (Parenthetically, it is unlikely that if (i) is true, it is only contingently true.) The same goes for (iii); if (i) and (iii) are true at all, it is very plausible that (i) and (iii) are necessary truths. If this is so, then if one holds (ii), one (without falling into logical inconsistency) cannot hold that one is reasonable in believing that (ii); rather, it will be the case that if (ii) is true, then no one's belief that (ii) is true is reasonable rather than not. Belief that (ii) will be epistemically self-defeating. It clearly seems a defect in a view that, were it true one could not reasonably believe it to be so. This suggests some such rule as:

(R5) *If conceptual system* **T** *is such that belief that* **T** *is true is epistemically self-defeating, then* **T** *is false.*

ASSESSMENT OF THEORIES AND MORAL KNOWLEDGE

If the argument of Chapter 5 is correct, there are ways of deciding between competing moral principles and competing ethical theories; it defended the view, broadly speaking, that there is moral knowledge. If this view is correct, we can add:

(R6) *If a conceptual system* **T** *entails that there is no moral knowledge, then* **T** *is false.*

One must be careful here; suppose **T** entails that a, or the, deity acts wrongly. It would not follow that the theory is wrong. What would have that effect would be **T** entailing that a moral principle which was known to be true was false, or that moral knowledge was impossible, or that there was no way of ever deciding between competing moral theories or ethical principles, or the like.

ONTOLOGICALLY SELF-DEFEATING THEORIES

One view about logic—a view called psychologism—holds a thesis which can be expressed along these lines: the "laws of logic" (e.g., *modus ponens*, or "*if* **p** *then* **q** and **p** imply **q**") are but generalizations concerning how people think. Thus, the theory goes, (1) "**P** and **P** *implies* **Q** imply **Q**" is true if and only if (2) "Whoever believes **P** and **P** *implies* **Q** also believes **Q**" is true, or the like. But, presumably, *(1) if and only if (2)* is true only if it meets some similar conditions; otherwise, its statement of (mutual) implication—namely *(1) if and only if (2)*—escapes psychologistic analysis. In sum: The statement *(1) if and only if (2)* asserts that (1) is true only given that (2) is true (and conversely); but *(1) if and only if (2)* itself, presumably, is intended to be true even though it is not believed by anyone except those who embrace psychologism.[2] So were psychologism true, one statement of mutual implication must be true after a fashion not provided for by psychologism.

The criticism is *separate* from the point that *(1) if and only if (2)* is clearly false; *modus ponens* is a valid form of inference whether people think in accord with it, or accept it, or not. The criticism made above is also separate from the point that if psychologism is to have rational support from such considerations, the reasoning involved here must be more than merely what people would happen to accept; it must be valid. But then again, psychologism will be false.

It seems, then, that psychologism is true if and only *(1) if and only if (2)* is true in a sense in which it, contrary to what psychologism intends, eludes psychologistic analysis. The *truth conditions* of a proposition **P** are simply whatever must exist in order for **P** to be true; psychologism seems unable to abide its own truth conditions. Such a view, we may say, is *ontologically self-defeating*. This suggests:

(R7) *If a conceptual system* **T** *is such that "***T** *is true" and "***T***'s truth conditions obtain" are incompatible, then* **T** *is false.*

SOLUTION-FAILURE AND THEORY ASSESSMENT

John Locke once offered a theory of perception which, in barest outlines, went like this. Suppose one perceives an elephant. There is then a *direct* object of perception—an idea or image of which one is immediately aware and which is private to oneself alone—and an *indirect* object of perception, the elephant itself. In cases of illusion

2. Who are not to be confused with psychologists; psychologism is a *philosophical*, not a *psychological*, theory.

or hallucination or the like, there is only the idea or image or direct object. As it were, one has direct acquaintance only with pictures of things, and never with things themselves. Locke later asked, as Berkeley did, the obvious question: on this view, how could one ever know that there are indirect objects of perception—that there are public physical objects? Other than as an escape from skepticism about physical objects, the view has little attraction; it was offered as an escape from, but instead led directly into, skepticism regarding the "external world." This suggests the following criterion:

(R8) *If the only rationale for* **T** *is that* **T** *solves problem* **P**, *and, given* **T**, **P** *remains,* **T** *should be rejected.*

ASSESSMENT AND PERCEPTUAL EVIDENCE

If the view concerning perceptual experience presented in Chapter 1 is correct, then we have good reason to think that there are physical objects (that there is an external world). Some religious traditions deny this, claiming that sensory experience in some sense is unworthy evidence and illusory, and that there is no "external world" at all. The suggestion, then, is not vacuous that:

(R9) *If* **T** *entails that sensory experience is never veridical, or that there is no external world, there is excellent reason for rejecting* **T**.

There seems, as well, to be evidence that historical events have occurred, and that in any straightforward sense this entails that time is not unreal. Yet some views have denied not merely the importance but even the occurrence of historical phenomena, though perhaps none has done so which did not base its denial on, or on some view which also entailed, the alleged unreality of the external world.

REFERENCE-RANGE AND THEORETICAL INADEQUACY

The reference range of a theory, let us say, is the range of data which, given its nature, it should be able to explain or illumine—the range of things which, given the theory, it ought not to leave as "surds." There is no general rule for telling what items fall within a theory's reference range, though no intellectual paralysis seems to set in when one considers what the reference range of a particular theory amounts to. It seems that:

(R10) *Any theory* **T** *which cannot explain or illumine data within* **T**'*s reference range is (in any form of* **T** *in which this is so) to be rejected.*

Moral disagreements, for example, seem to be in just this manner a stumbling block and a snare to ethical noncognitivism.

THEORIES AND DATA

There are ranges of data which seem relatively theory-free (or theory-shared), at least with respect to any very plausible theory (perceptual data, e.g., of a sort one might refer to as contained within "reflective perceptual common sense"), though of course if "secondary qualities" are "mind-dependent" reflections of "primary qualities" and mathematics really "the language of nature" such "perceptual common sense" may be considerably more malleable, or at any rate less representational of the nature of things, than "reflective ethical common sense." Not all of this data need come from within a theory's reference range, and in any case, there is point to something along the lines of:

(R11) *If a conceptual system* **T** *contradicts well-confirmed data* **D**, *then if* **T** *cannot justify so doing,* **T** *is (probably) false.*

AD HOC HYPOTHESES

Some theories advertise their weakness by requiring *ad hoc* hypotheses. Suppose that there is excellent reason to think that proposition **P** is true, that theory **T** as it stands entails **not-P**, and that **T** *entails* **not-P** can be avoided if one adds some hypothesis **H** to **T** which changes **T** sufficiently to avoid **P**'s falsifying **T**, though **H** has no other role in **T** and no credentials besides saving **T** from that fate. Then **H** is *ad hoc* relative to **T**. Perhaps the epistemic state of affairs just described is one in which **T** is rendered highly suspicious—one in which **T**'s need of **H** in order to avoid falsification, like internal bleeding, is (when it surfaces) a sign of deeper troubles. If so, the way to put things is something like:

(R12) *If* **T** *requires one or more ad hoc hypotheses,* **T** *is epistemically defective in ways perhaps not yet plain.*

Of course, it is possible to debate whether a hypothesis really is *ad hoc*.

REMARKS CONCERNING THE CRITERIA

Several things seem true about (R1–R12): (i) there are other criteria for assessing conceptual systems besides (R1–R12); (ii) a theory, or conceptual system, or world view, which violates any of (R1–R12) is refuted, or at least needs revision, if it is to be accepted; (iii) none of (R1–R12) requires that a theory be predictive in order for it to be checked, along falsificationist lines, by considering whether it violates them (that **T** *entails* **P** does not mean that **T** *predicts* **P**); (iv) even if one expands "perceptual certification" and "logical certification" greatly in any natural way, they will not include all of (R1–R12), which include epistemic criteria neither broadly perceptual nor broadly logical; (v) (R1–R12) contain nothing to prevent them from, or limit them to, applying to religious conceptual systems.

CONCLUSION

A world view which explains or illumines the data within its relevance range, has some experiential support, and falls prey to none of (R1–R12) and their kin is (thus far) in good epistemic position. It seems unlikely that theism falls prey to any of (R1–R12). It has some experiential support and explains and illumines data within its relevance range. So theism, including Christian theism, apparently is in good epistemic position. For anything that has been argued here, however, various views incompatible with theism also may be in good epistemic position. The same is true of most, if not all, arguments for theism, though this is not usually stated. One question that remains is: how, exactly, *does* theism, and Christianity in particular, relate to the data presented by various disciplines? What are its implications, if any, for anthropology or psychology or history, and how do those implications fare? Do they fit with and integrate what is known? Are they fruitful? Another question that remains is: what are the implications, in these areas, of various other world views, religious and otherwise, and how do these implications fare? Raising these questions underlines the limited range of the current inquiry, whose purpose has been to defend the cognitive status of religious conceptual systems in general, and Christian monotheism in particular, and to do so in a way which outlined an approach to dealing with the rational assessment of such systems.

Perhaps the case for the cognitive status of religious conceptual systems has been made. If so, the next step would be to engage in the rational assessment of various religious (and nonreligious) conceptual systems ("Eastern" as well as "Western") along the lines suggested in the current chapter. That step lies beyond the boundaries of this volume, whose purpose has been to show that this step can be taken—that the epistemic ground is firm at least to the point where that step is the next.

SUGGESTIONS FOR FURTHER READING

Bromiley, Geoffrey W. *Historical Theology.* Grand Rapids, MI: Eerdmans, 1978.

Clark, Gordon H. *A Christian View of Men and Things.* Grand Rapids, MI: Eerdmans, 1952.

Coplestone, Frederick. *Aquinas.* Harmondsworth, England: Penguin, 1967.

_____. *A History of Philosophy.* Westminster, MD: The Newman Bookshop, 1946-53.

Perhaps the best general history of philosophy in English.

Hepburn, Ronald W. *Christianity and Paradox: Critical Studies in Twentieth-Century Theology.* New York: Pegasus, 1968.

Henry, Carl F. H. *God, Revelation and Authority.* Waco, TX: Word Books, 1976-83.

A discussion of a wide range of interconnections among theology, philosophy, and other disciplines.

_____. *Remaking the Modern Mind.* Grand Rapids, MI: Eerdmans, 1946.

Holmes, Arthur F. *All Truth Is God's Truth.* Grand Rapids, MI: Eerdmans, 1977.

_____. *Contours of a World View.* Grand Rapids, MI: Eerdmans, 1983.

_____. *The Idea of a Christian College.* Grand Rapids, MI: Eerdmans, 1975.

Hopkins, Jasper, and Richardson, Herbert W., ed. and trans. *Anselm of Canterbury.* 2d ed. New York: Mellen Press, 1975.

Markus, R. A., ed. *Augustine.* Garden City, NY: Doubleday-Anchor, 1972.

Mitchell, Basil. *The Justification of Religious Belief.* New York: Macmillan, 1973.

Nash, Ronald, ed. *The Philosophy of Gordon H. Clark.* Philadelphia: Presbyterian and Reformed Press, 1968.

Oates, Whitney J., ed. *The Basic Writings of St. Augustine.* New York: Random House, 1948.

Orr, James. *The Christian View of God and the World.* Grand Rapids, MI: Eerdmans, 1954.

Pegis, Anton C., ed. *The Basic Writings of St. Thomas Aquinas.* New York: Random House, 1945.

Penelhum, Terence. *Problems of Religious Knowledge.* London: Macmillan, 1971.

Reischauer, August Karl. *The Nature and Truth of the Great Religions.* Tokyo: Tuttle, 1967.

Yandell, Keith E. "Miracles, Epistemology, and Hume's Barrier." *International Journal for Philosophy of Religion,* 13 (1976).

———. "Religious Experience and Rational Appraisal." *Religious Studies,* 10 (June 1974): 173-87.

APPENDIX

THEORETICAL CONTEXTS, EXPERIENTIAL EVIDENCE, AND RELATIVE PLAUSIBILITY: AN ALTERNATIVE ACCOUNT

One might argue the matter differently concerning Axiom (A5)*.

One might claim that if **A1** and **A2** are equiplausible, and **A2** is evidence-canceling regarding experience **E** and **C**, whereas **A1** is not, then one simply does not know what to make of **E**; one does not know whether **E** provides evidence for **C** or not. The argument goes as follows. Suppose Ralph ingests a pill which immediately produces two effects. It completely paralyzes him, and it causes him to seem to see a pheasant in his garden if he is looking at his garden through a window. As it happens, he is looking at his garden through a window when he ingests the pill. But Ralph knows that half the time there is a pheasant visible in his garden anyway, and it may be that the experience he is now having—that of perceptually seeming to see a pheasant—has exactly the phenomenological "filling" it has because he is seeing a real pheasant in his garden. The problem is that he would be having the experience he is now having even were it the case that now the garden is empty of all wildlife. There are two explanations of Ralph's current visual experience: (A1) Ralph is seeing a real pheasant, and (A2) Ralph seems to see a pheasant that is not there (and does so due to his having ingested the pill). In his paralyzed state, Ralph cannot open the window and see whether the bird is still there, or walk out to see if he hears as well as sees it. Under these conditions, Ralph is condemned to wonder whether his experience is pill-caused (and so *not* evidence) or *not* pill-caused (and so evidence). The problem is not whether *There is a pheasant in the garden,* or even *Ralph now sees a real pheasant,* is compatible with *Ralph's pill causes experiences in which he seems to see a pheasant and Ralph took a pill;* there is no incompatibility there at all. What is relevantly true, however, is this: *If Ralph took the pill, then his present experience of seeming to see a pheasant is not evidence that there is a real pheasant that he sees.* The reason for this is simply that, even if *no* pheasant now occupies his garden, Ralph will have an experience with the "perceptual phenomenological filling" which his present experience possesses. This is so even if the explanation expressed by *Ralph's pill is the cause of his current visual experience* is not more than equiplausible with *A pheasant in the garden is the cause of Ralph's current visual experience.*

Suppose that it is the case that *If there is really a pheasant in the garden, Ralph will see it whether he has taken the pill or not* and *The odds of there being a pheasant in the garden now are exactly 50/50.* Then (A1) is indeed equiplausible with (A2). But, for all that, Ralph's current visual experience is not evidence that a pheasant now graces the garden for the simple but sufficient reason that he would be having an experience with the very phenomenology (or very *sort* of phenomenology, at any rate) of the experience he is having even were there no pheasant there.

Analogously with numinous experience, the argument continues: if *Ralph has an experience in which he seems to encounter God* is true at time **t**, and there is equiplausibility between the explanations *God caused this experience* and *Ralph's desire for a cosmic Father-figure caused this experience,* and the latter explanation is evidence-canceling, then Ralph's experience is not evidence that God exists. It is not evidence that God exists because *ex hypothesi* he would have the experience at **t** even were God not to play any causal role in its occurrence.

If this line of reasoning is correct, then (A5)* should be replaced by (A5)** which reads: *If explanation* **A1** *of one's experience* **E** *is at least as plausible as explanation* **A2,** *where if* **A2** *rather than* **A1** *is true, then* **E** *is veridical with respect to* **E** *and* **C,** *and one knows this, then even though* **E** *meets the relevance conditions with respect to* **C,** *one has no better reason to accept than not to accept* **C.**

If one replaces (A5)* by (A5)**, one will need a further step in the argument, namely **(N):** There is no evidence-canceling explanation of numinous experiences—i.e., there are at least some numinous experiences regarding which no evidence-canceling explanations obtain.

Perhaps the most plausible line of reasoning in **(N)**'s favor begins by noting that a one-or-more-membered set **S** of explanations of numinous experience **E** is evidence-canceling only if **S** is competitive with the claim **G** that *God is the object (and so is part of the cause) of* **E**. **S** and **G** will be competitive only if **S** by itself is sufficient in the sense previously discussed—only if the truth of both **S** and **G** yields causal duplication regarding **E**.